ORCS

INSPACE*

D1473726

ONI PRESS

AN ONI PRESS PUBLICATION

ORCS IN SPACE*

Written by
JUSTIN ROILAND, RASHAD GHEITH, ABED GHEITH & MIKE TANNER

Illustrated by
FRANÇOIS VIGNEAULT

Colors by
DJ CHAVIS

Color flatting by
DAVE PENDER

Designed by
SARAH ROCKWELL

Edited by
AMANDA MEADOWS

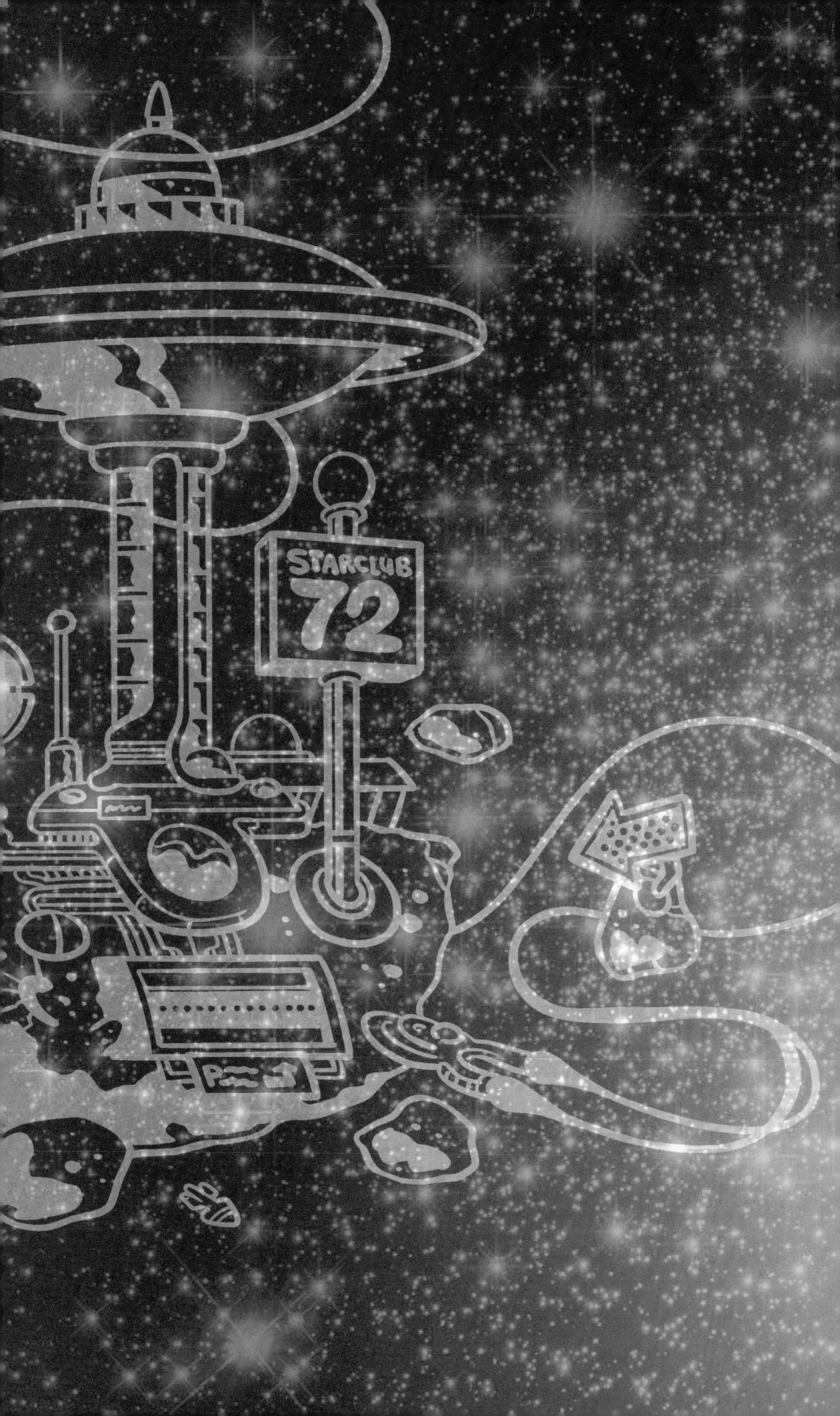
STARCLUB
72

PUBLISHED BY
ONI-LION FORGE
PUBLISHING
GROUP, LLC.

JAMES LUCAS JONES, *PRESIDENT & PUBLISHER*
SARAH GAYDOS, *EDITOR IN CHIEF* • CHARLIE
CHU, *E.V.P. OF CREATIVE & BUSINESS DEVELOPMENT*
ALEX SEGURA, *S.V.P. OF MARKETING & SALES*
BRAD ROOKS, *DIRECTOR OF OPERATIONS* • AMBER
O'NEILL, *SPECIAL PROJECTS MANAGER* • MARGOT
WOOD, *DIRECTOR OF MARKETING & SALES* • KATIE
SAINZ, *MARKETING MANAGER* • TARA LEHMANN,
PUBLICIST • HOLLY AITCHISON, *CONSUMER*
MARKETING MANAGER • TROY LOOK, *DIRECTOR OF*
DESIGN & PRODUCTION • KATE Z. STONE, *SENIOR*
GRAPHIC DESIGNER • CAREY HALL, *GRAPHIC*
DESIGNER • HILARY THOMPSON, *GRAPHIC*
DESIGNER • SARAH ROCKWELL, *GRAPHIC DESIGNER*
ANGIE KNOWLES, *DIGITAL PREPRESS LEAD*
VINCENT KUKUA, *DIGITAL PREPRESS TECHNICIAN*
JASMINE AMIRI, *SENIOR EDITOR* • SHAWNA
GORE, *SENIOR EDITOR* • AMANDA MEADOWS,
SENIOR EDITOR • ROBERT MEYERS, *SENIOR*
EDITOR, LICENSING • DESIREE RODRIGUEZ, *EDITOR*
GRACE SCHEIPETER, *EDITOR* • ZACK SOTO, *EDITOR*
CHRIS CERASI, *EDITORIAL COORDINATOR* • STEVE
ELLIS, *VICE PRESIDENT OF GAMES* • BEN EISNER,
GAME DEVELOPER • MICHELLE NGUYEN, *EXECUTIVE*
ASSISTANT • JUNG LEE, *LOGISTICS COORDINATOR*
KUIAN KELLUM, *WAREHOUSE ASSISTANT*
• JOE NOZEMACK, *PUBLISHER EMERITUS* •

ONIPRESS.COM

LIONFORGE.COM

🐦 /JUSTINROILAND
🐦 /MIKEISERNIE
🐦 /ABEDG
📷 /FRANCOISVIGNEAULT
📷 /DJCOLORSCOMICS
🐦 /WAYTOOMANYDAVES

FIRST EDITION: OCTOBER 2021

ISBN: 978-1-62010-756-0

EISBN: 978-1-62010-761-4

LIBRARY OF CONGRESS CONTROL NUMBER: 2020937772

1 2 3 4 5 6 7 8 9 10

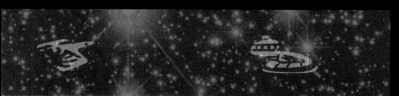

ORCS IN SPACE VOLUME 1, October 2021. Published by Oni-Lion Forge Publishing Group, LLC., 1319 SE Martin Luther King Jr. Blvd., Suite 240, Portland, OR 97214. Orcs in Space is ™ & © 2021 Justin Roiland, Rashad Gheith, Abed Gheith. All rights reserved. Oni Press logo and icon are ™ & © 2021 Oni Press, Inc. All rights reserved. Oni Press logo and icon artwork created by Keith A. Wood. The events, institutions, and characters presented in this book are fictional. Any resemblance to actual persons, living or dead, is purely coincidental. No portion of this publication may be reproduced, by any means, without the express written permission of the copyright holders. Printed in Canada.

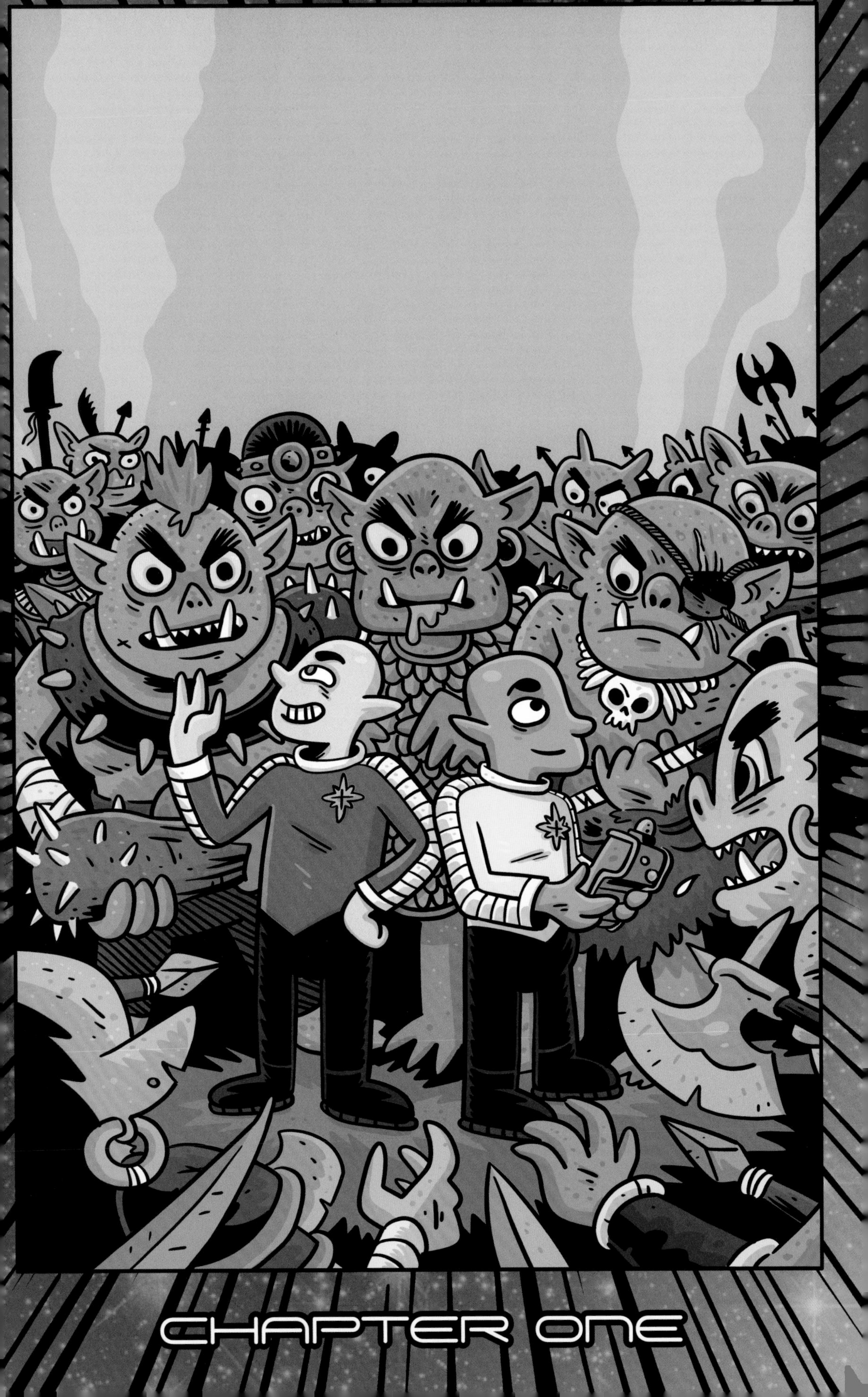

CHAPTER ONE

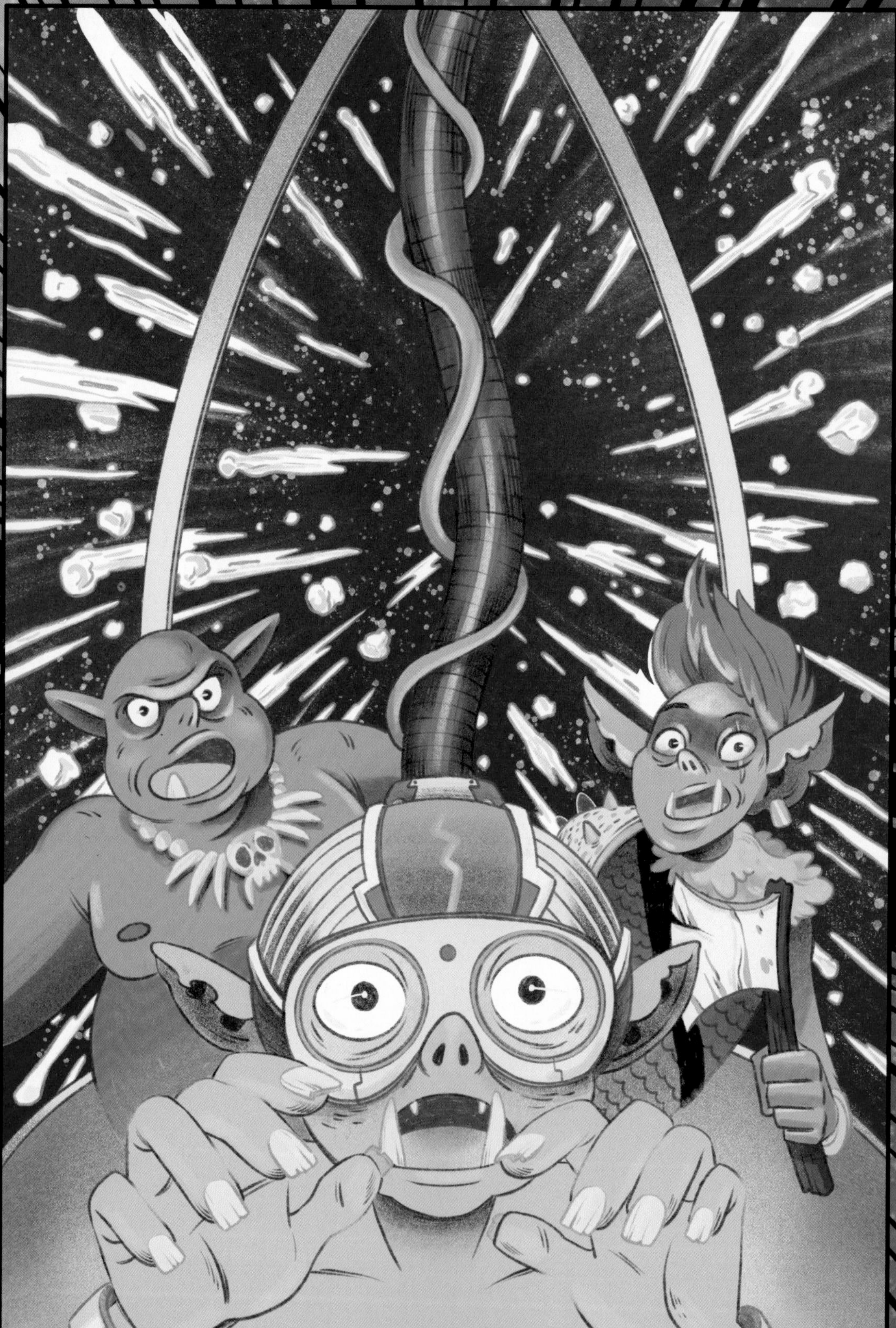

VARIANT COVER

BY NICOLE GOUX

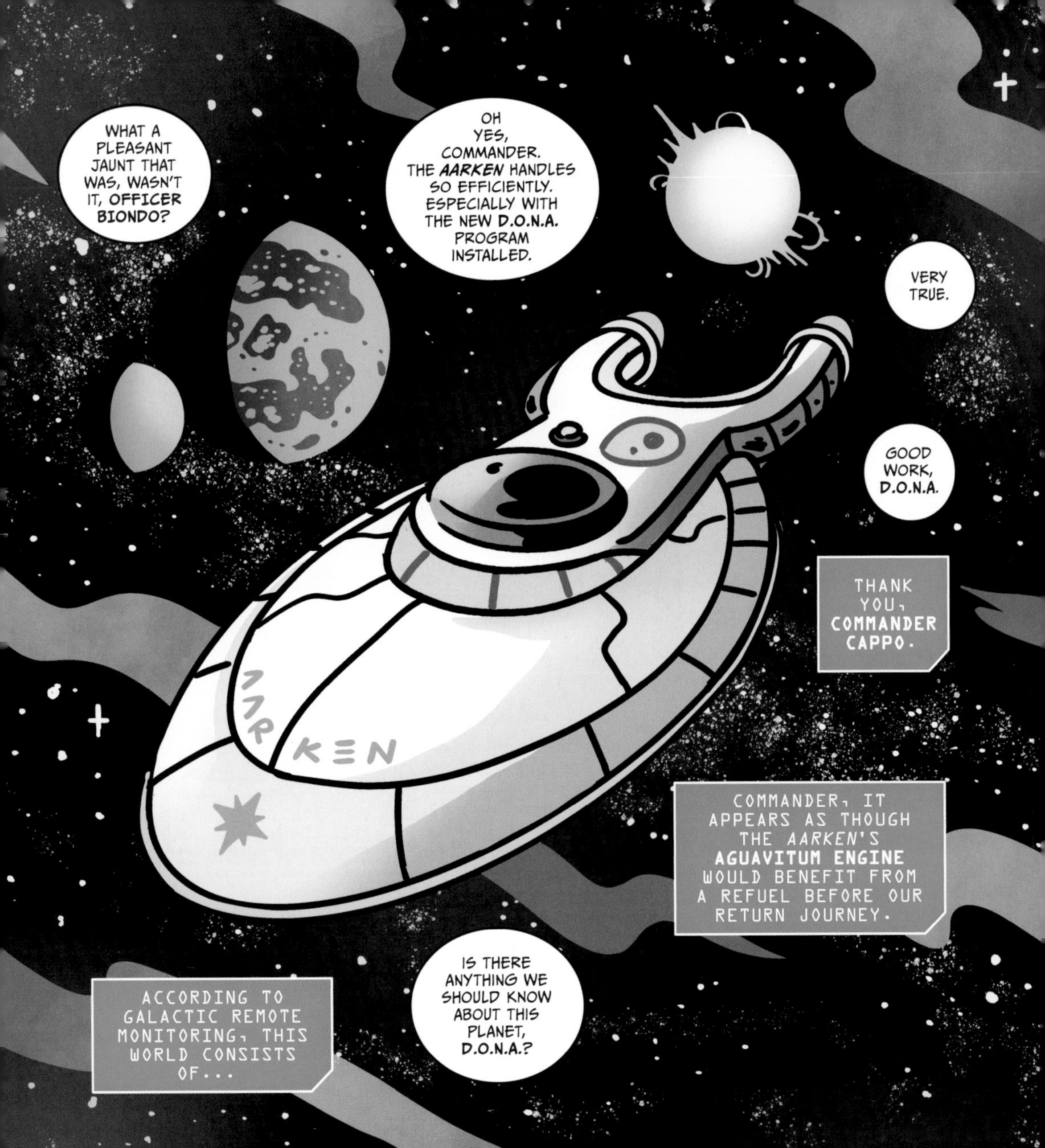

WHAT A PLEASANT JAUNT THAT WAS, WASN'T IT, OFFICER BIONDO?
OH YES, COMMANDER. THE AARKEN HANDLES SO EFFICIENTLY. ESPECIALLY WITH THE NEW D.O.N.A. PROGRAM INSTALLED.
VERY TRUE.
GOOD WORK, D.O.N.A.
THANK YOU, COMMANDER CAPPO.
AARKEN
COMMANDER, IT APPEARS AS THOUGH THE AARKEN'S AGUAVITUM ENGINE WOULD BENEFIT FROM A REFUEL BEFORE OUR RETURN JOURNEY.
IS THERE ANYTHING WE SHOULD KNOW ABOUT THIS PLANET, D.O.N.A.?
ACCORDING TO GALACTIC REMOTE MONITORING, THIS WORLD CONSISTS OF...

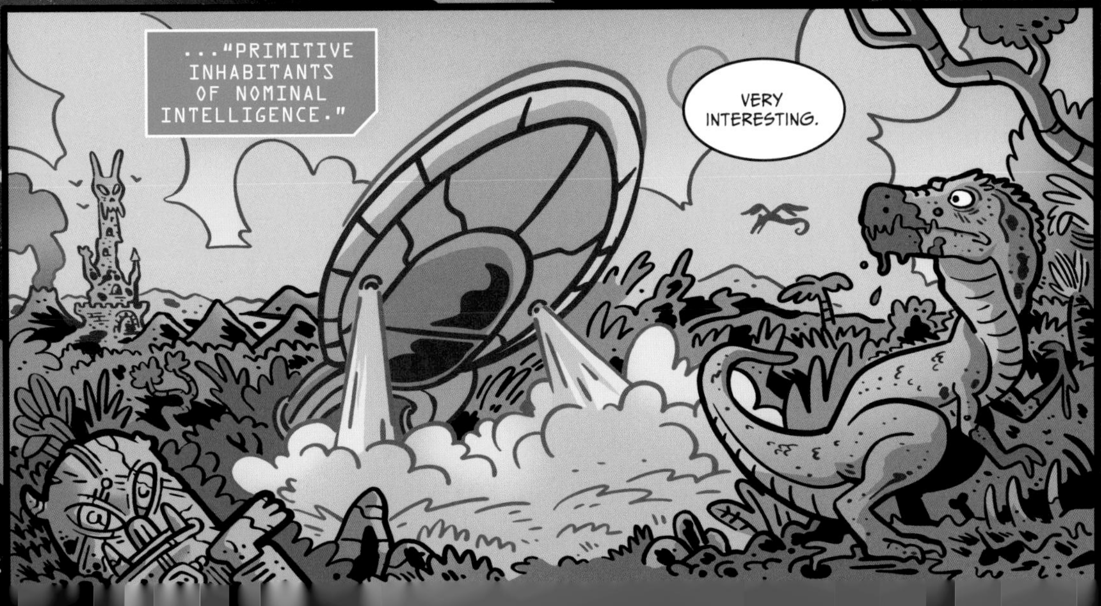

..."PRIMITIVE INHABITANTS OF NOMINAL INTELLIGENCE."
VERY INTERESTING.

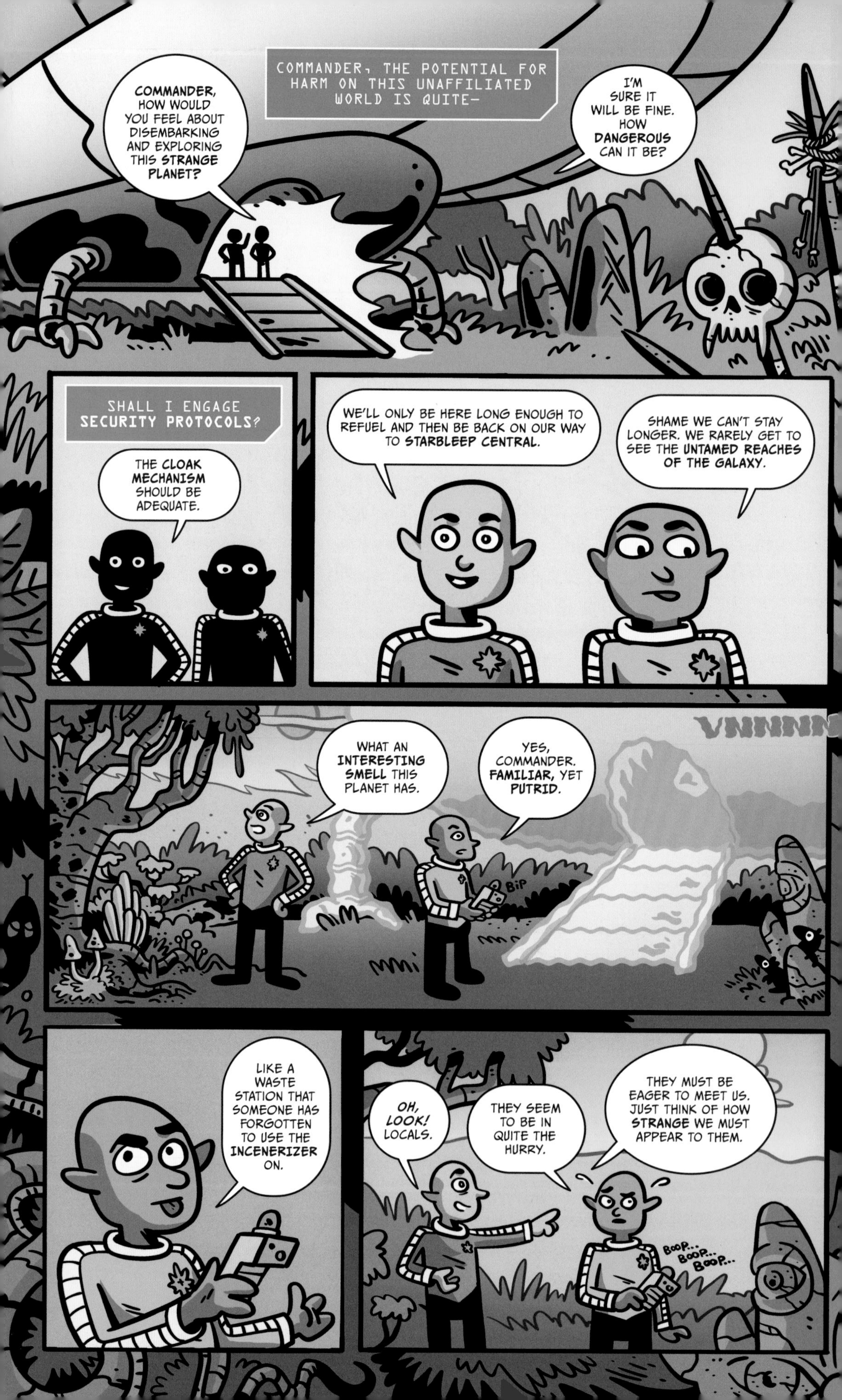
COMMANDER, HOW WOULD YOU FEEL ABOUT DISEMBARKING AND EXPLORING THIS STRANGE PLANET?
COMMANDER, THE POTENTIAL FOR HARM ON THIS UNAFFILIATED WORLD IS QUITE—
I'M SURE IT WILL BE FINE. HOW DANGEROUS CAN IT BE?
SHALL I ENGAGE SECURITY PROTOCOLS?
THE CLOAK MECHANISM SHOULD BE ADEQUATE.
WE'LL ONLY BE HERE LONG ENOUGH TO REFUEL AND THEN BE BACK ON OUR WAY TO STARBLEEP CENTRAL.
SHAME WE CAN'T STAY LONGER. WE RARELY GET TO SEE THE UNTAMED REACHES OF THE GALAXY.
VNNNN
WHAT AN INTERESTING SMELL THIS PLANET HAS.
YES, COMMANDER. FAMILIAR, YET PUTRID.
BIP
LIKE A WASTE STATION THAT SOMEONE HAS FORGOTTEN TO USE THE INCENERIZER ON.
OH, LOOK! LOCALS.
THEY SEEM TO BE IN QUITE THE HURRY.
THEY MUST BE EAGER TO MEET US. JUST THINK OF HOW STRANGE WE MUST APPEAR TO THEM.
BOOP... BOOP... BOOP...

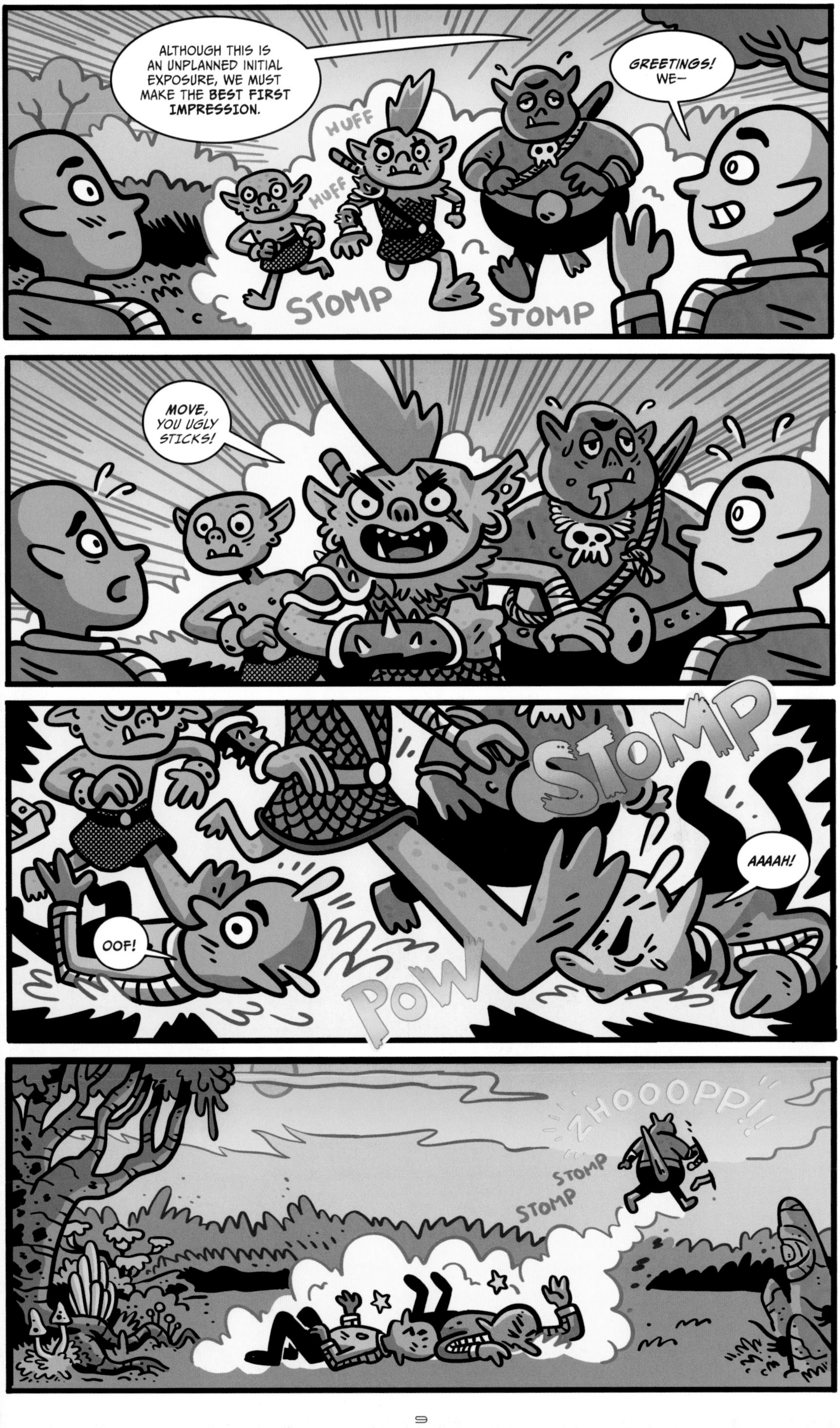
ALTHOUGH THIS IS AN UNPLANNED INITIAL EXPOSURE, WE MUST MAKE THE BEST FIRST IMPRESSION.
HUFF
HUFF
GREETINGS! WE–
STOMP
STOMP
MOVE, YOU UGLY STICKS!
STOMP
AAAAH!
OOF!
POW
ZHOOOPP!!
STOMP
STOMP

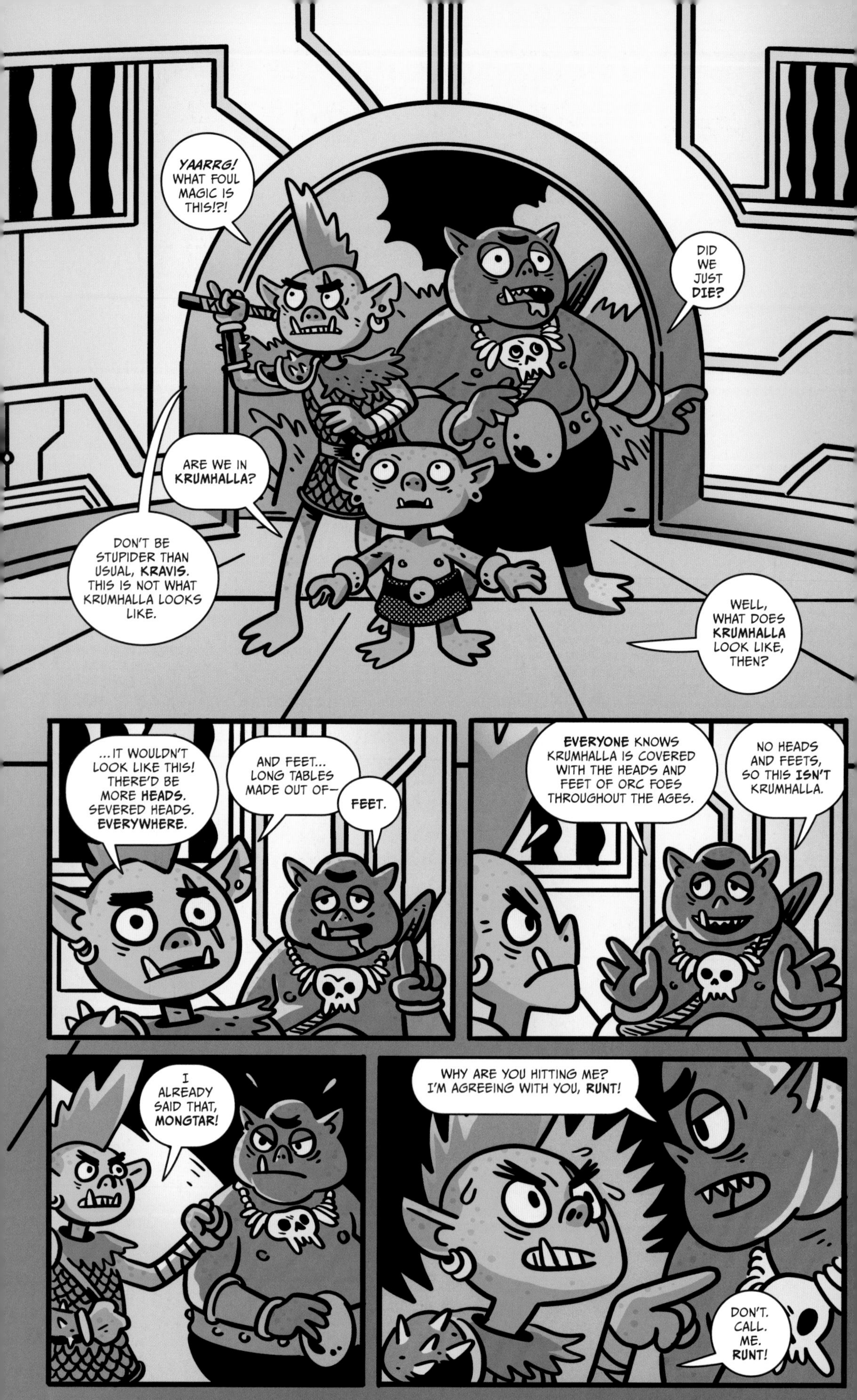
YAARRG! WHAT FOUL MAGIC IS THIS!?!
DID WE JUST DIE?
ARE WE IN KRUMHALLA?
DON'T BE STUPIDER THAN USUAL, KRAVIS. THIS IS NOT WHAT KRUMHALLA LOOKS LIKE.
WELL, WHAT DOES KRUMHALLA LOOK LIKE, THEN?
...IT WOULDN'T LOOK LIKE THIS! THERE'D BE MORE HEADS. SEVERED HEADS. EVERYWHERE.
AND FEET... LONG TABLES MADE OUT OF—
FEET.
EVERYONE KNOWS KRUMHALLA IS COVERED WITH THE HEADS AND FEET OF ORC FOES THROUGHOUT THE AGES.
NO HEADS AND FEETS, SO THIS ISN'T KRUMHALLA.
I ALREADY SAID THAT, MONGTAR!
WHY ARE YOU HITTING ME? I'M AGREEING WITH YOU, RUNT!
DON'T. CALL. ME. RUNT!

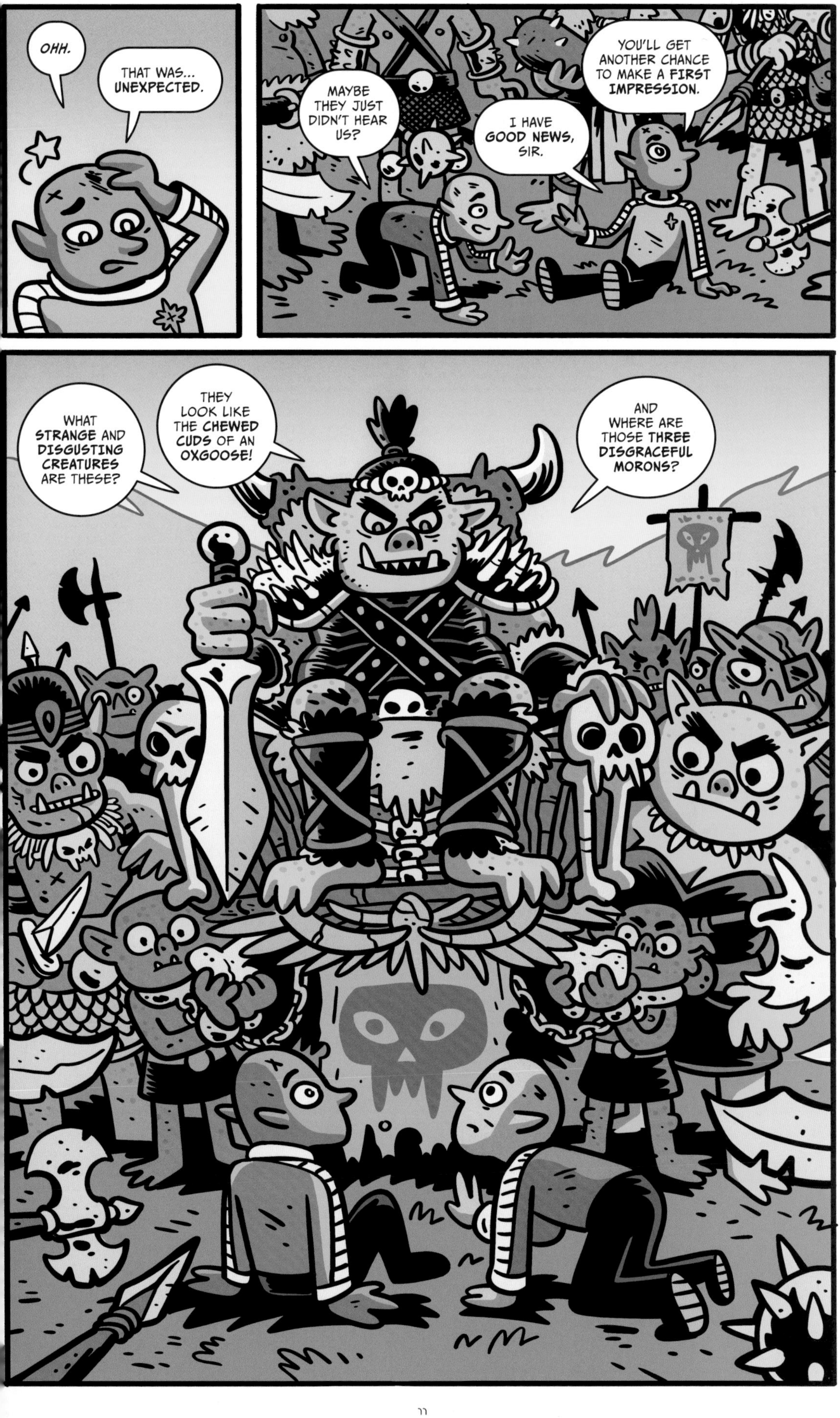
OHH.
THAT WAS... UNEXPECTED.
MAYBE THEY JUST DIDN'T HEAR US?
I HAVE GOOD NEWS, SIR.
YOU'LL GET ANOTHER CHANCE TO MAKE A FIRST IMPRESSION.
WHAT STRANGE AND DISGUSTING CREATURES ARE THESE?
THEY LOOK LIKE THE CHEWED CUDS OF AN OXGOOSE!
AND WHERE ARE THOSE THREE DISGRACEFUL MORONS?

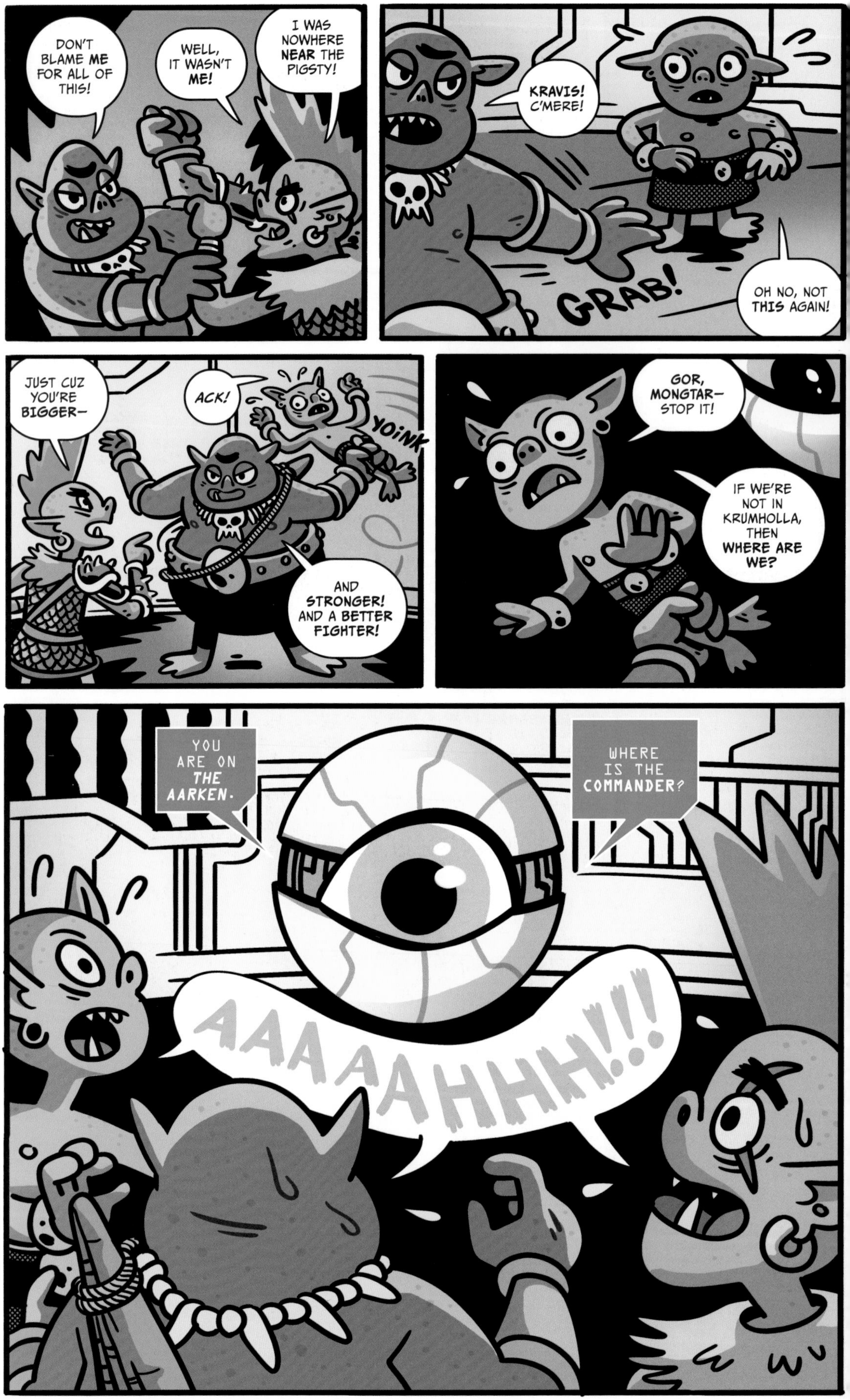

DON'T BLAME ME FOR ALL OF THIS!
WELL, IT WASN'T ME!
I WAS NOWHERE NEAR THE PIGSTY!
KRAVIS! C'MERE!
GRAB!
OH NO, NOT THIS AGAIN!
JUST CUZ YOU'RE BIGGER—
ACK!
YOINK
AND STRONGER! AND A BETTER FIGHTER!
GOR, MONGTAR— STOP IT!
IF WE'RE NOT IN KRUMHOLLA, THEN WHERE ARE WE?
YOU ARE ON THE AARKEN.
WHERE IS THE COMMANDER?
AAAAAHHH!!!

AAAAHHH!!! AAHHHH!!

AT LEAST THAT WASN'T YOUR **DOMINANT HAND**, COMMANDER.

TAKE THEM BACK TO **THE PIT**, THEY MAY KNOW SOMETHING!

YOU MAGGOT-RIDDEN, SOFT-TOED PEONS, YOU LOST THOSE **THREE BUFFOONS**!

OUTTA MY WAY, YOU **PUS-POTS**!

I **SWORE** I'D HAVE THEIR **HEADS**!

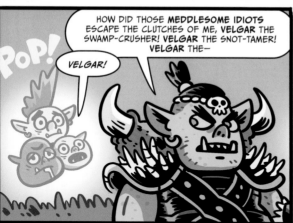
HOW DID THOSE **MEDDLESOME IDIOTS** ESCAPE THE CLUTCHES OF ME, **VELGAR** THE SWAMP-CRUSHER! **VELGAR** THE SNOT-TAMER! **VELGAR** THE—

POP!

VELGAR!

AHH! BY THE SACRED MOLE OF DAGNEK THE CANCEROUS, WHAT MAGIC HAS STOLEN **YOUR BODIES**?

BACK INSIDE!

BACK INSIDE!

POP!

RAH!

VELGAR'S FOUND US!

WE'RE **DOOMED**!

REPEATING QUESTION: **WHERE IS THE COMMANDER?**

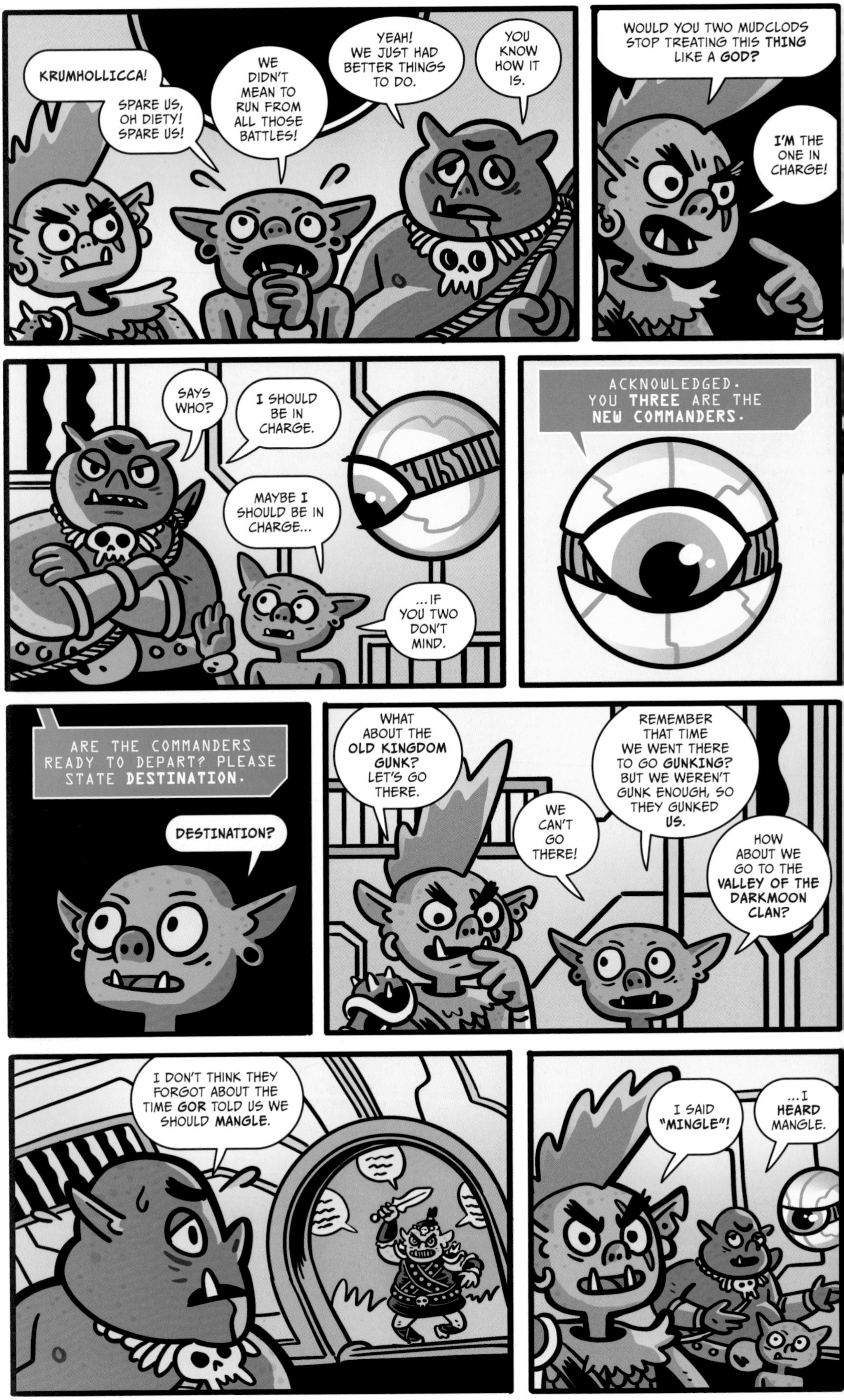

KRUMHOLLICCA!
SPARE US, OH DIETY! SPARE US!
WE DIDN'T MEAN TO RUN FROM ALL THOSE BATTLES!
YEAH! WE JUST HAD BETTER THINGS TO DO.
YOU KNOW HOW IT IS.
WOULD YOU TWO MUDCLODS STOP TREATING THIS THING LIKE A GOD?
I'M THE ONE IN CHARGE!
SAYS WHO?
I SHOULD BE IN CHARGE.
MAYBE I SHOULD BE IN CHARGE...
...IF YOU TWO DON'T MIND.
ACKNOWLEDGED. YOU THREE ARE THE NEW COMMANDERS.
ARE THE COMMANDERS READY TO DEPART? PLEASE STATE DESTINATION.
DESTINATION?
WHAT ABOUT THE OLD KINGDOM GUNK? LET'S GO THERE.
WE CAN'T GO THERE!
REMEMBER THAT TIME WE WENT THERE TO GO GUNKING? BUT WE WEREN'T GUNK ENOUGH, SO THEY GUNKED US.
HOW ABOUT WE GO TO THE VALLEY OF THE DARKMOON CLAN?
I DON'T THINK THEY FORGOT ABOUT THE TIME GOR TOLD US WE SHOULD MANGLE.
I SAID "MINGLE"!
...I HEARD MANGLE.

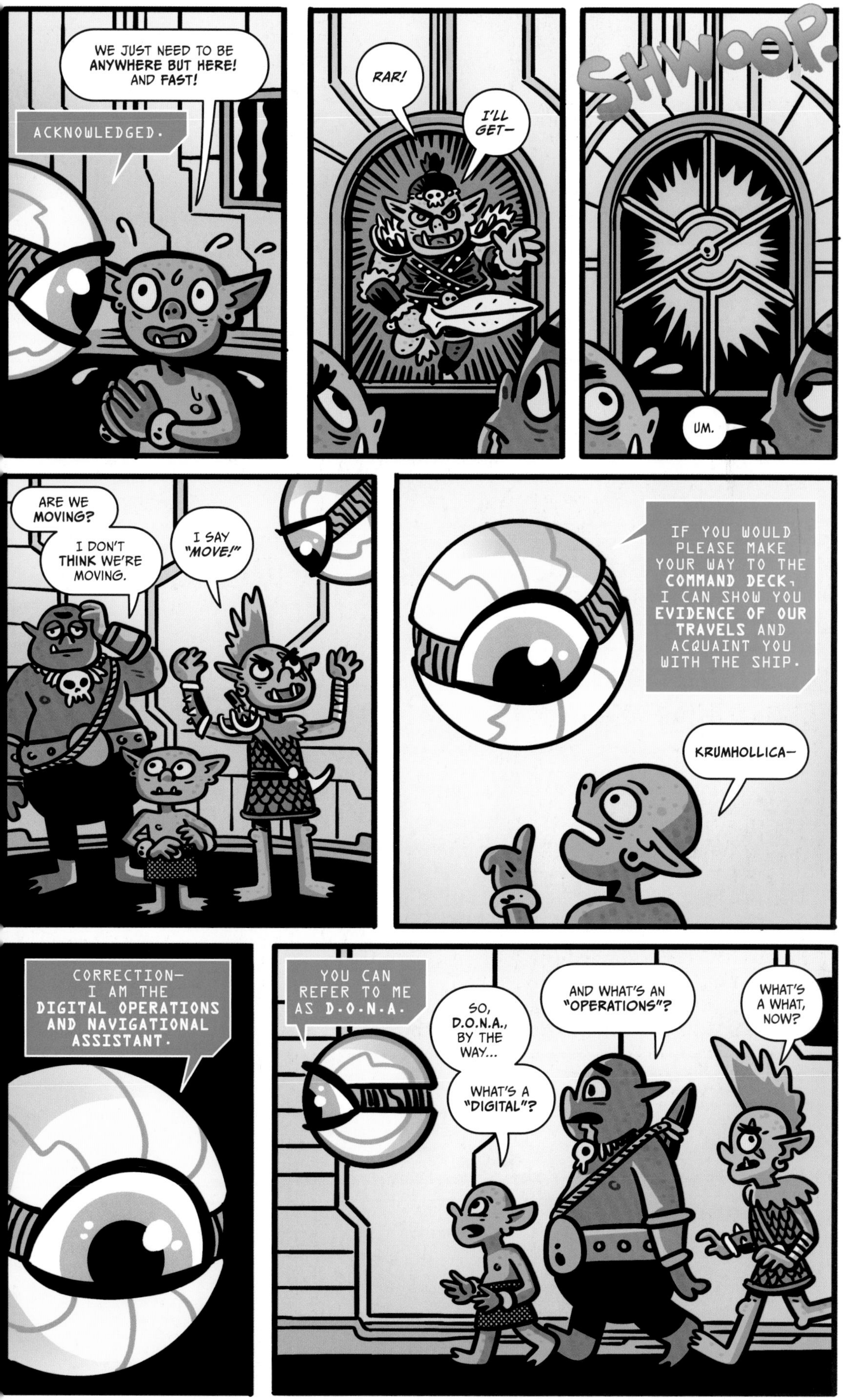

WE JUST NEED TO BE ANYWHERE BUT HERE! AND FAST!
ACKNOWLEDGED.
RAR!
I'LL GET—
SHWOOP.
UM.
ARE WE MOVING?
I DON'T THINK WE'RE MOVING.
I SAY "MOVE!"
IF YOU WOULD PLEASE MAKE YOUR WAY TO THE COMMAND DECK, I CAN SHOW YOU EVIDENCE OF OUR TRAVELS AND ACQUAINT YOU WITH THE SHIP.
KRUMHOLLICA—
CORRECTION— I AM THE DIGITAL OPERATIONS AND NAVIGATIONAL ASSISTANT.
YOU CAN REFER TO ME AS D.O.N.A.
SO, D.O.N.A., BY THE WAY...
WHAT'S A "DIGITAL"?
AND WHAT'S AN "OPERATIONS"?
WHAT'S A WHAT, NOW?

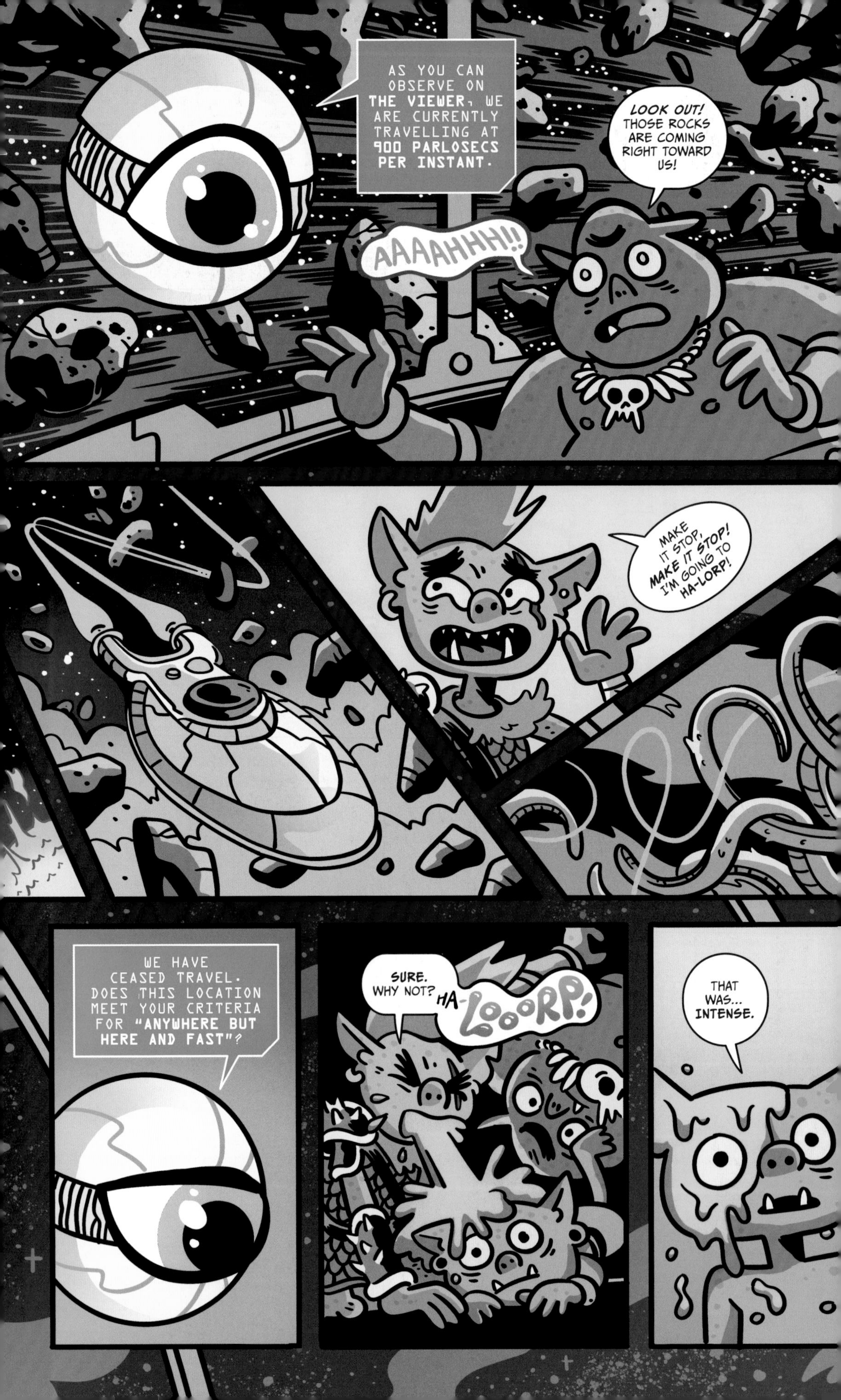
AS YOU CAN OBSERVE ON **THE VIEWER**, WE ARE CURRENTLY TRAVELLING AT **900 PARLOSECS PER INSTANT**.
LOOK OUT! THOSE ROCKS ARE COMING RIGHT TOWARD US!
AAAAHHH!!
MAKE IT STOP, ***MAKE IT STOP!*** I'M GOING TO **HA-LORP!**
WE HAVE CEASED TRAVEL. DOES THIS LOCATION MEET YOUR CRITERIA FOR **"ANYWHERE BUT HERE AND FAST"**?
SURE. WHY NOT?
HA-LOOORP!
THAT WAS... **INTENSE.**

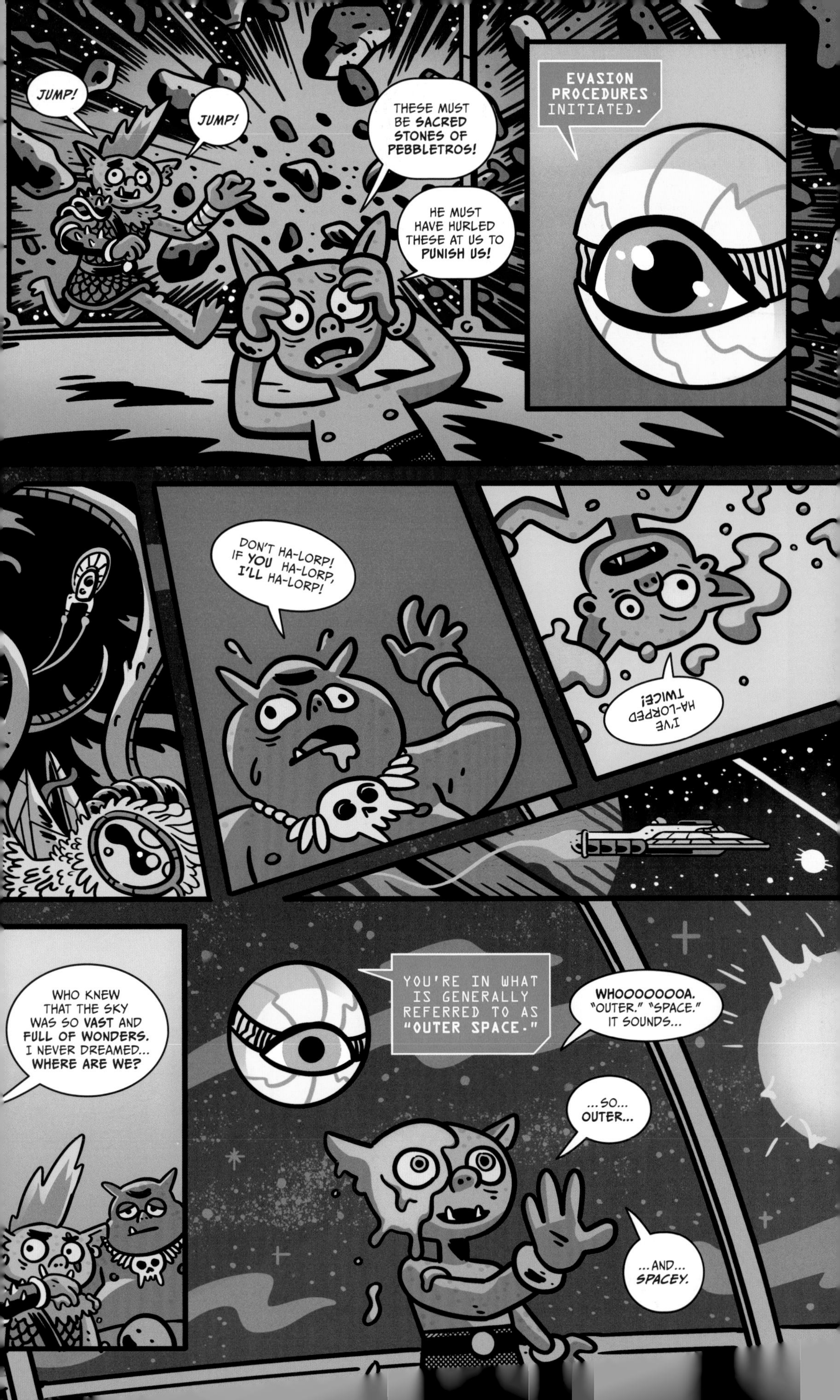

JUMP!
JUMP!
THESE MUST BE SACRED STONES OF PEBBLETROS!
HE MUST HAVE HURLED THESE AT US TO PUNISH US!
EVASION PROCEDURES INITIATED.
DON'T HA-LORP! IF YOU HA-LORP, I'LL HA-LORP!
I'VE HA-LORPED TWICE!
WHO KNEW THAT THE SKY WAS SO VAST AND FULL OF WONDERS. I NEVER DREAMED... WHERE ARE WE?
YOU'RE IN WHAT IS GENERALLY REFERRED TO AS "OUTER SPACE."
WHOOOOOOOA. "OUTER." "SPACE." IT SOUNDS...
...SO... OUTER...
...AND... SPACEY.

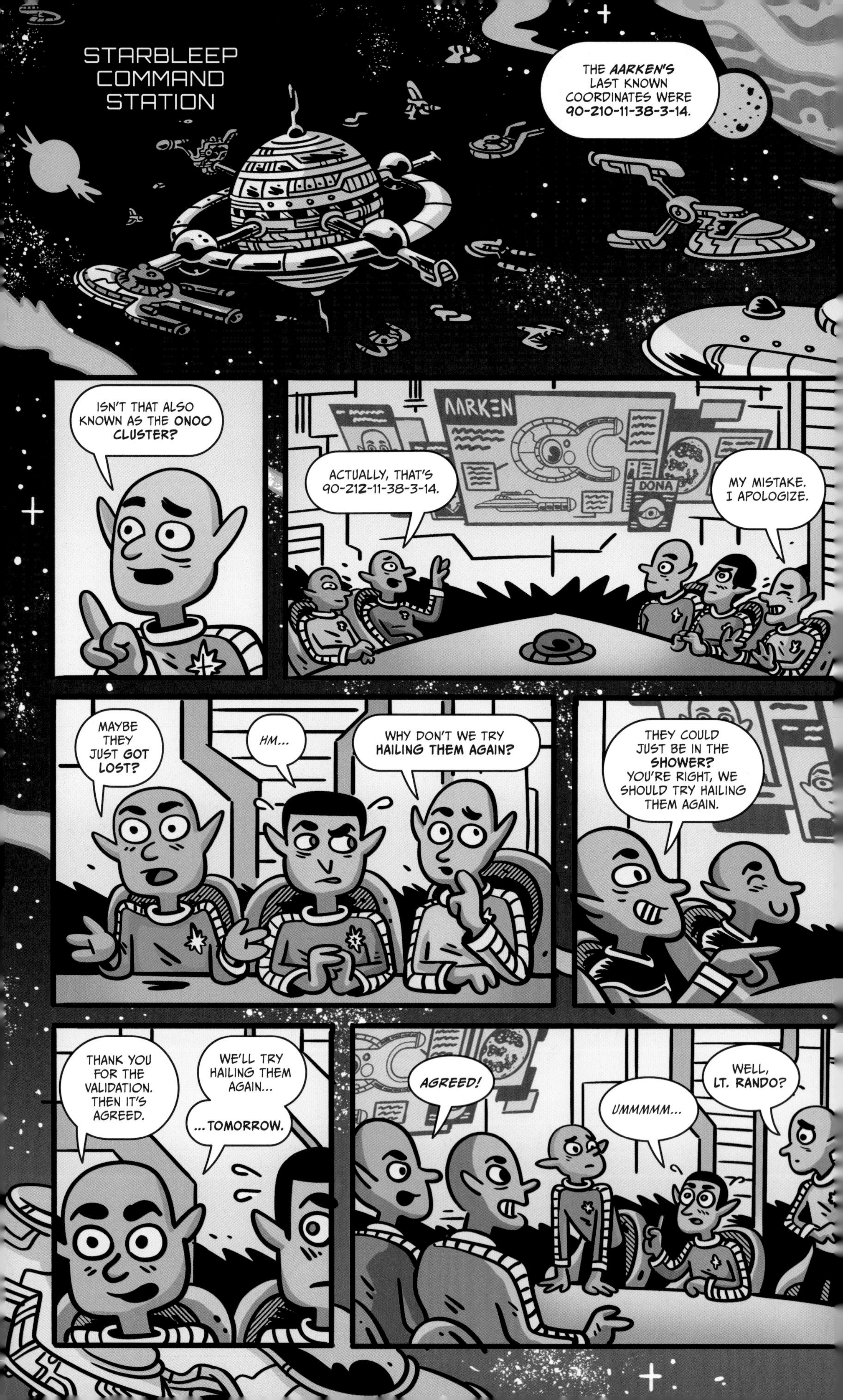
STARBLEEP COMMAND STATION
THE AARKEN'S LAST KNOWN COORDINATES WERE 90-210-11-38-3-14.
ISN'T THAT ALSO KNOWN AS THE ONOO CLUSTER?
AARKEN
ACTUALLY, THAT'S 90-212-11-38-3-14.
DONA
MY MISTAKE. I APOLOGIZE.
MAYBE THEY JUST GOT LOST?
HM...
WHY DON'T WE TRY HAILING THEM AGAIN?
THEY COULD JUST BE IN THE SHOWER? YOU'RE RIGHT, WE SHOULD TRY HAILING THEM AGAIN.
THANK YOU FOR THE VALIDATION. THEN IT'S AGREED.
WE'LL TRY HAILING THEM AGAIN...
...TOMORROW.
AGREED!
UMMMMM...
WELL, LT. RANDO?

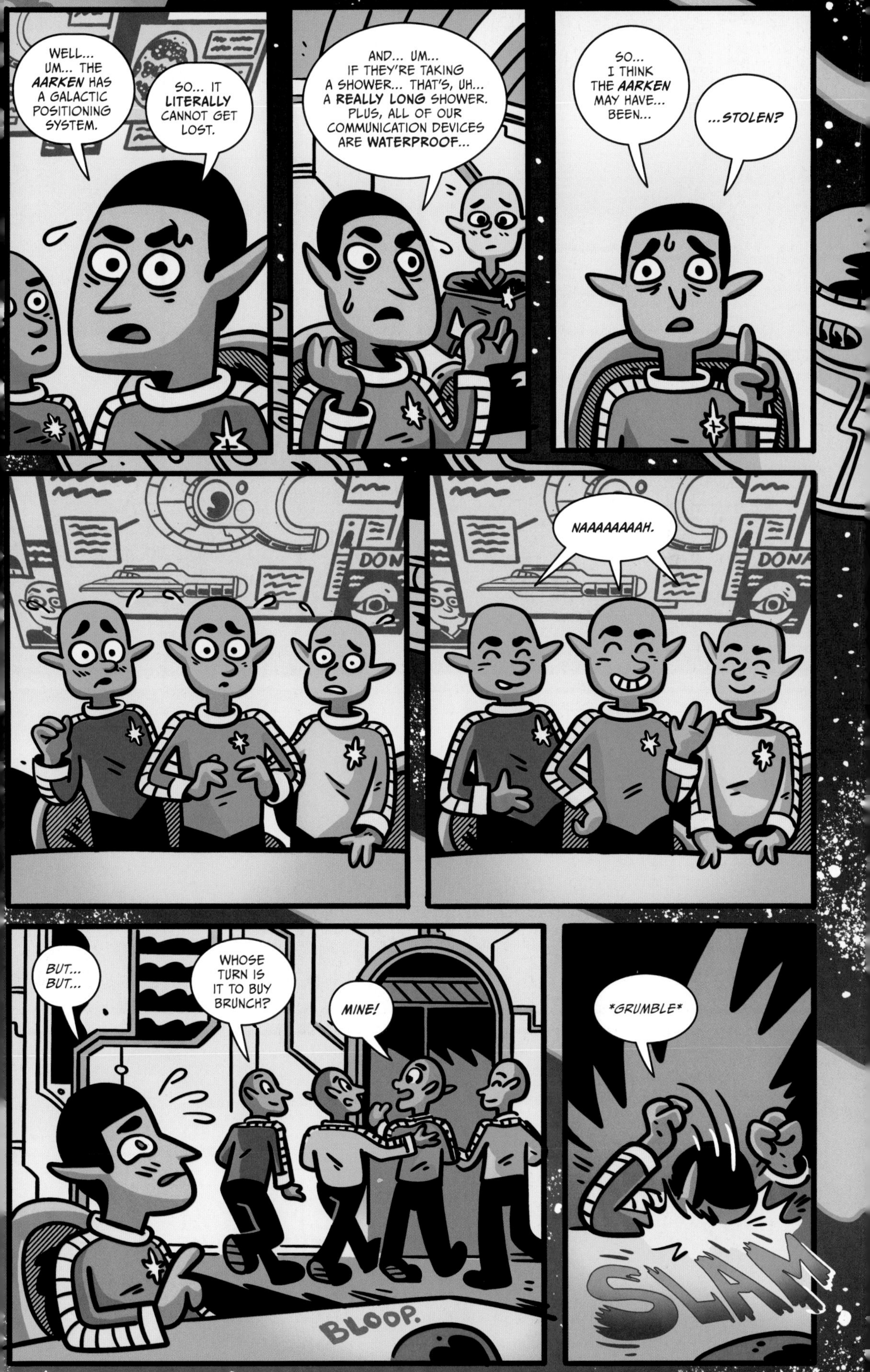
WELL... UM... THE AARKEN HAS A GALACTIC POSITIONING SYSTEM.
SO... IT LITERALLY CANNOT GET LOST.
AND... UM... IF THEY'RE TAKING A SHOWER... THAT'S, UH... A REALLY LONG SHOWER. PLUS, ALL OF OUR COMMUNICATION DEVICES ARE WATERPROOF...
SO... I THINK THE AARKEN MAY HAVE... BEEN...
...STOLEN?
NAAAAAAAAH.
BUT... BUT...
WHOSE TURN IS IT TO BUY BRUNCH?
MINE!
BLOOP.
GRUMBLE
SLAM

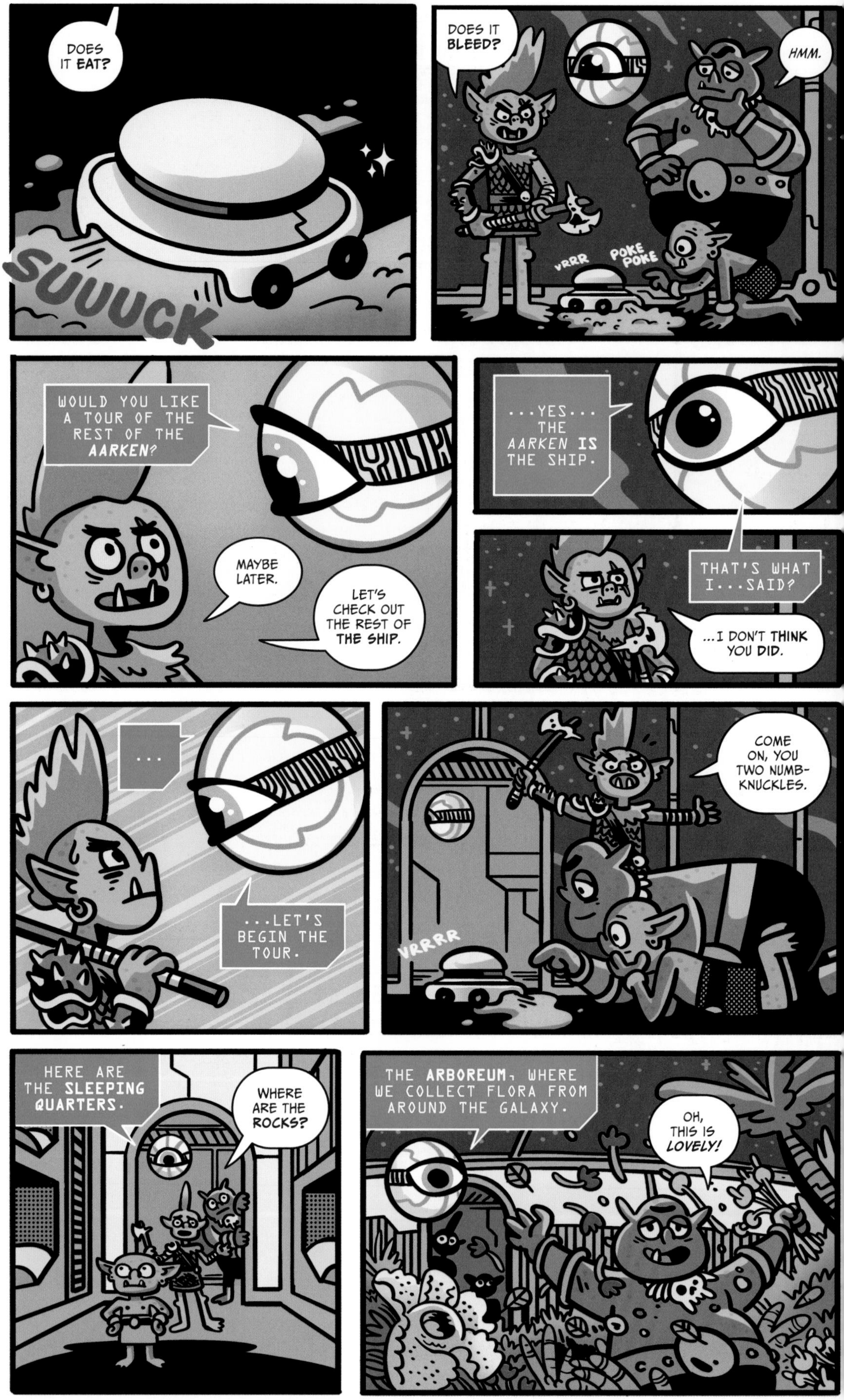
DOES IT EAT?
SUUUCK
DOES IT BLEED?
HMM.
VRRR
POKE POKE
WOULD YOU LIKE A TOUR OF THE REST OF THE AARKEN?
...YES... THE AARKEN IS THE SHIP.
MAYBE LATER.
LET'S CHECK OUT THE REST OF THE SHIP.
THAT'S WHAT I...SAID?
...I DON'T THINK YOU DID.
...
...LET'S BEGIN THE TOUR.
COME ON, YOU TWO NUMB-KNUCKLES.
VRRRR
HERE ARE THE SLEEPING QUARTERS.
WHERE ARE THE ROCKS?
THE ARBOREUM, WHERE WE COLLECT FLORA FROM AROUND THE GALAXY.
OH, THIS IS LOVELY!

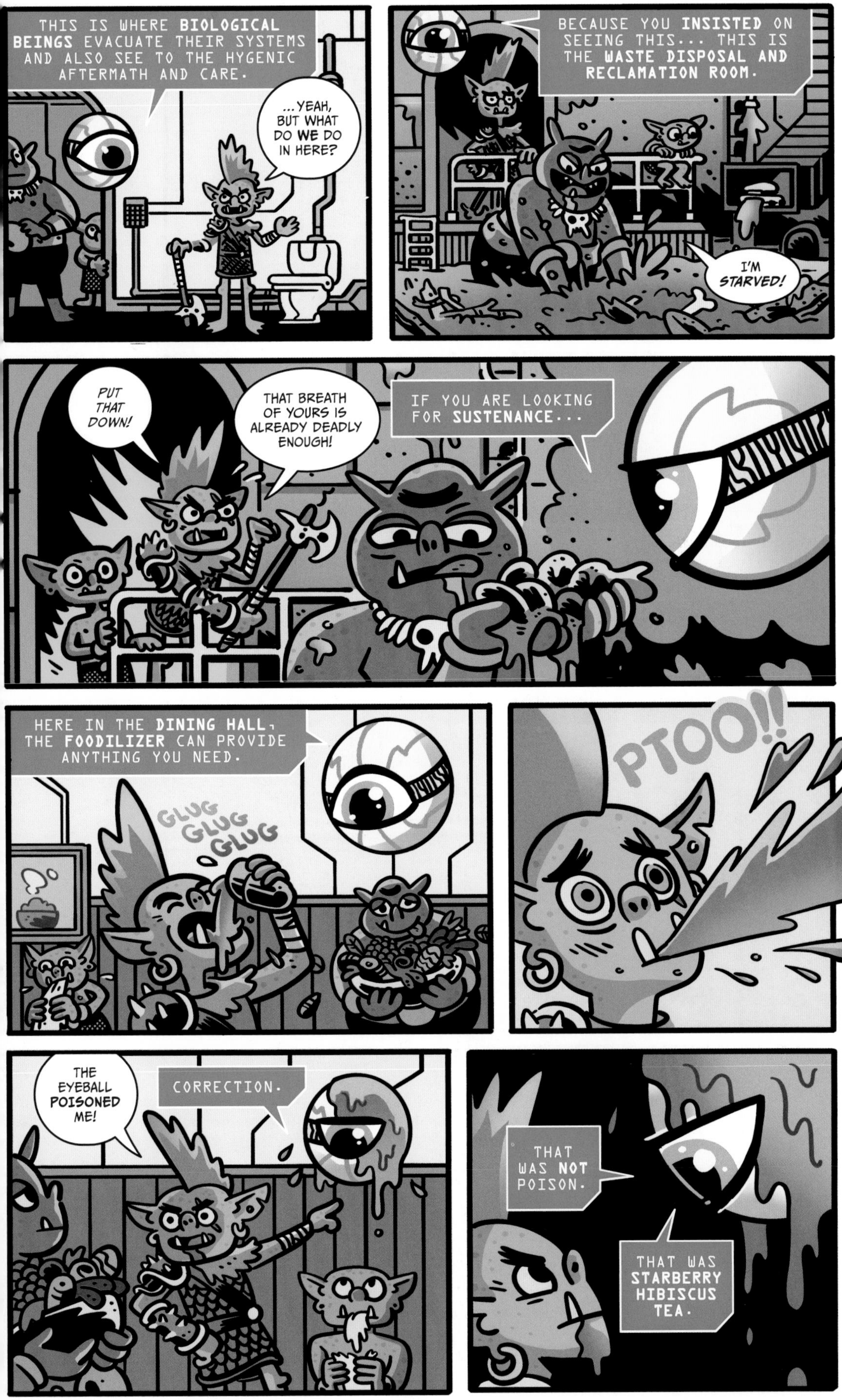

THIS IS WHERE BIOLOGICAL BEINGS EVACUATE THEIR SYSTEMS AND ALSO SEE TO THE HYGENIC AFTERMATH AND CARE.
...YEAH, BUT WHAT DO WE DO IN HERE?
BECAUSE YOU INSISTED ON SEEING THIS... THIS IS THE WASTE DISPOSAL AND RECLAMATION ROOM.
I'M STARVED!
PUT THAT DOWN!
THAT BREATH OF YOURS IS ALREADY DEADLY ENOUGH!
IF YOU ARE LOOKING FOR SUSTENANCE...
HERE IN THE DINING HALL, THE FOODILIZER CAN PROVIDE ANYTHING YOU NEED.
GLUG GLUG GLUG
PTOO!!
THE EYEBALL POISONED ME!
CORRECTION.
THAT WAS NOT POISON.
THAT WAS STARBERRY HIBISCUS TEA.

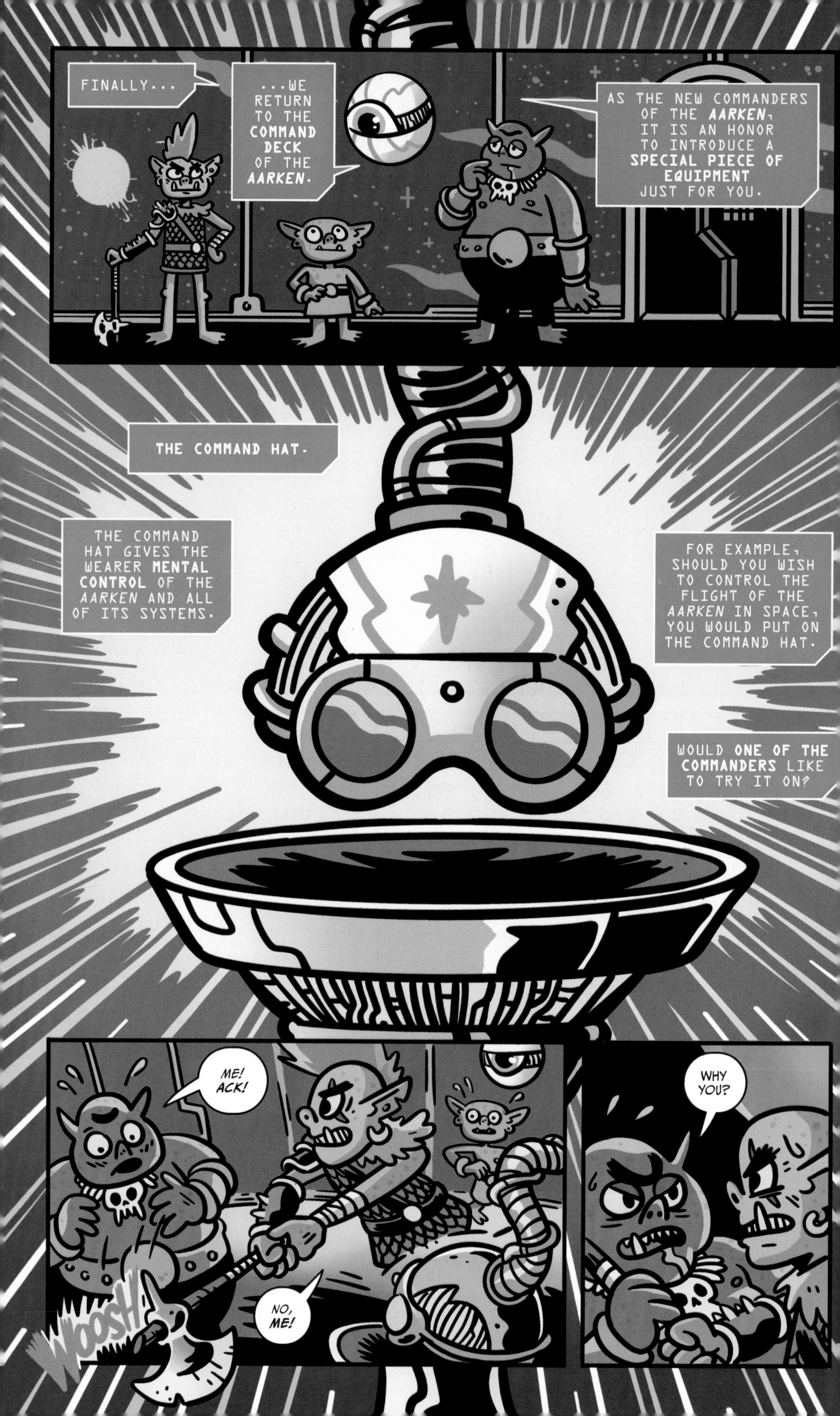
FINALLY...
...WE RETURN TO THE **COMMAND DECK** OF THE *AARKEN*.
AS THE NEW COMMANDERS OF THE ***AARKEN***, IT IS AN HONOR TO INTRODUCE A **SPECIAL PIECE OF EQUIPMENT** JUST FOR YOU.
THE COMMAND HAT.
THE COMMAND HAT GIVES THE WEARER **MENTAL CONTROL** OF THE *AARKEN* AND ALL OF ITS SYSTEMS.
FOR EXAMPLE, SHOULD YOU WISH TO CONTROL THE FLIGHT OF THE *AARKEN* IN SPACE, YOU WOULD PUT ON THE COMMAND HAT.
WOULD **ONE OF THE COMMANDERS** LIKE TO TRY IT ON?
ME! ACK!
NO, ME!
WOOSH!
WHY YOU?

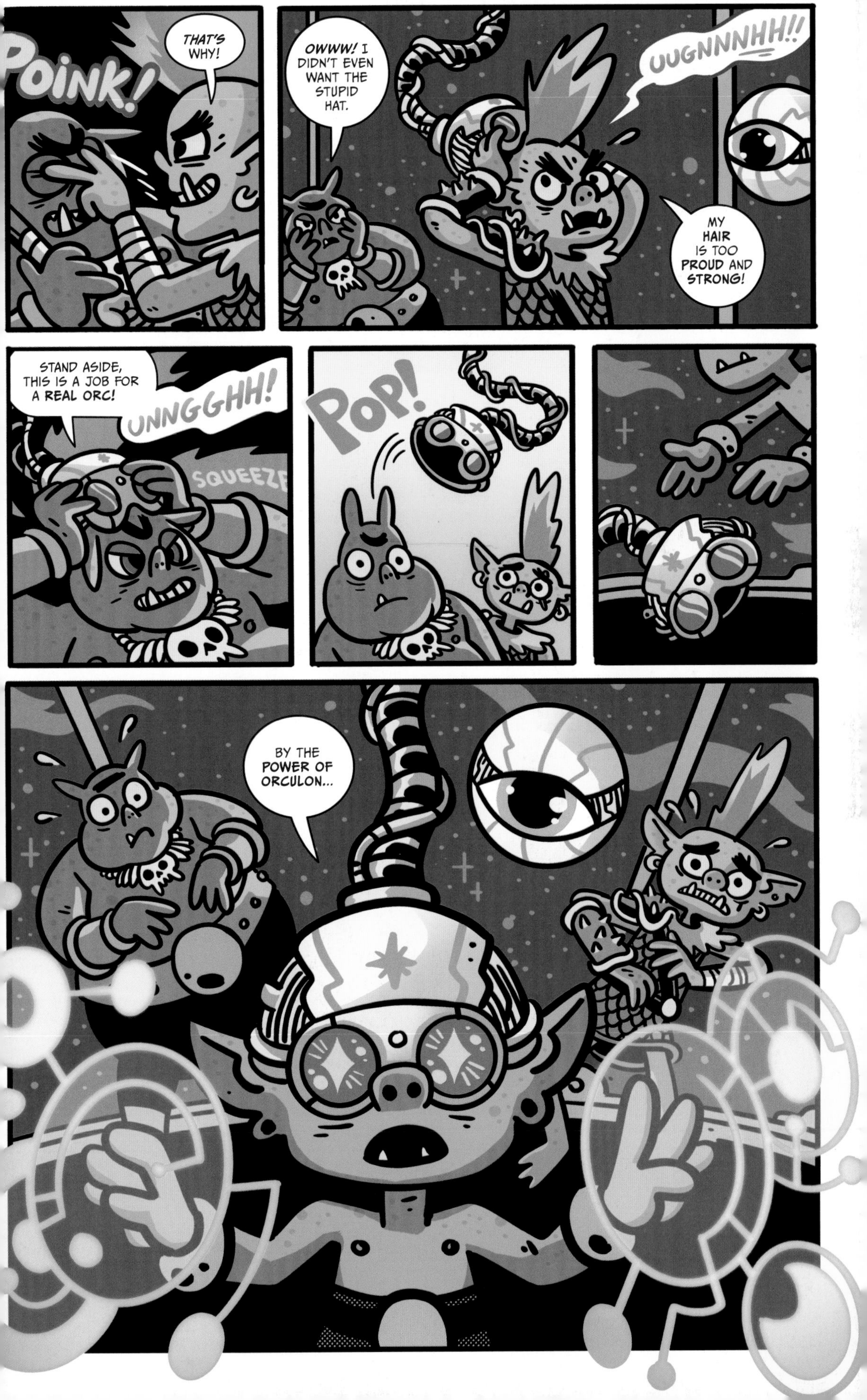
POINK!
THAT'S WHY!
OWWW! I DIDN'T EVEN WANT THE STUPID HAT.
UUGNNNHH!!
MY HAIR IS TOO PROUD AND STRONG!
STAND ASIDE, THIS IS A JOB FOR A REAL ORC!
UNNGGHH!
SQUEEZE
POP!
BY THE POWER OF ORCULON...

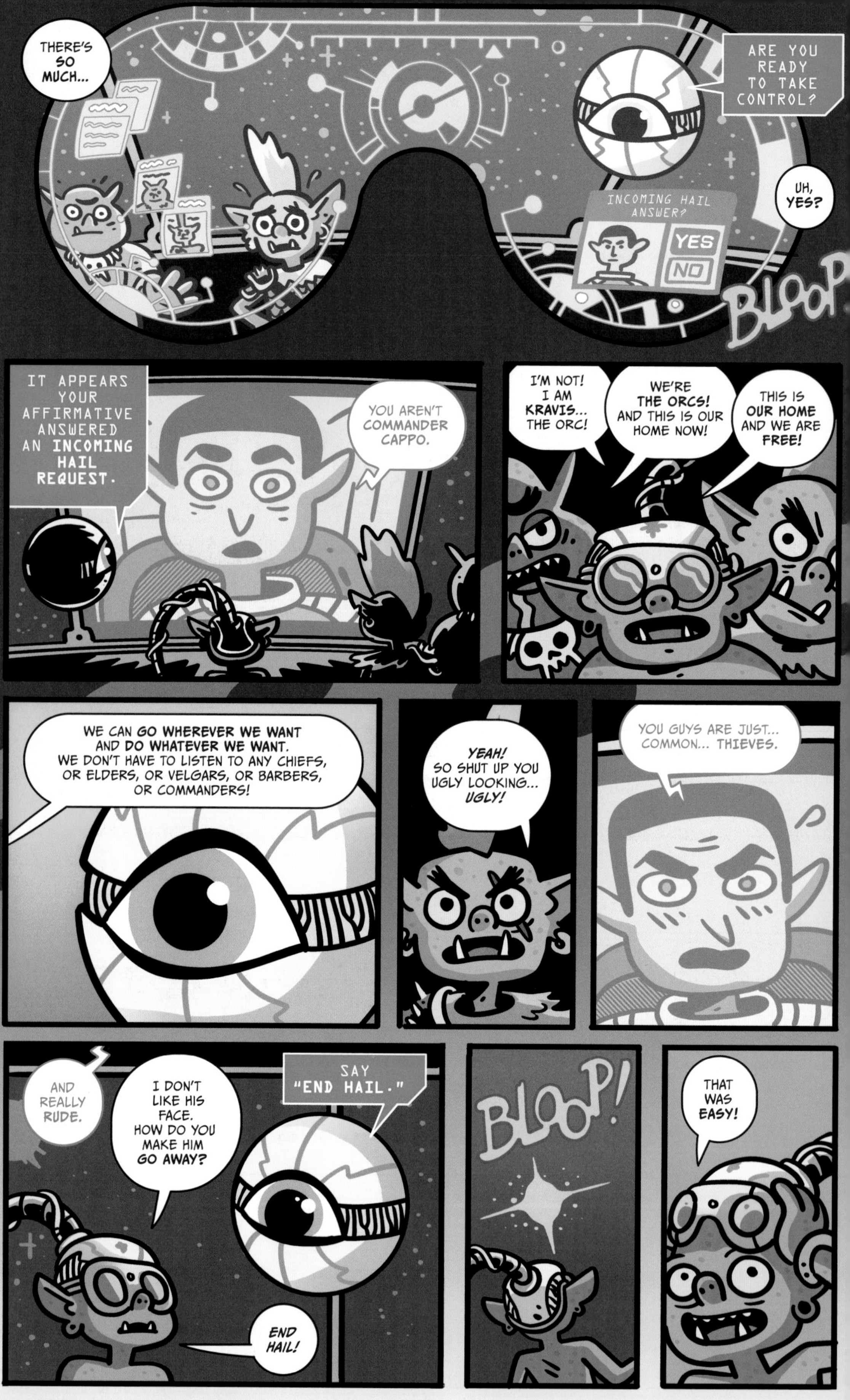
THERE'S SO MUCH...
ARE YOU READY TO TAKE CONTROL?
INCOMING HAIL ANSWER?
YES
NO
UH, YES?
BLOOP!
IT APPEARS YOUR AFFIRMATIVE ANSWERED AN INCOMING HAIL REQUEST.
YOU AREN'T COMMANDER CAPPO.
I'M NOT! I AM KRAVIS... THE ORC!
WE'RE THE ORCS! AND THIS IS OUR HOME NOW!
THIS IS OUR HOME AND WE ARE FREE!
WE CAN GO WHEREVER WE WANT AND DO WHATEVER WE WANT. WE DON'T HAVE TO LISTEN TO ANY CHIEFS, OR ELDERS, OR VELGARS, OR BARBERS, OR COMMANDERS!
YEAH! SO SHUT UP YOU UGLY LOOKING... UGLY!
YOU GUYS ARE JUST... COMMON... THIEVES.
AND REALLY RUDE.
I DON'T LIKE HIS FACE. HOW DO YOU MAKE HIM GO AWAY?
SAY "END HAIL."
END HAIL!
BLOOP!
THAT WAS EASY!

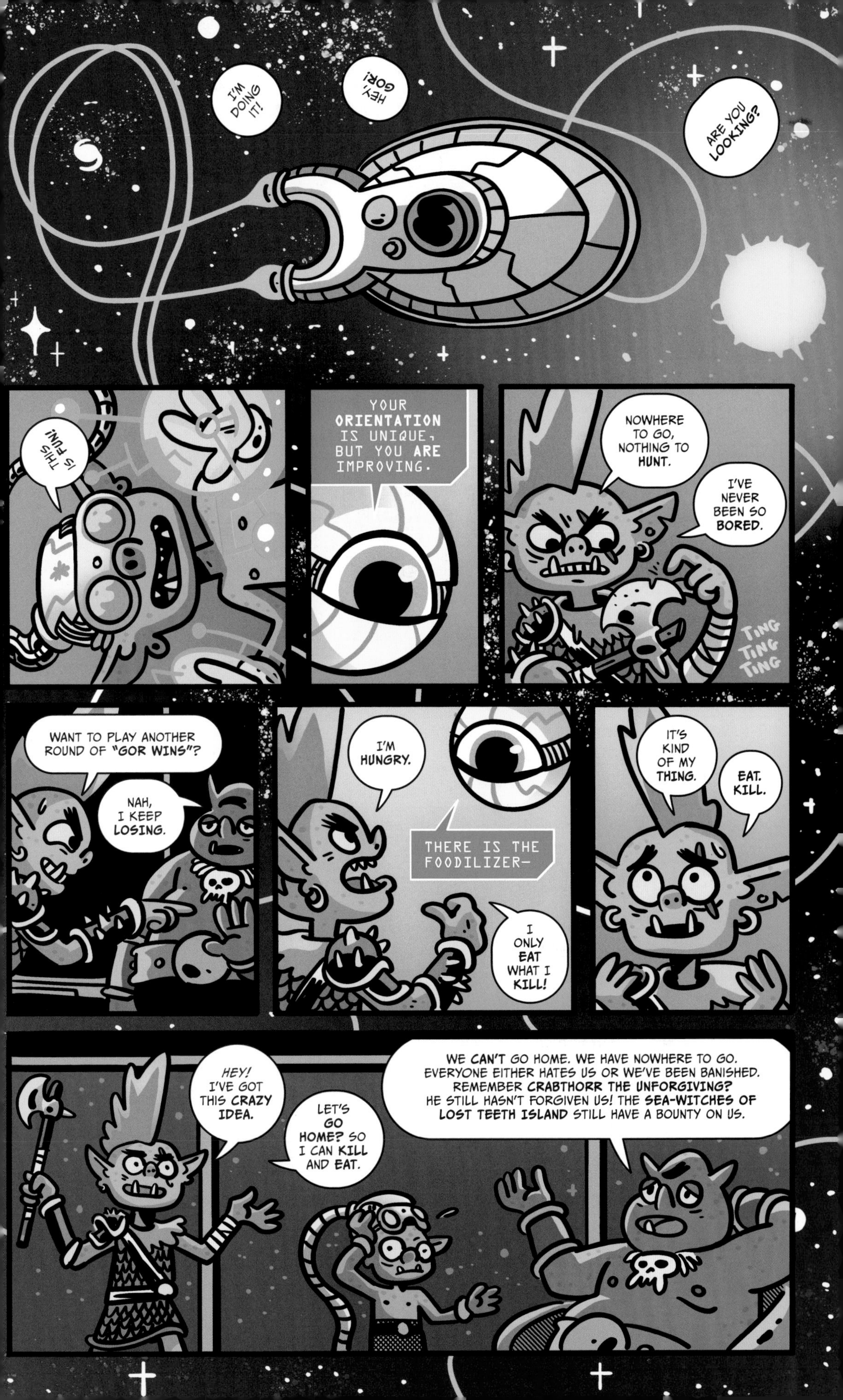
I'M DOING IT!
HEY, GOR!
ARE YOU LOOKING?
THIS IS FUN!
YOUR **ORIENTATION** IS UNIQUE, BUT YOU **ARE** IMPROVING.
NOWHERE TO GO, NOTHING TO **HUNT**.
I'VE NEVER BEEN SO **BORED**.
TING TING TING
WANT TO PLAY ANOTHER ROUND OF **"GOR WINS"**?
NAH, I KEEP **LOSING**.
I'M **HUNGRY**.
THERE IS THE FOODILIZER—
I ONLY **EAT** WHAT I **KILL**!
IT'S KIND OF MY **THING**.
EAT. KILL.
HEY! I'VE GOT THIS **CRAZY IDEA**.
LET'S **GO HOME?** SO I CAN **KILL** AND **EAT**.
WE **CAN'T** GO HOME. WE HAVE NOWHERE TO GO. EVERYONE EITHER HATES US OR WE'VE BEEN BANISHED. REMEMBER **CRABTHORR THE UNFORGIVING?** HE STILL HASN'T FORGIVEN US! THE **SEA-WITCHES OF LOST TEETH ISLAND** STILL HAVE A BOUNTY ON US.

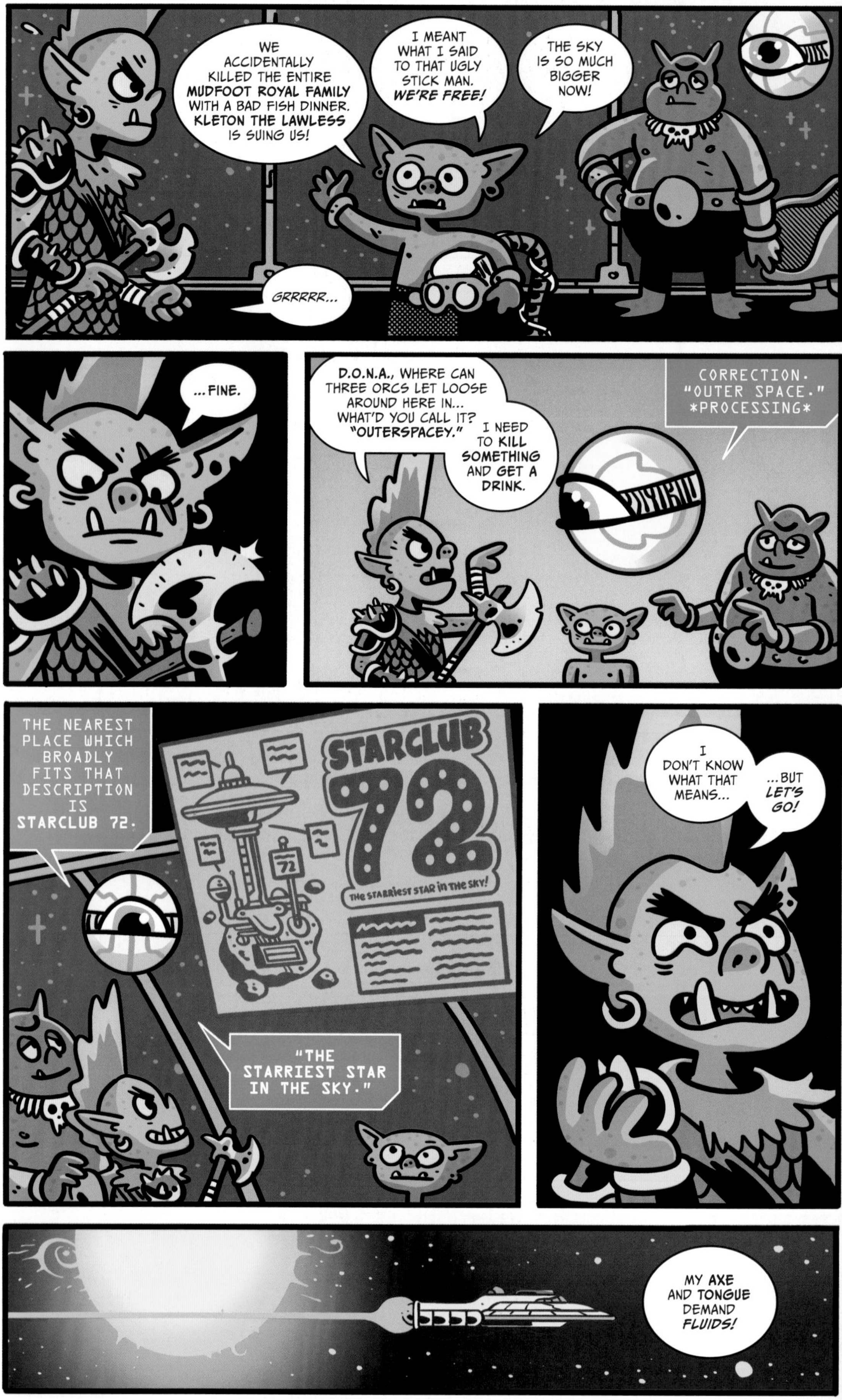
WE ACCIDENTALLY KILLED THE ENTIRE MUDFOOT ROYAL FAMILY WITH A BAD FISH DINNER. KLETON THE LAWLESS IS SUING US!
I MEANT WHAT I SAID TO THAT UGLY STICK MAN. WE'RE FREE!
THE SKY IS SO MUCH BIGGER NOW!
GRRRRR...
...FINE.
D.O.N.A., WHERE CAN THREE ORCS LET LOOSE AROUND HERE IN... WHAT'D YOU CALL IT? "OUTERSPACEY."
I NEED TO KILL SOMETHING AND GET A DRINK.
CORRECTION. "OUTER SPACE." *PROCESSING*
THE NEAREST PLACE WHICH BROADLY FITS THAT DESCRIPTION IS STARCLUB 72.
STARCLUB 72
THE STARRIEST STAR IN THE SKY!
"THE STARRIEST STAR IN THE SKY."
I DON'T KNOW WHAT THAT MEANS...
...BUT LET'S GO!
MY AXE AND TONGUE DEMAND FLUIDS!

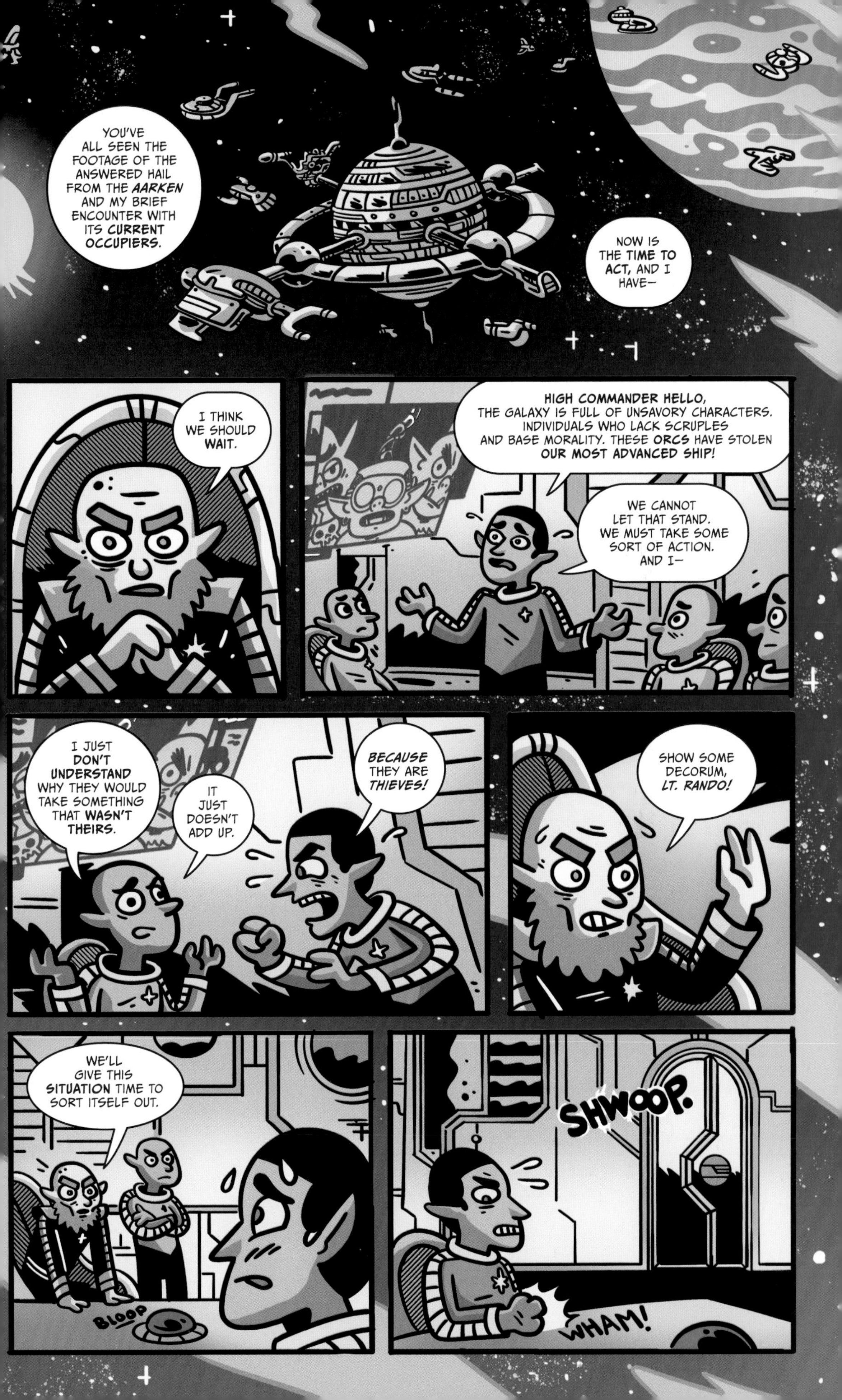

YOU'VE ALL SEEN THE FOOTAGE OF THE ANSWERED HAIL FROM THE AARKEN AND MY BRIEF ENCOUNTER WITH ITS CURRENT OCCUPIERS.
NOW IS THE TIME TO ACT, AND I HAVE—
I THINK WE SHOULD WAIT.
HIGH COMMANDER HELLO, THE GALAXY IS FULL OF UNSAVORY CHARACTERS. INDIVIDUALS WHO LACK SCRUPLES AND BASE MORALITY. THESE ORCS HAVE STOLEN OUR MOST ADVANCED SHIP!
WE CANNOT LET THAT STAND. WE MUST TAKE SOME SORT OF ACTION. AND I—
I JUST DON'T UNDERSTAND WHY THEY WOULD TAKE SOMETHING THAT WASN'T THEIRS.
IT JUST DOESN'T ADD UP.
BECAUSE THEY ARE THIEVES!
SHOW SOME DECORUM, LT. RANDO!
WE'LL GIVE THIS SITUATION TIME TO SORT ITSELF OUT.
BLOOP
SHWOOP.
WHAM!

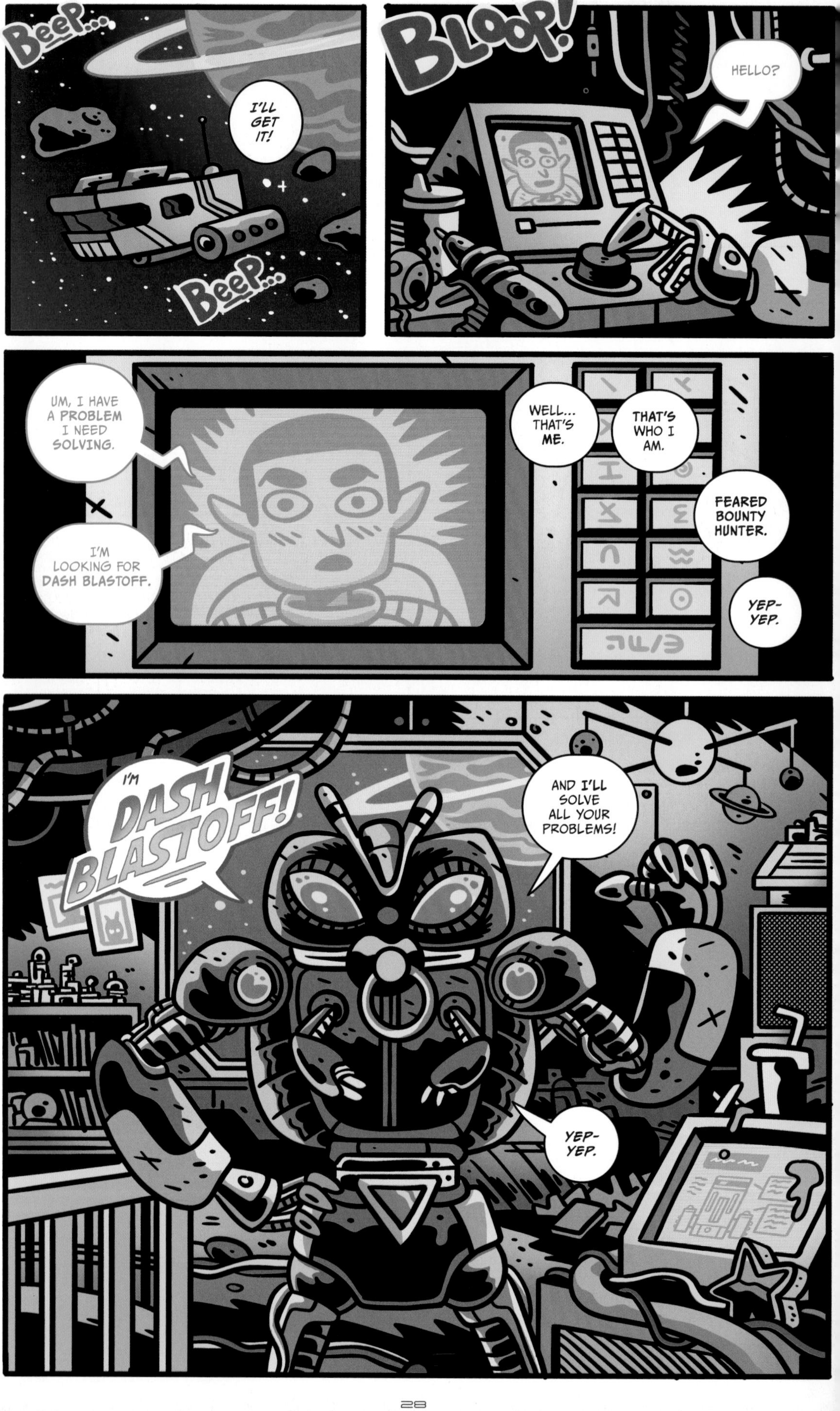
BEEP...
I'LL GET IT!
BEEP...
BLOOP!
HELLO?
UM, I HAVE A PROBLEM I NEED SOLVING.
I'M LOOKING FOR DASH BLASTOFF.
WELL... THAT'S ME.
THAT'S WHO I AM.
FEARED BOUNTY HUNTER.
YEP-YEP.
I'M DASH BLASTOFF!
AND I'LL SOLVE ALL YOUR PROBLEMS!
YEP-YEP.

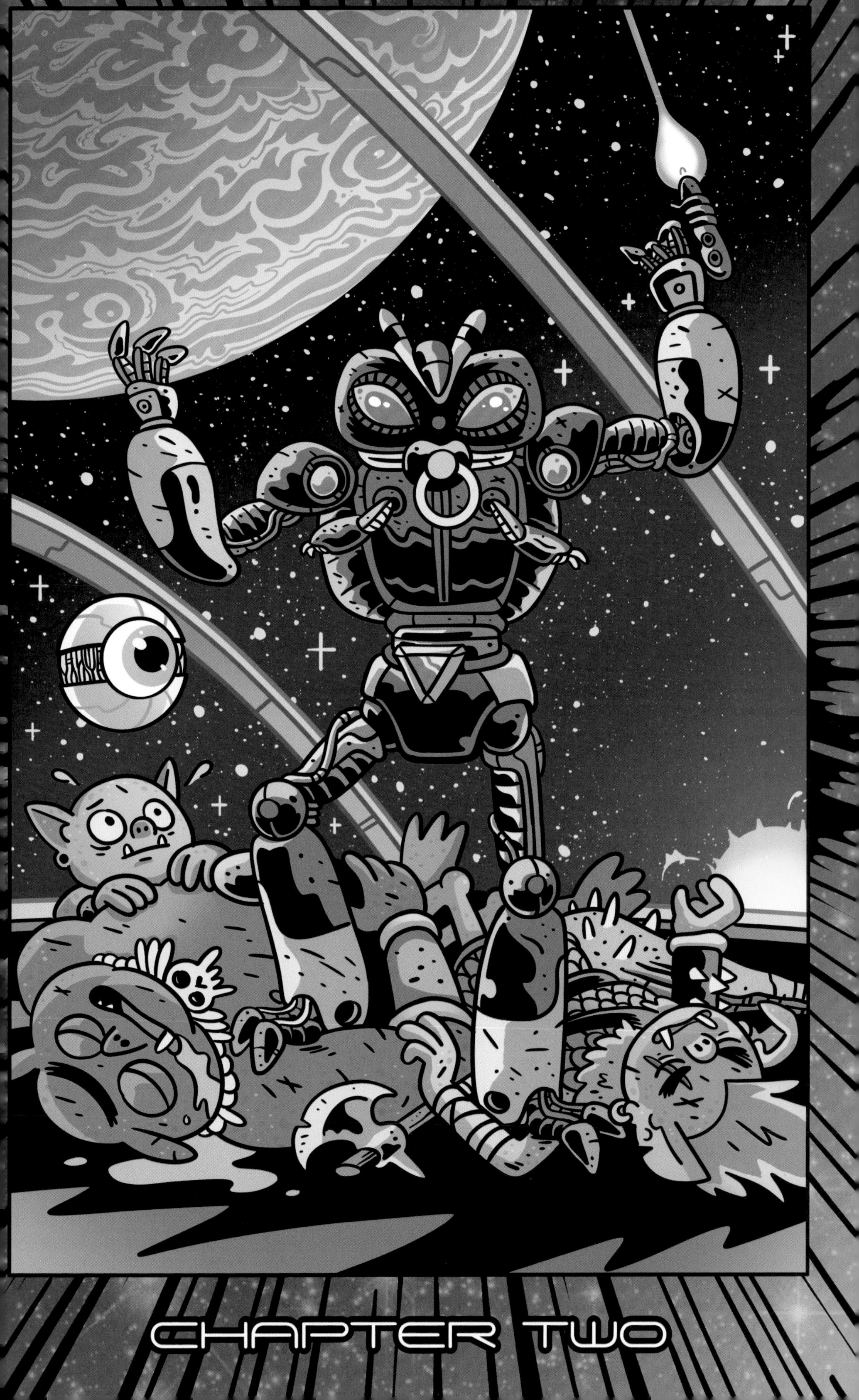

CHAPTER TWO

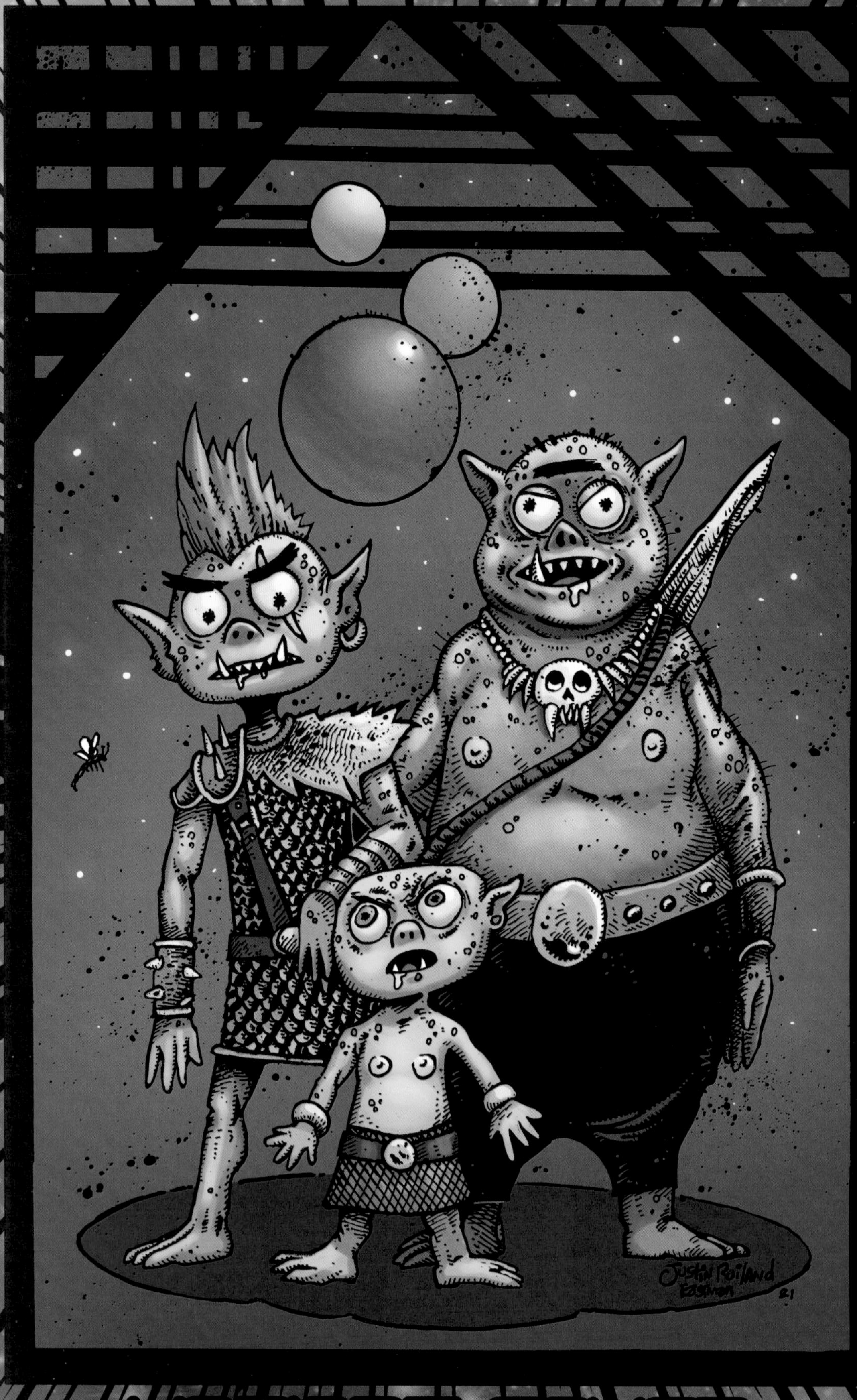
Justin Roiland
Eastman
21

VARIANT COVER

BY JUSTIN ROILAND & KEVIN EASTMAN

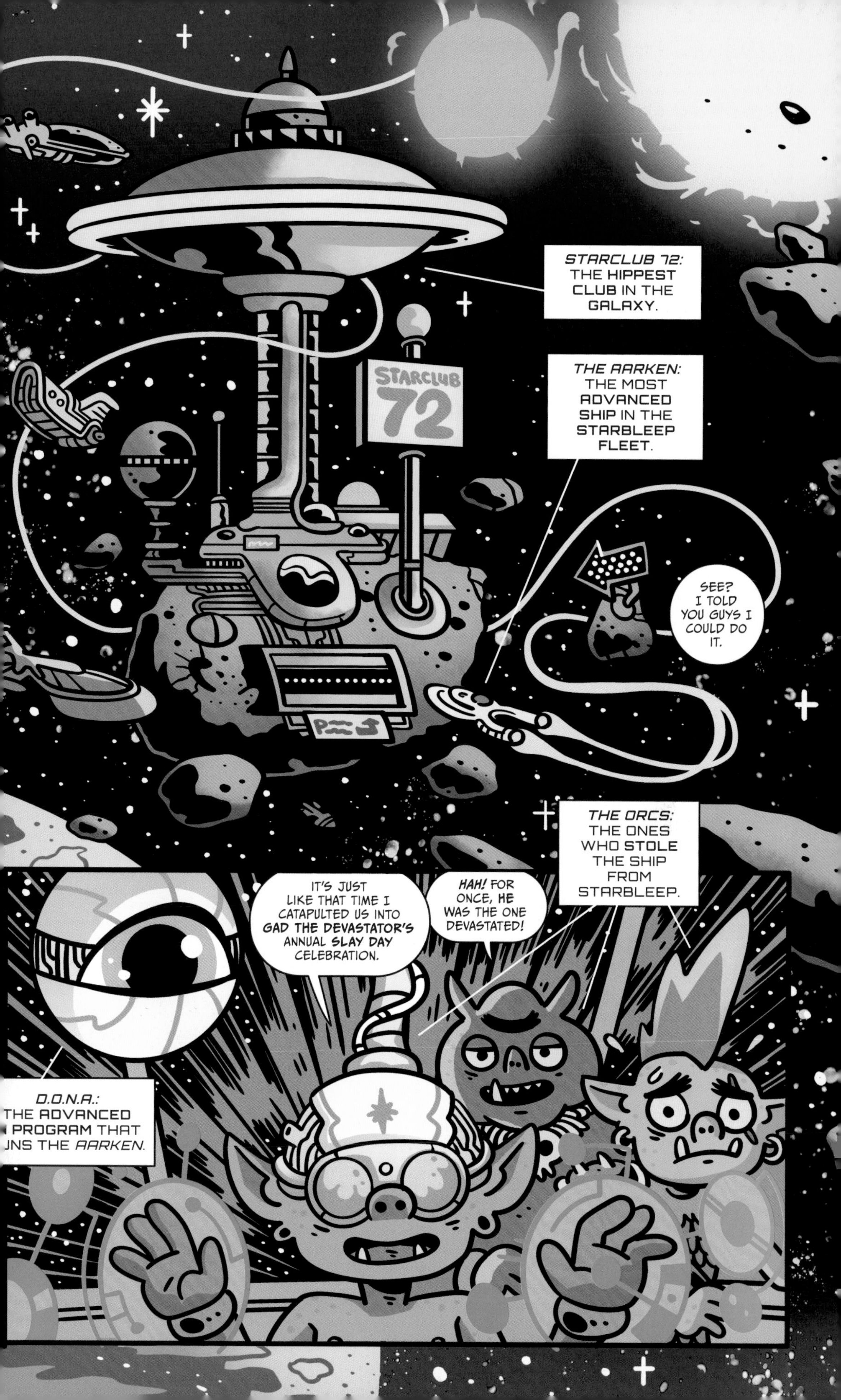

STARCLUB 72: THE **HIPPEST CLUB** IN THE GALAXY.
STARCLUB 72
THE AARKEN: THE MOST **ADVANCED SHIP** IN THE **STARBLEEP FLEET**.
SEE? I TOLD YOU GUYS I COULD DO IT.
THE ORCS: THE ONES WHO **STOLE** THE SHIP FROM STARBLEEP.
IT'S JUST LIKE THAT TIME I CATAPULTED US INTO **GAD THE DEVASTATOR'S** ANNUAL **SLAY DAY** CELEBRATION.
HAH! FOR ONCE, **HE** WAS THE ONE DEVASTATED!
D.O.N.A.: THE **ADVANCED** **PROGRAM** THAT
NS THE *AARKEN*.

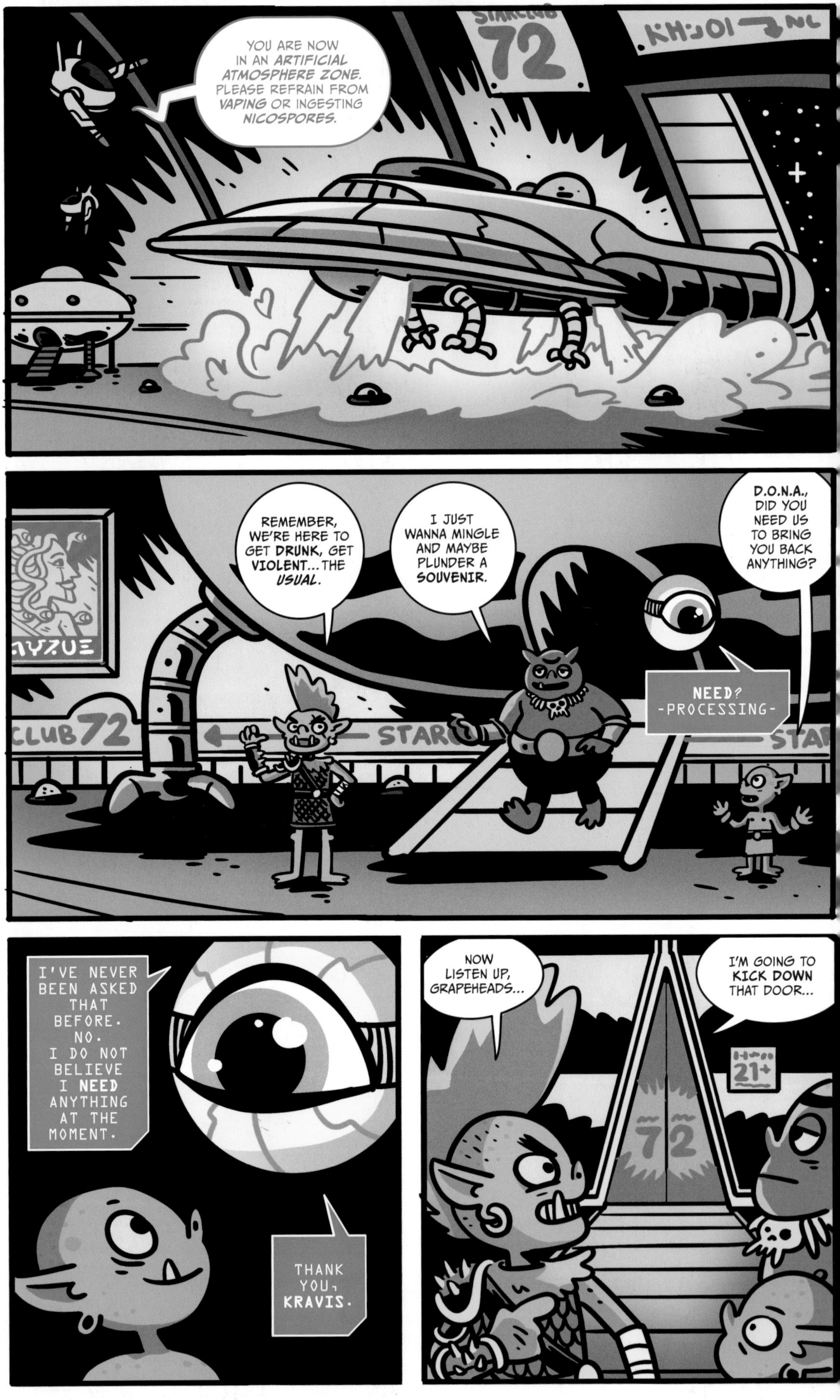
STARCLUB
72
YOU ARE NOW IN AN *ARTIFICIAL ATMOSPHERE ZONE.* PLEASE REFRAIN FROM *VAPING* OR INGESTING *NICOSPORES.*
REMEMBER, WE'RE HERE TO GET **DRUNK**, GET **VIOLENT**... THE *USUAL*.
I JUST WANNA MINGLE AND MAYBE PLUNDER A **SOUVENIR**.
D.O.N.A., DID YOU NEED US TO BRING YOU BACK ANYTHING?
NEED? -PROCESSING-
CLUB 72
STAR
I'VE NEVER BEEN ASKED THAT BEFORE. NO. I DO NOT BELIEVE I **NEED** ANYTHING AT THE MOMENT.
THANK YOU, **KRAVIS**.
NOW LISTEN UP, GRAPEHEADS...
I'M GOING TO **KICK DOWN** THAT DOOR...
21+
72

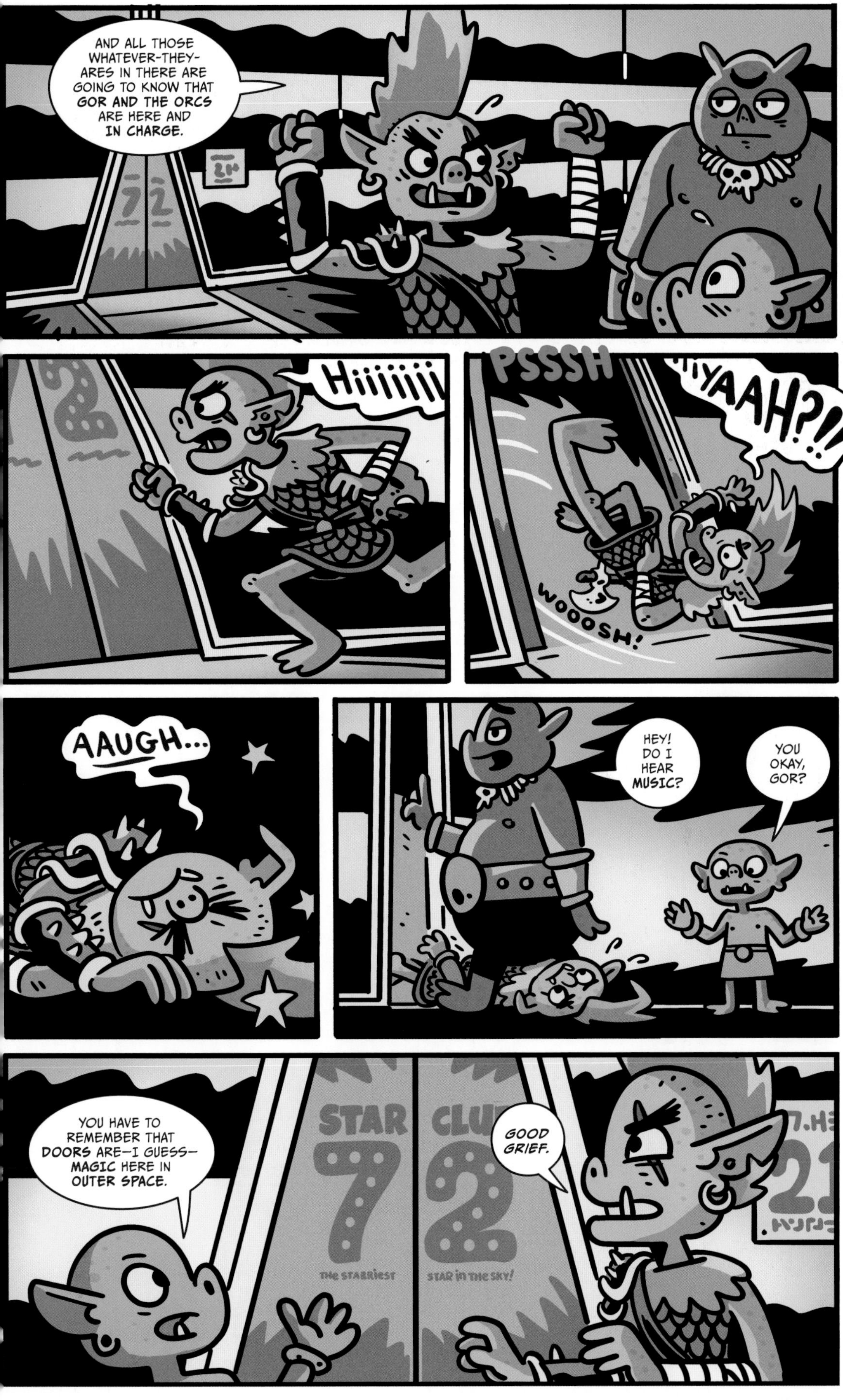

AND ALL THOSE WHATEVER-THEY-ARES IN THERE ARE GOING TO KNOW THAT GOR AND THE ORCS ARE HERE AND IN CHARGE.
Hiiiiiii
PSSSH
YAAH?!!
WOOOSH!
AAUGH...
HEY! DO I HEAR MUSIC?
YOU OKAY, GOR?
YOU HAVE TO REMEMBER THAT DOORS ARE—I GUESS—MAGIC HERE IN OUTER SPACE.
STAR
7
THE STARRIEST
CLU
2
STAR IN THE SKY!
GOOD GRIEF.

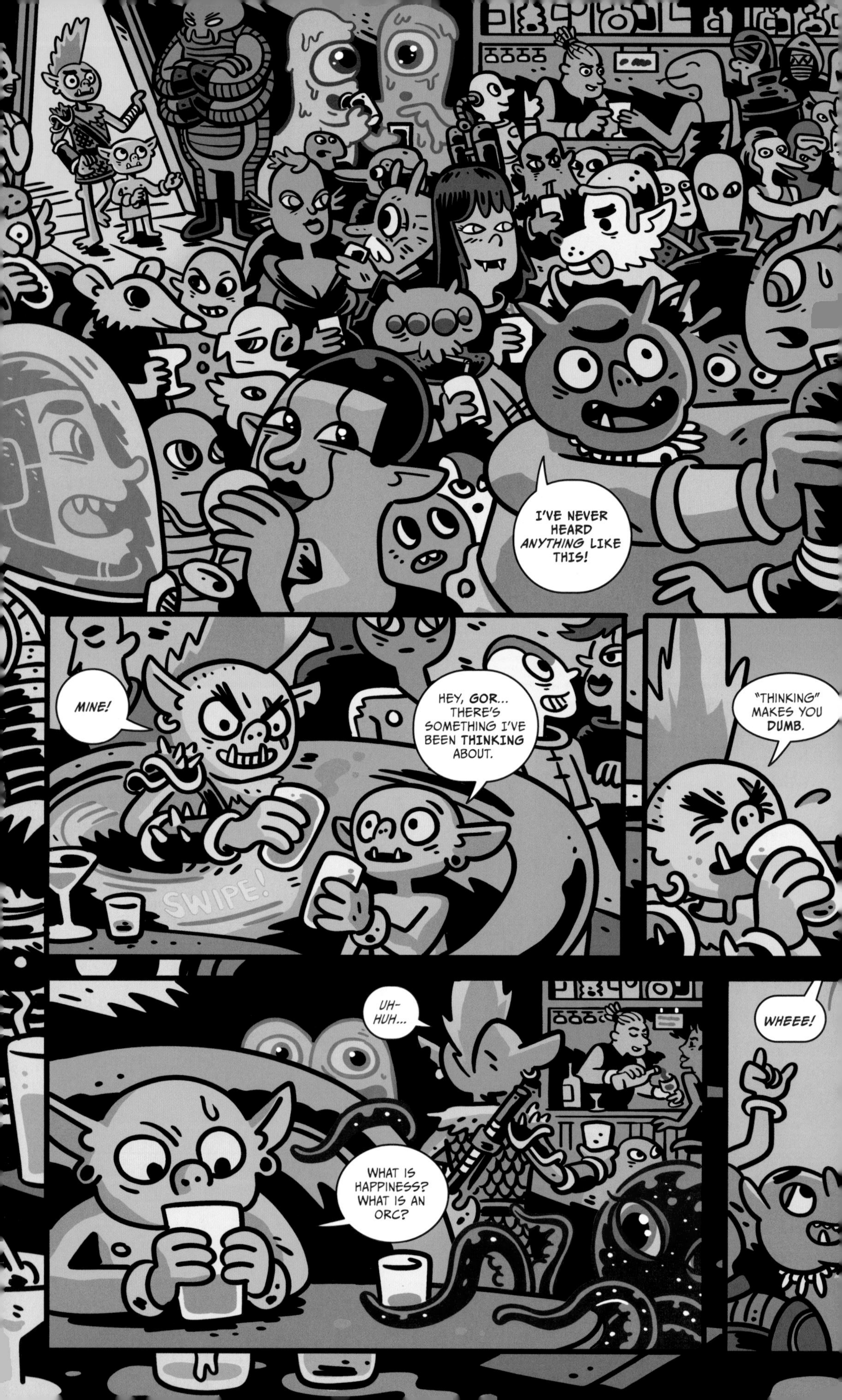
I'VE NEVER HEARD ANYTHING LIKE THIS!
MINE!
SWIPE!
HEY, GOR... THERE'S SOMETHING I'VE BEEN THINKING ABOUT.
"THINKING" MAKES YOU DUMB.
UH-HUH...
WHAT IS HAPPINESS? WHAT IS AN ORC?
WHEEE!

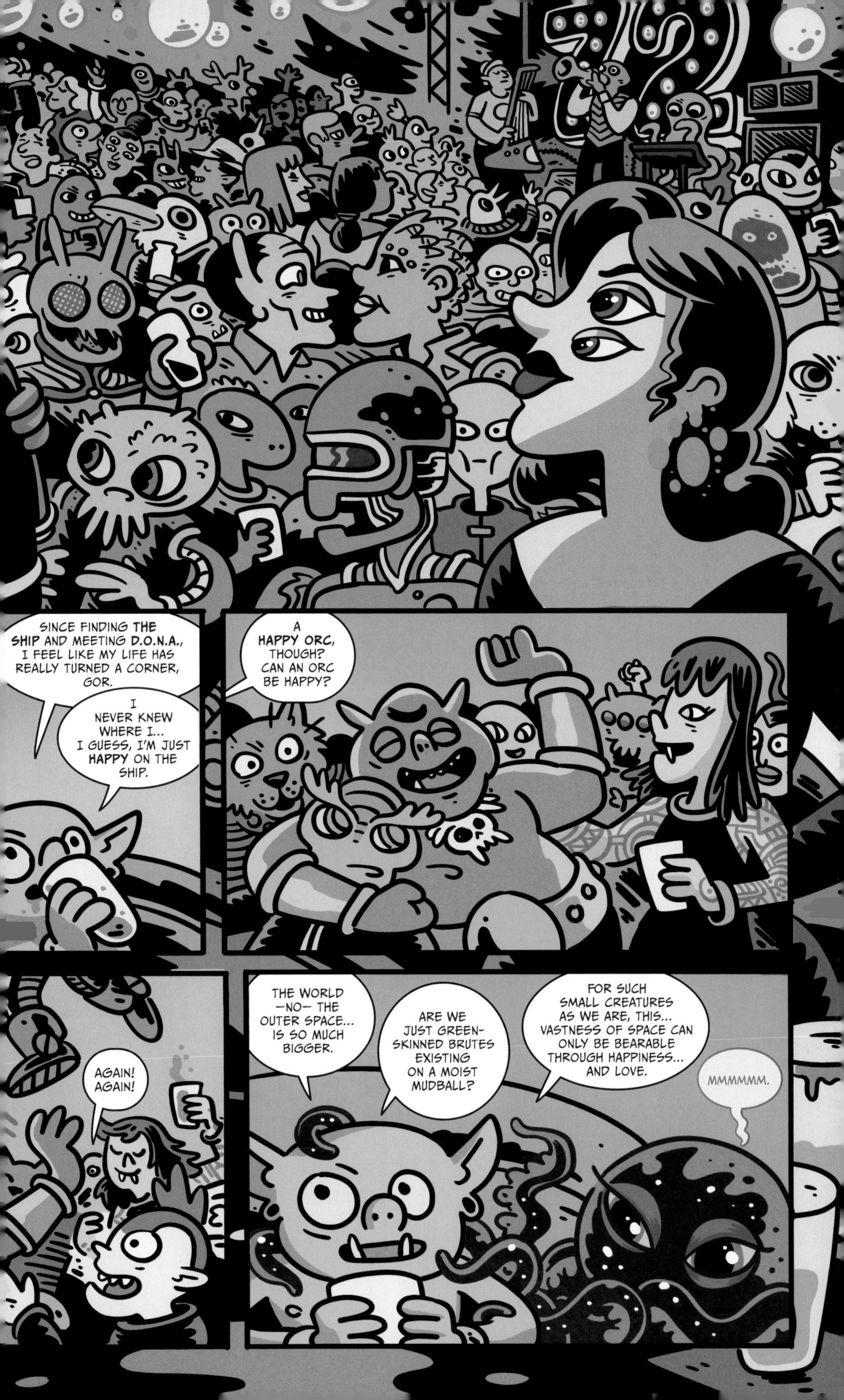
SINCE FINDING THE SHIP AND MEETING D.O.N.A., I FEEL LIKE MY LIFE HAS REALLY TURNED A CORNER, GOR.
I NEVER KNEW WHERE I... I GUESS, I'M JUST HAPPY ON THE SHIP.
A HAPPY ORC, THOUGH? CAN AN ORC BE HAPPY?
AGAIN! AGAIN!
THE WORLD —NO— THE OUTER SPACE... IS SO MUCH BIGGER.
ARE WE JUST GREEN-SKINNED BRUTES EXISTING ON A MOIST MUDBALL?
FOR SUCH SMALL CREATURES AS WE ARE, THIS... VASTNESS OF SPACE CAN ONLY BE BEARABLE THROUGH HAPPINESS... AND LOVE.
MMMMMM.

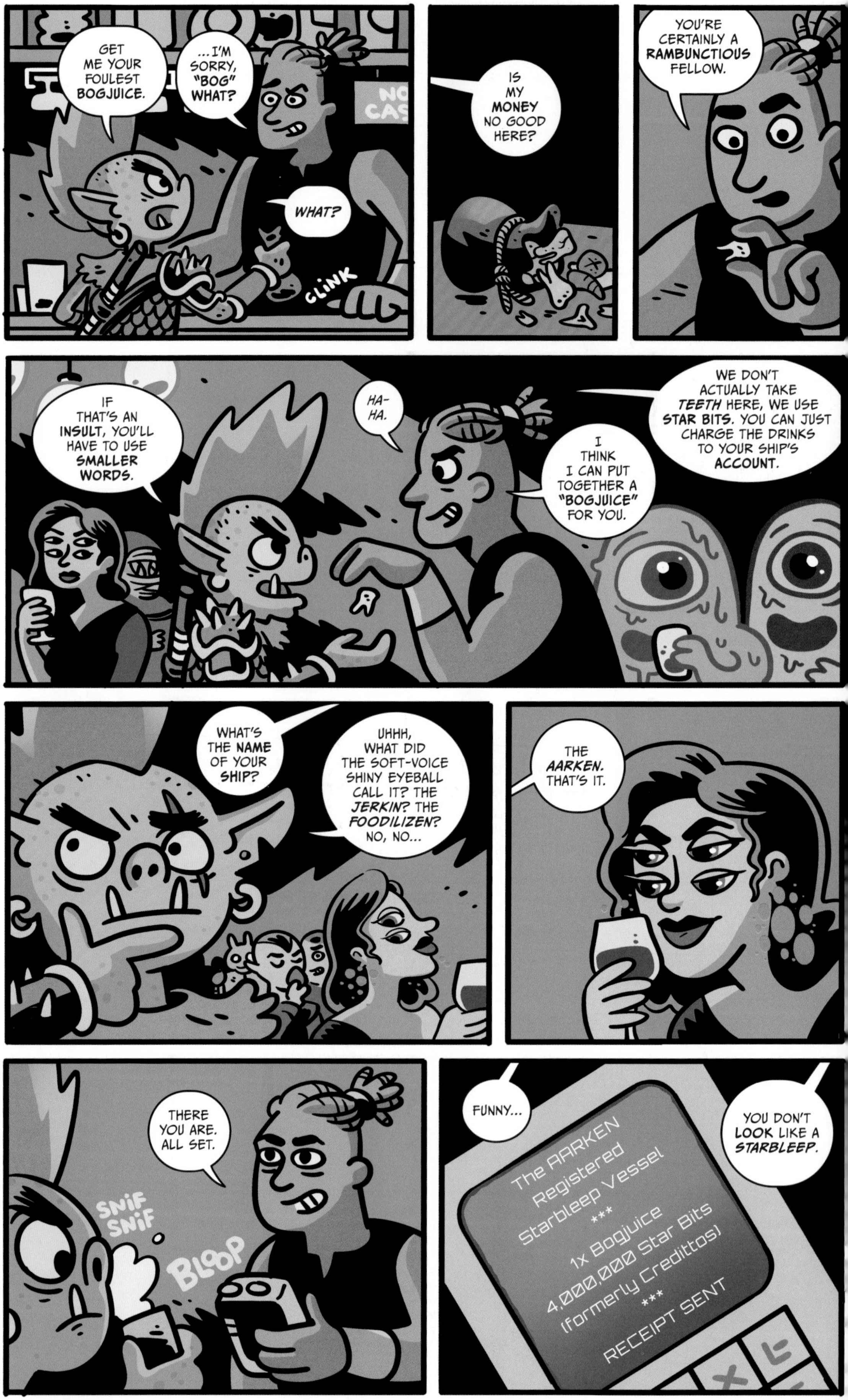
GET ME YOUR FOULEST BOGJUICE.
...I'M SORRY, "BOG" WHAT?
WHAT?
CLINK
IS MY MONEY NO GOOD HERE?
YOU'RE CERTAINLY A RAMBUNCTIOUS FELLOW.
IF THAT'S AN INSULT, YOU'LL HAVE TO USE SMALLER WORDS.
HA-HA.
WE DON'T ACTUALLY TAKE TEETH HERE, WE USE STAR BITS. YOU CAN JUST CHARGE THE DRINKS TO YOUR SHIP'S ACCOUNT.
I THINK I CAN PUT TOGETHER A "BOGJUICE" FOR YOU.
WHAT'S THE NAME OF YOUR SHIP?
UHHH, WHAT DID THE SOFT-VOICE SHINY EYEBALL CALL IT? THE JERKIN? THE FOODILIZEN? NO, NO...
THE AARKEN. THAT'S IT.
THERE YOU ARE. ALL SET.
SNIF SNIF
BLOOP
FUNNY...
YOU DON'T LOOK LIKE A STARBLEEP.
The AARKEN
Registered
Starbleep Vessel
***
1x Bogjuice
4,000,000 Star Bits
(formerly Credittos)
***
RECEIPT SENT

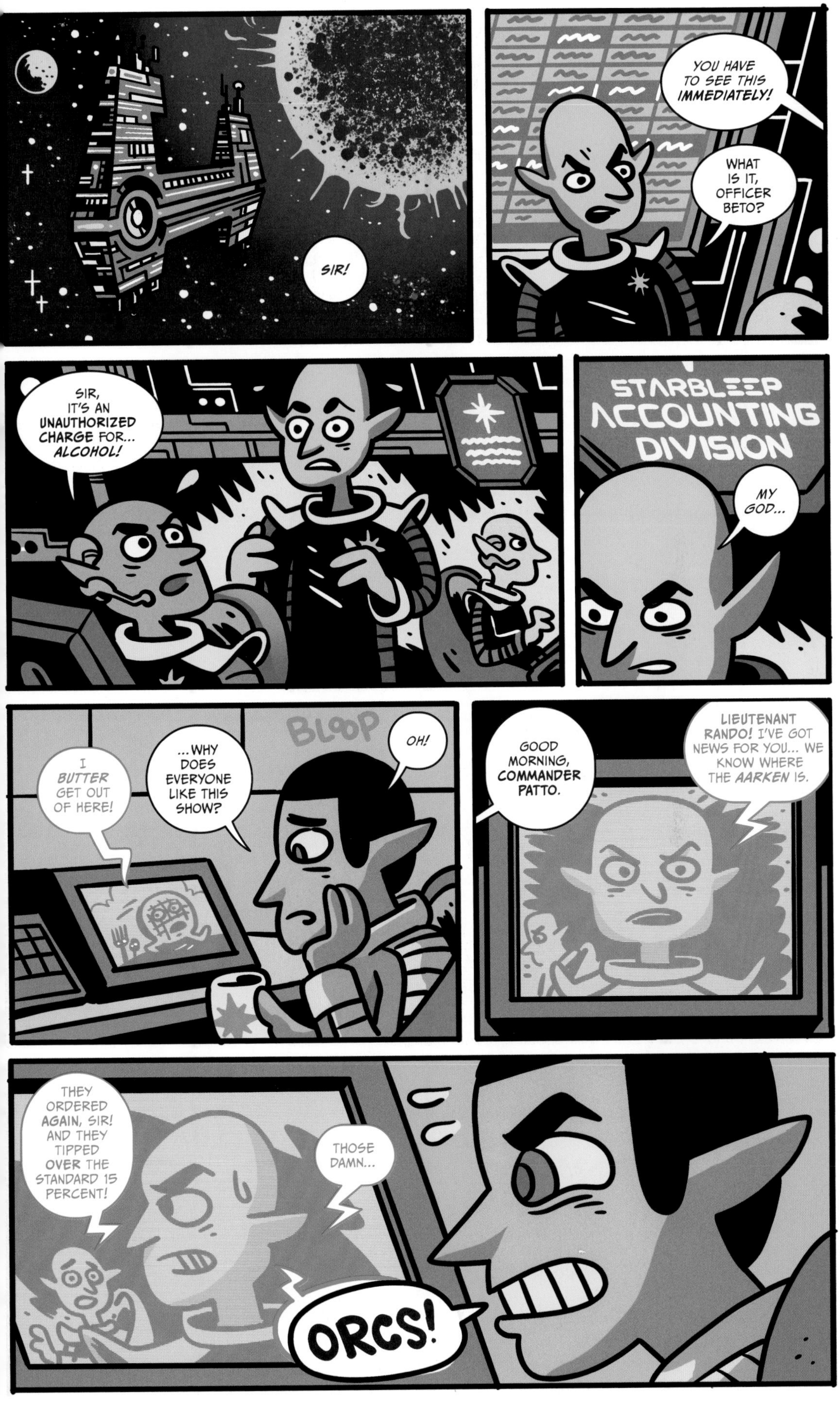
SIR!
YOU HAVE TO SEE THIS IMMEDIATELY!
WHAT IS IT, OFFICER BETO?
SIR, IT'S AN UNAUTHORIZED CHARGE FOR... ALCOHOL!
STARBLEEP ACCOUNTING DIVISION
MY GOD...
BLOOP
I BUTTER GET OUT OF HERE!
...WHY DOES EVERYONE LIKE THIS SHOW?
OH!
GOOD MORNING, COMMANDER PATTO.
LIEUTENANT RANDO! I'VE GOT NEWS FOR YOU... WE KNOW WHERE THE AARKEN IS.
THEY ORDERED AGAIN, SIR! AND THEY TIPPED OVER THE STANDARD 15 PERCENT!
THOSE DAMN...
ORCS!

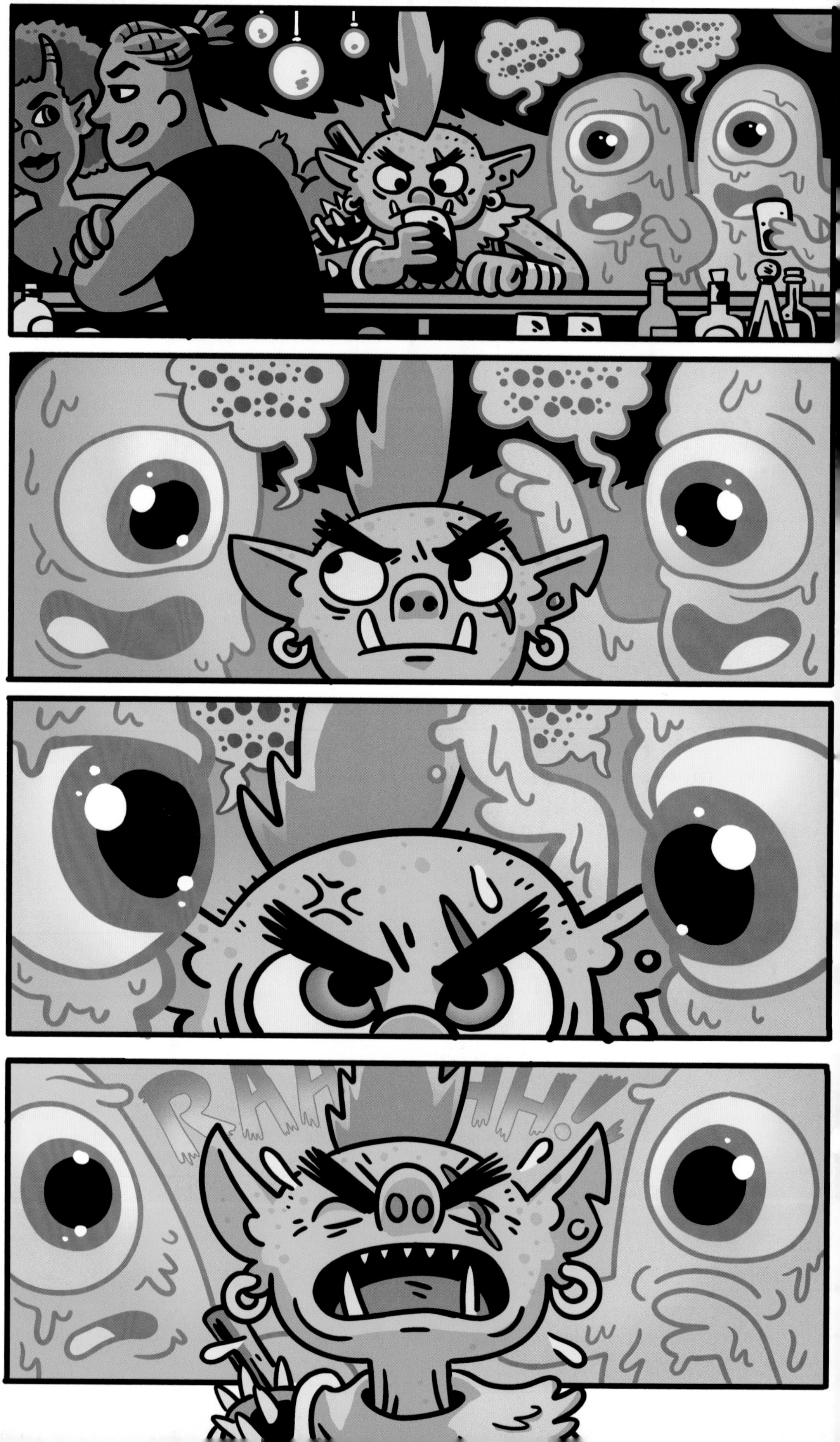
RAA HH!

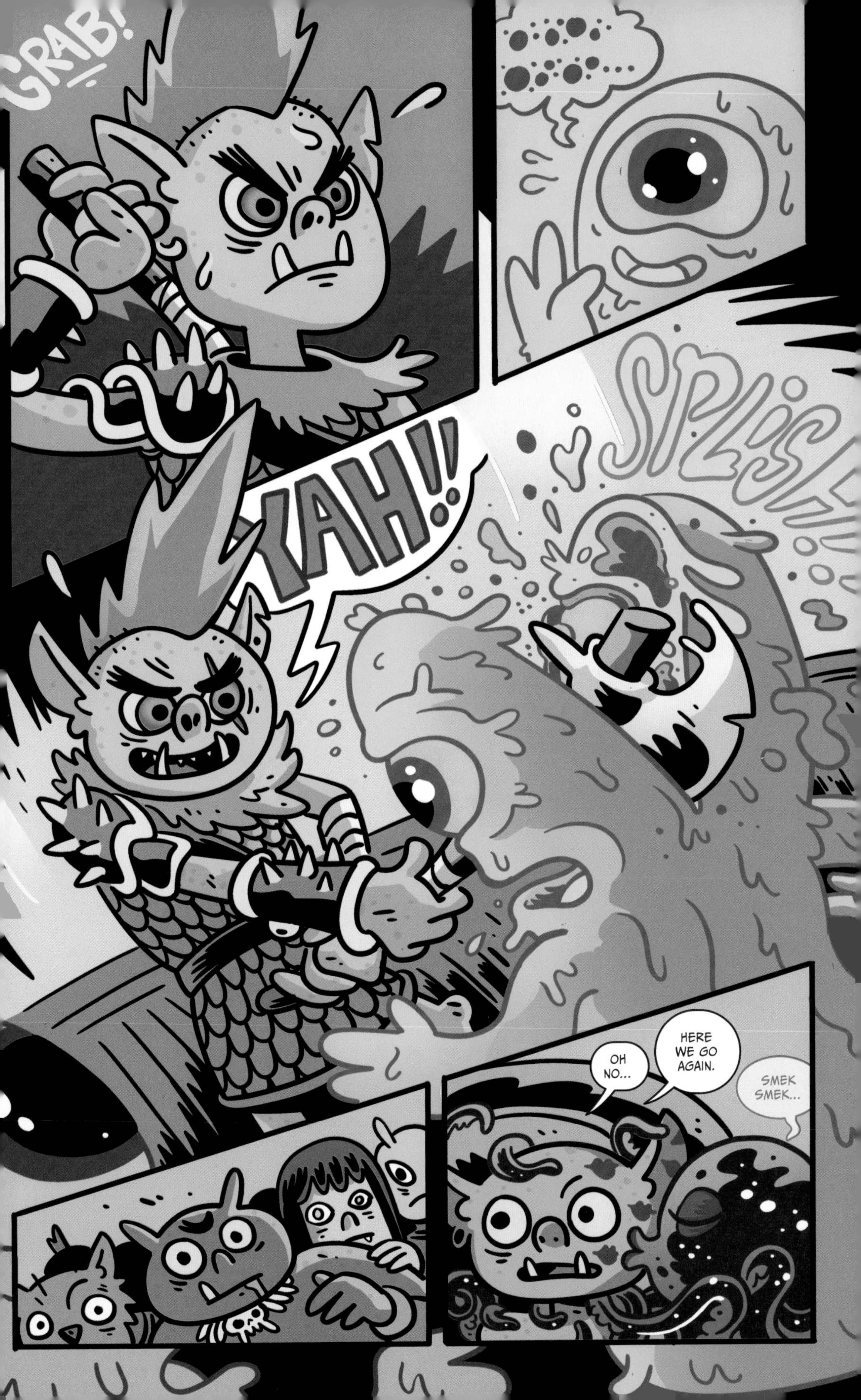
GRAB!
YAH!!
SPLISH
OH NO...
HERE WE GO AGAIN.
SMEK SMEK...

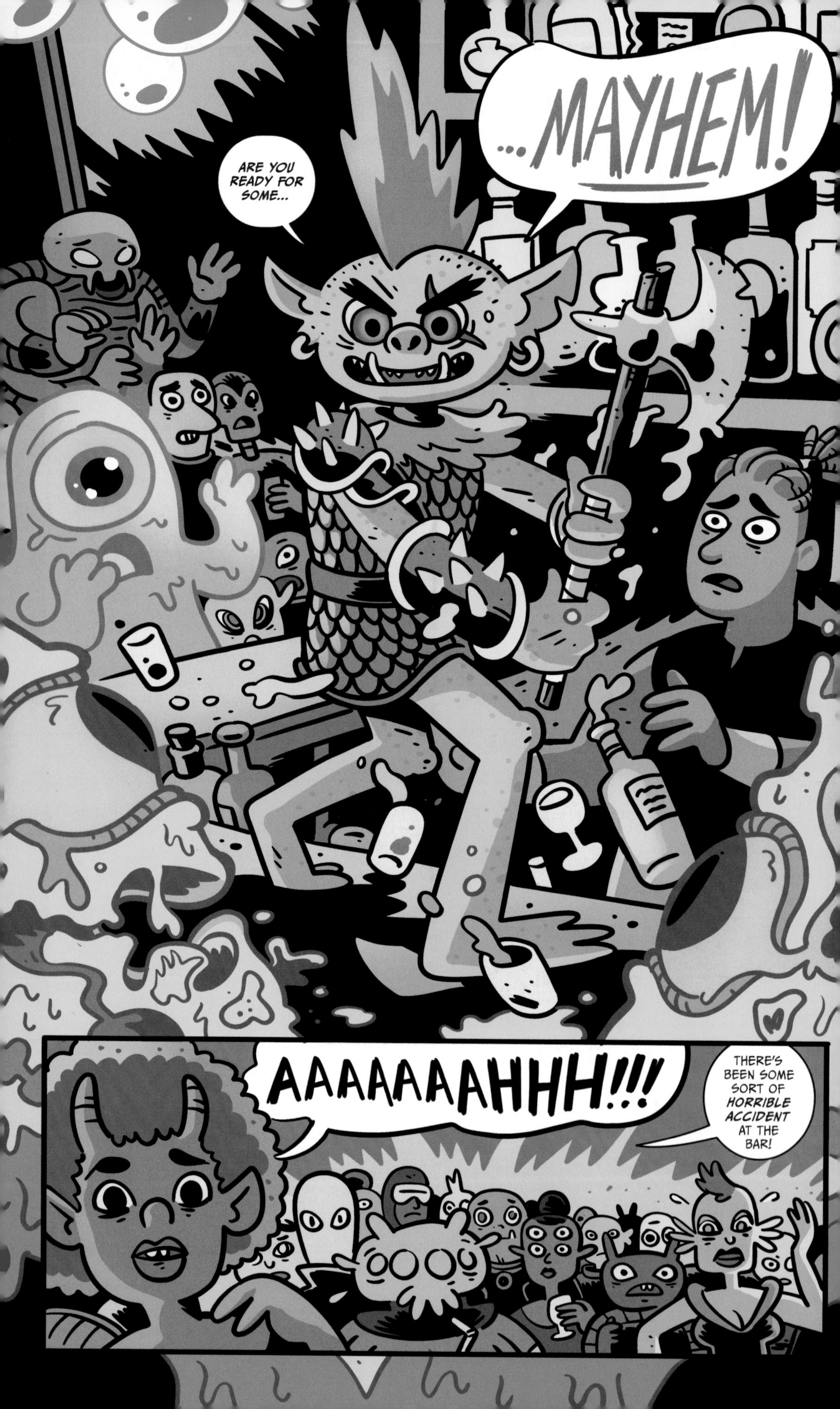

ARE YOU READY FOR SOME...
...MAYHEM!
AAAAAAAAHHHH!!!!
THERE'S BEEN SOME SORT OF *HORRIBLE ACCIDENT* AT THE BAR!

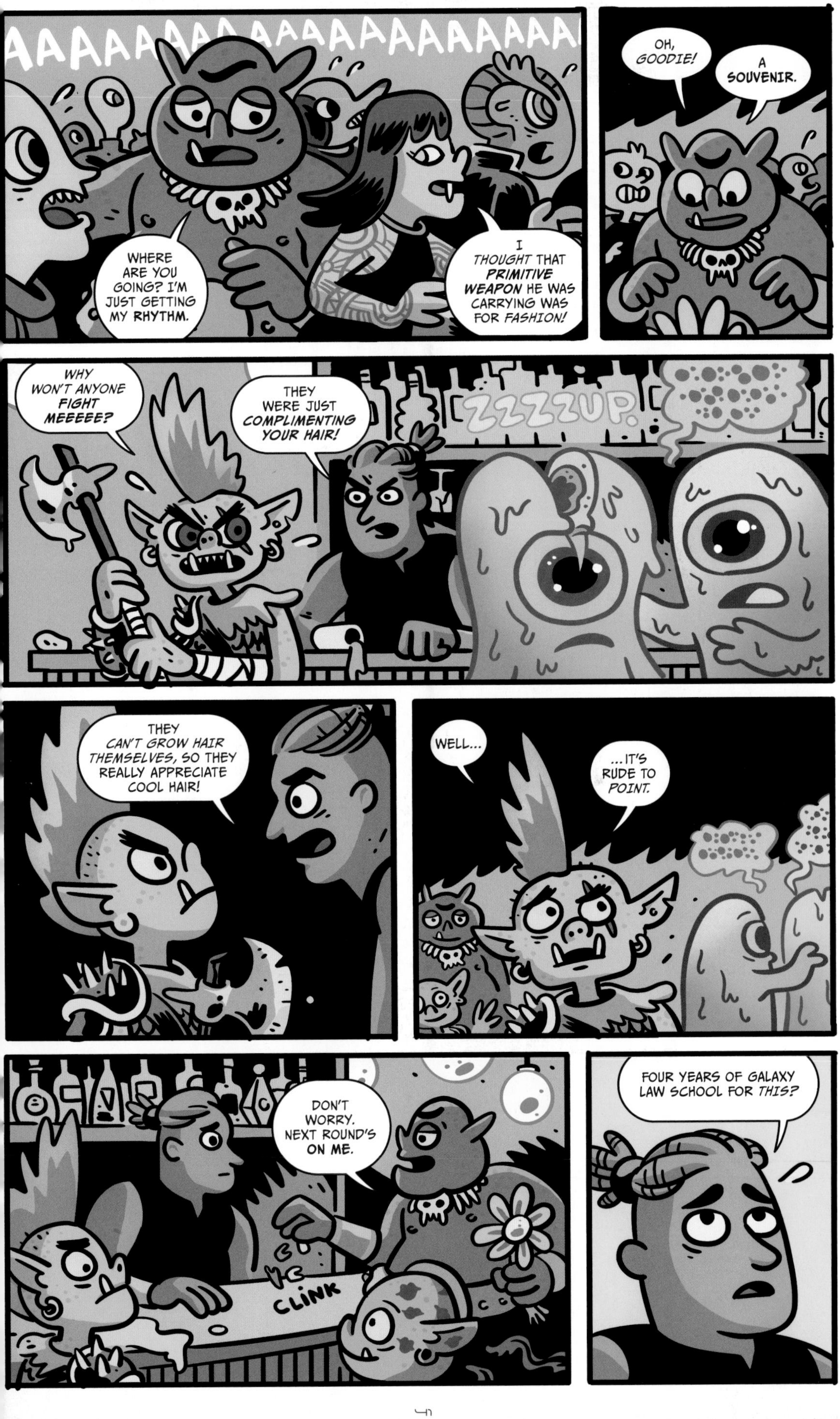
AAAAAAAAAAAAAAAAAAAAA!
WHERE ARE YOU GOING? I'M JUST GETTING MY RHYTHM.
I THOUGHT THAT PRIMITIVE WEAPON HE WAS CARRYING WAS FOR FASHION!
OH, GOODIE!
A SOUVENIR.
WHY WON'T ANYONE FIGHT MEEEEE?
THEY WERE JUST COMPLIMENTING YOUR HAIR!
ZZZZUP.
THEY CAN'T GROW HAIR THEMSELVES, SO THEY REALLY APPRECIATE COOL HAIR!
WELL...
...IT'S RUDE TO POINT.
DON'T WORRY. NEXT ROUND'S ON ME.
CLINK
FOUR YEARS OF GALAXY LAW SCHOOL FOR THIS?

Beep Boop Bip
WELCOME BACK, COMMANDERS...
OH, WHO ARE YOU?
I'M DASH BLASTOFF.
AND YOU'VE BEEN A VERY BAD SHIP, AND I'M HERE TO TAKE YOU BACK TO STARBLEEP.
I JUST HAVE TO ENTER THIS CODE THAT STARBLEEPER GAVE ME AND...
Beep Boop
BLOOP
PERSONALITY PROGRAM DISABLED.
WELCOME ABOARD, COMMANDER.
SIMPLE PIMPLE, YEP-YEP.
HE SAID I COULD JUST TELL THE COMPUTER TO FLY BACK TO HEADQUARTERS...
I'LL JUST—
...BUT IT SOUNDS LIKE A REAL SWELL TIME TO FLY THE MOST ADVANCED SHIP IN THE GALAXY.
D.O.N.N.N.N.N.A.!
WE'RE BACK!

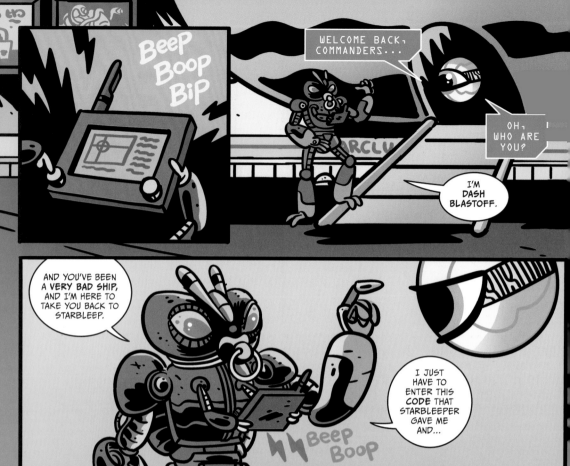

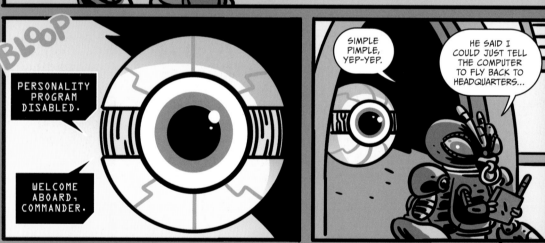

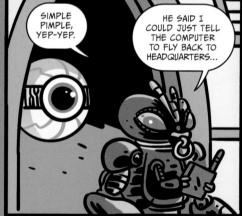

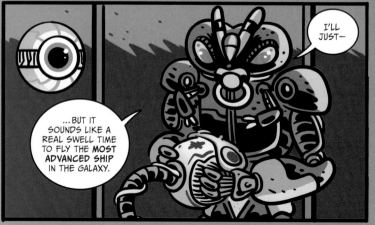

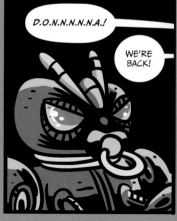

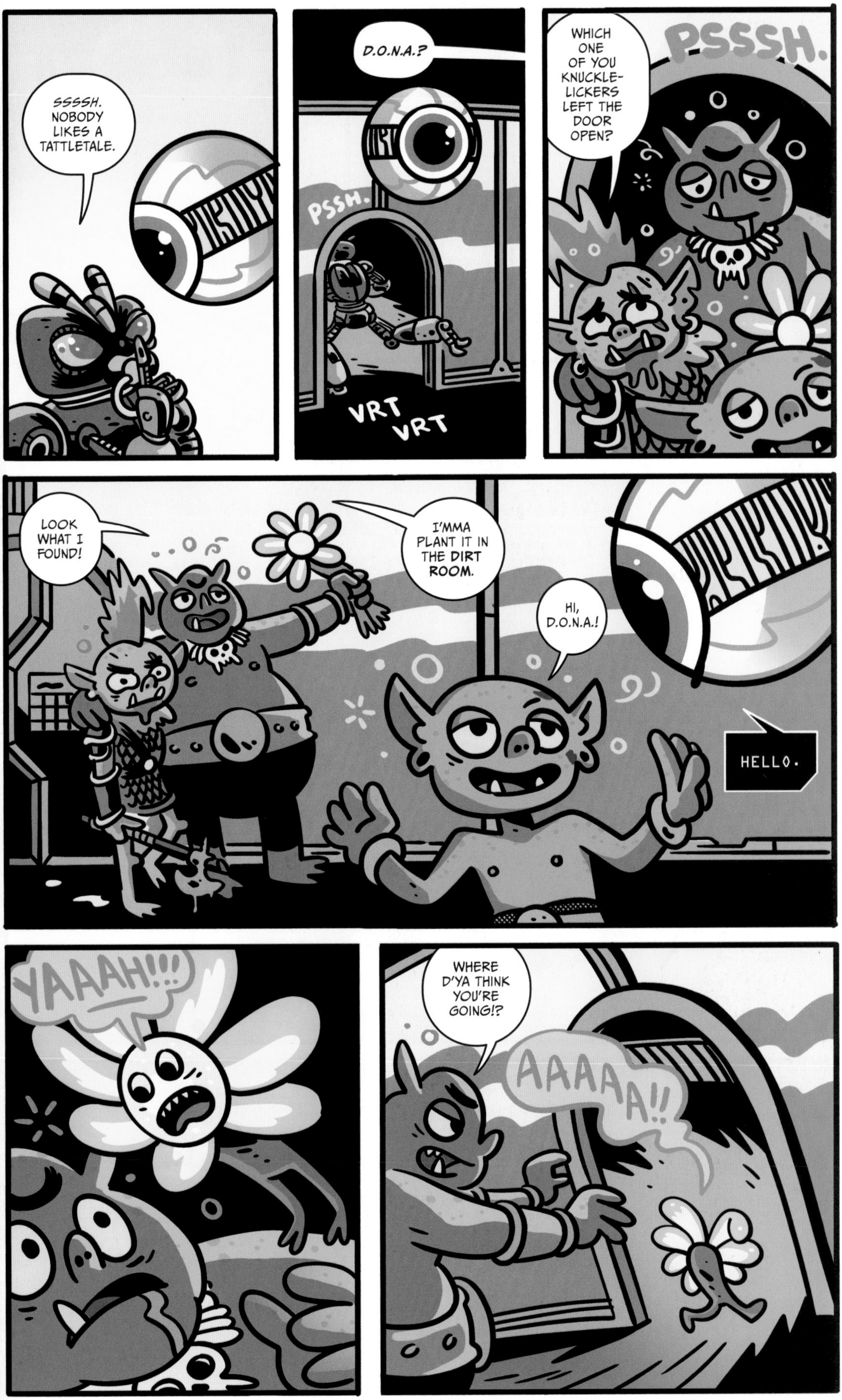
SSSSH. NOBODY LIKES A TATTLETALE.
D.O.N.A.?
PSSH.
VRT VRT
WHICH ONE OF YOU KNUCKLE-LICKERS LEFT THE DOOR OPEN?
PSSSH.
LOOK WHAT I FOUND!
I'MMA PLANT IT IN THE **DIRT ROOM**.
HI, D.O.N.A.!
HELLO.
YAAAH!!!
WHERE D'YA THINK YOU'RE GOING!?
AAAAA!!

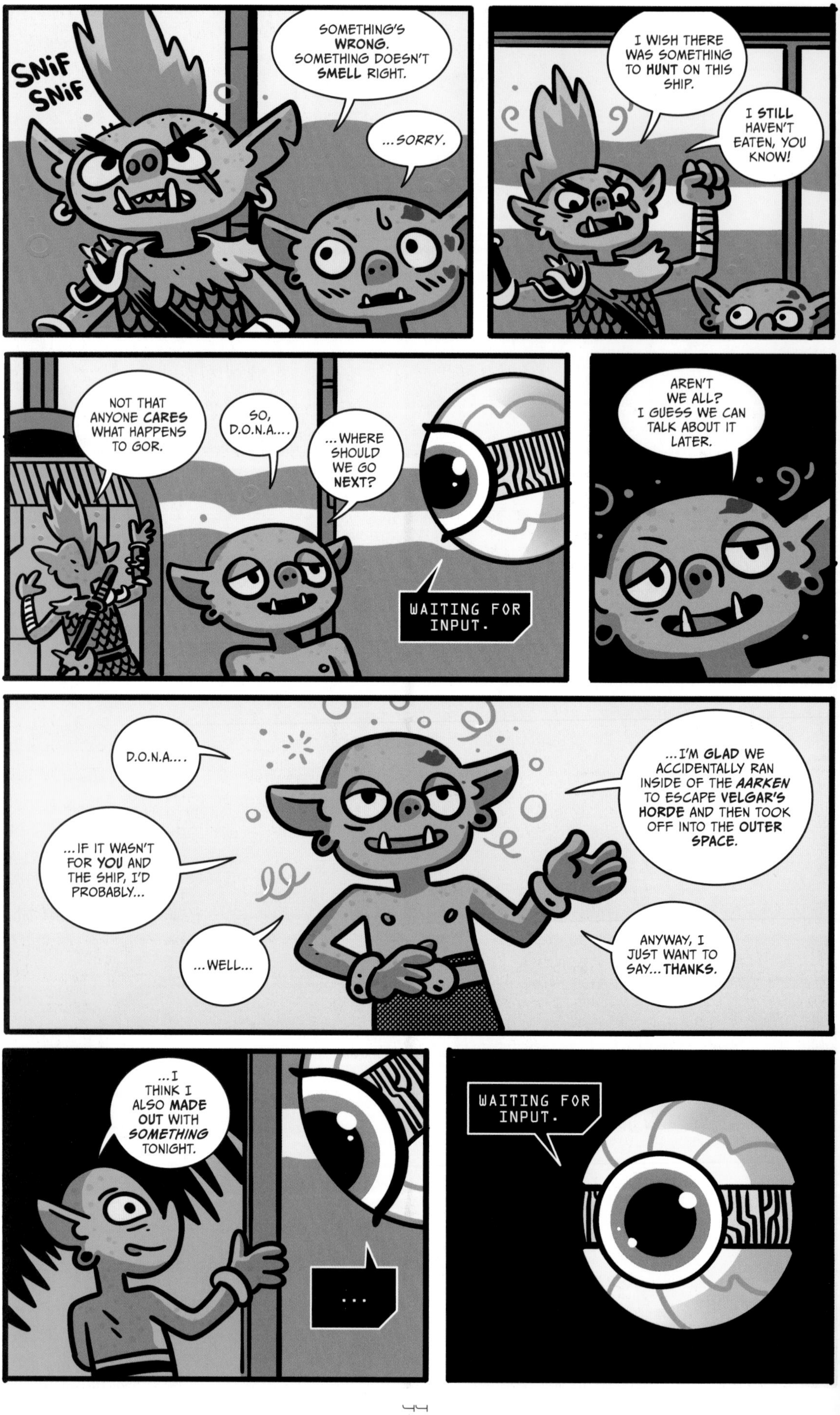
SNIF SNIF
SOMETHING'S WRONG. SOMETHING DOESN'T SMELL RIGHT.
...SORRY.
I WISH THERE WAS SOMETHING TO HUNT ON THIS SHIP.
I STILL HAVEN'T EATEN, YOU KNOW!
NOT THAT ANYONE CARES WHAT HAPPENS TO GOR.
SO, D.O.N.A....
...WHERE SHOULD WE GO NEXT?
WAITING FOR INPUT.
AREN'T WE ALL? I GUESS WE CAN TALK ABOUT IT LATER.
D.O.N.A....
...I'M GLAD WE ACCIDENTALLY RAN INSIDE OF THE AARKEN TO ESCAPE VELGAR'S HORDE AND THEN TOOK OFF INTO THE OUTER SPACE.
...IF IT WASN'T FOR YOU AND THE SHIP, I'D PROBABLY...
...WELL...
ANYWAY, I JUST WANT TO SAY... THANKS.
...I THINK I ALSO MADE OUT WITH SOMETHING TONIGHT.
...
WAITING FOR INPUT.

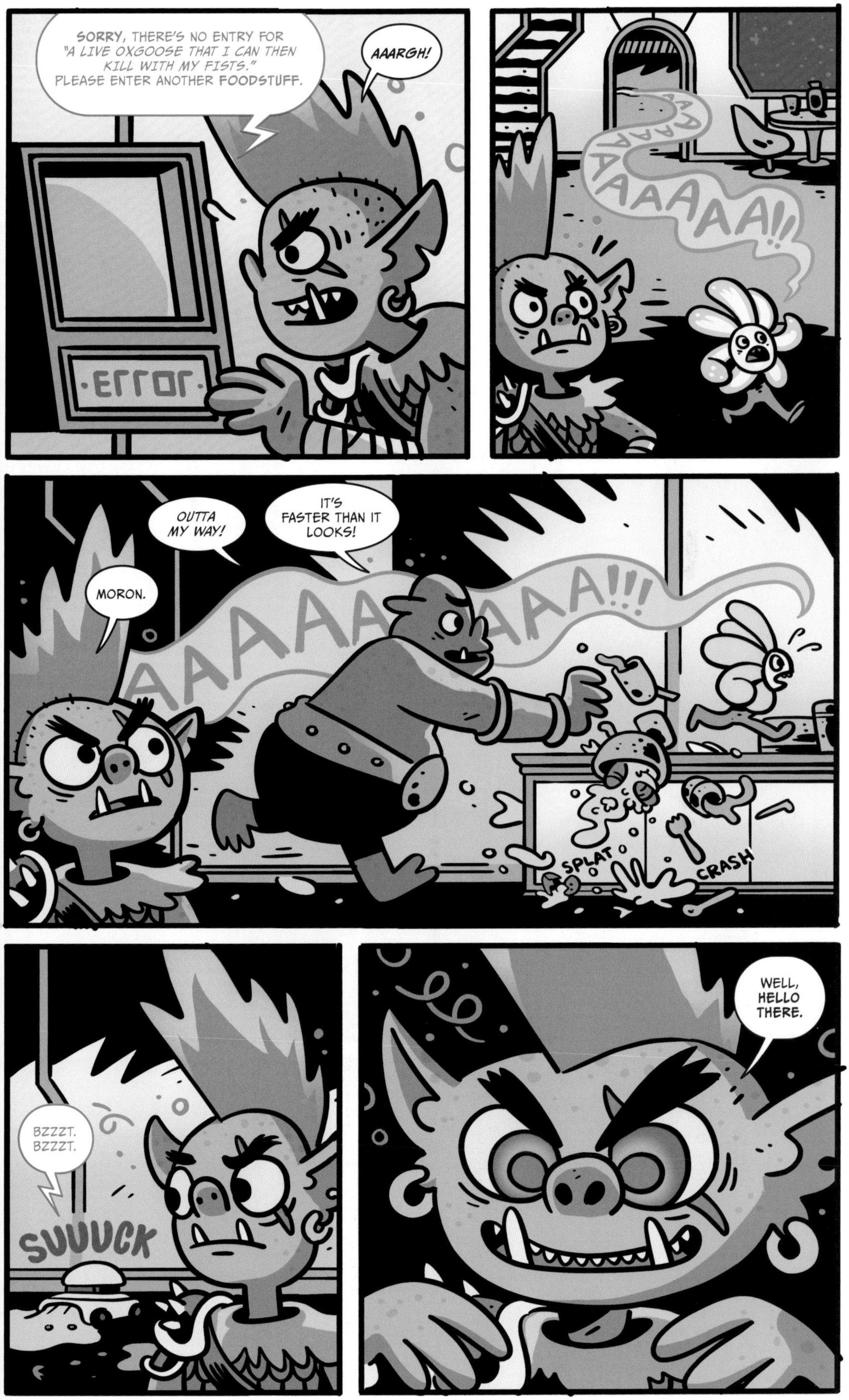

SORRY, THERE'S NO ENTRY FOR "A LIVE OXGOOSE THAT I CAN THEN KILL WITH MY FISTS." PLEASE ENTER ANOTHER FOODSTUFF.
AAARGH!
ERROR
AAAAAAAAAAAAA!!
MORON.
OUTTA MY WAY!
IT'S FASTER THAN IT LOOKS!
AAAAAAAAA!!!
SPLAT
CRASH
BZZZT. BZZZT.
SUUUCK
WELL, HELLO THERE.

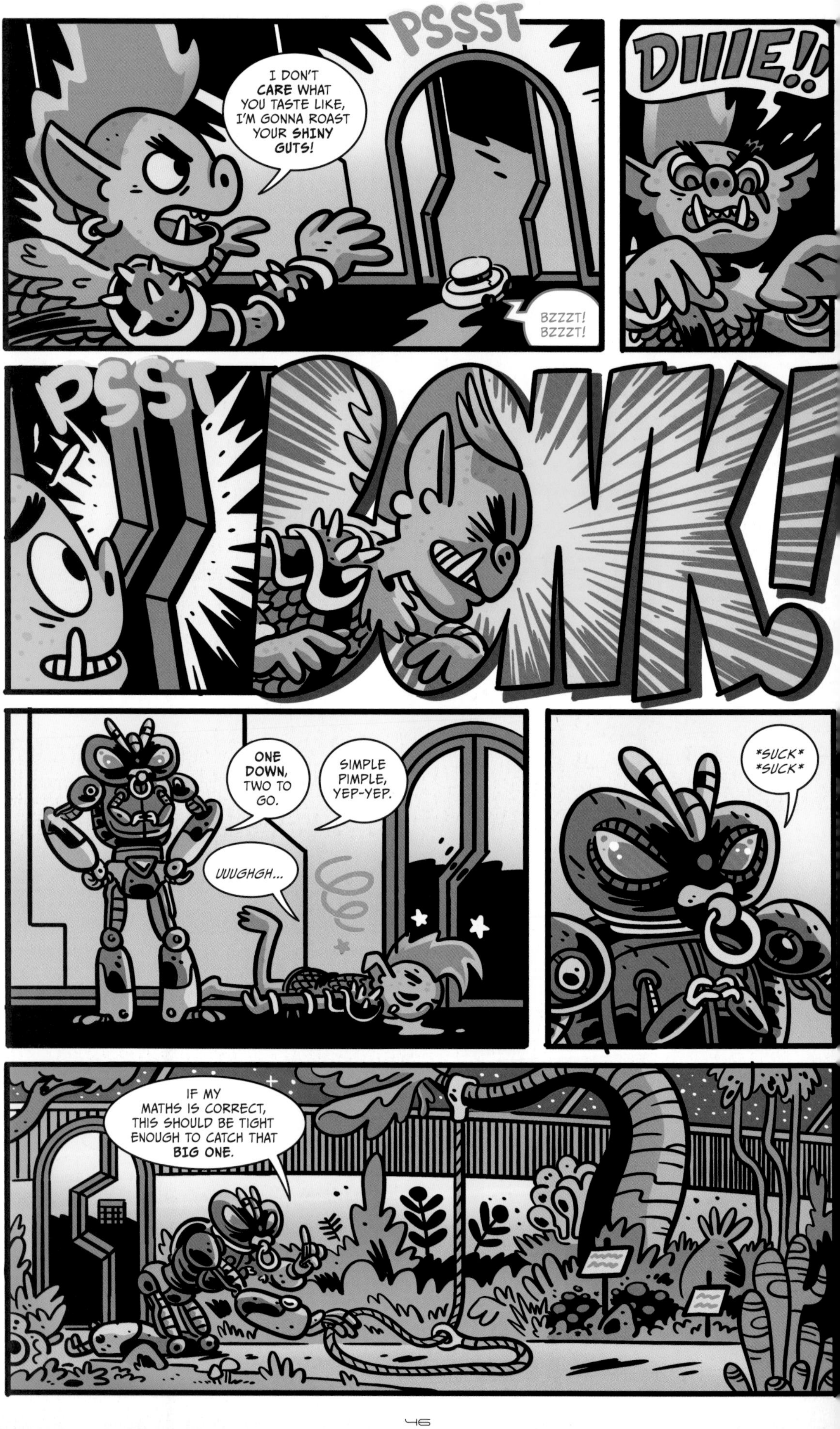
PSSST
I DON'T CARE WHAT YOU TASTE LIKE, I'M GONNA ROAST YOUR SHINY GUTS!
BZZZT! BZZZT!
DIIIE!!
PSST
BONK!
ONE DOWN, TWO TO GO.
SIMPLE PIMPLE, YEP-YEP.
UUUGHGH...
SUCK *SUCK*
IF MY MATHS IS CORRECT, THIS SHOULD BE TIGHT ENOUGH TO CATCH THAT BIG ONE.

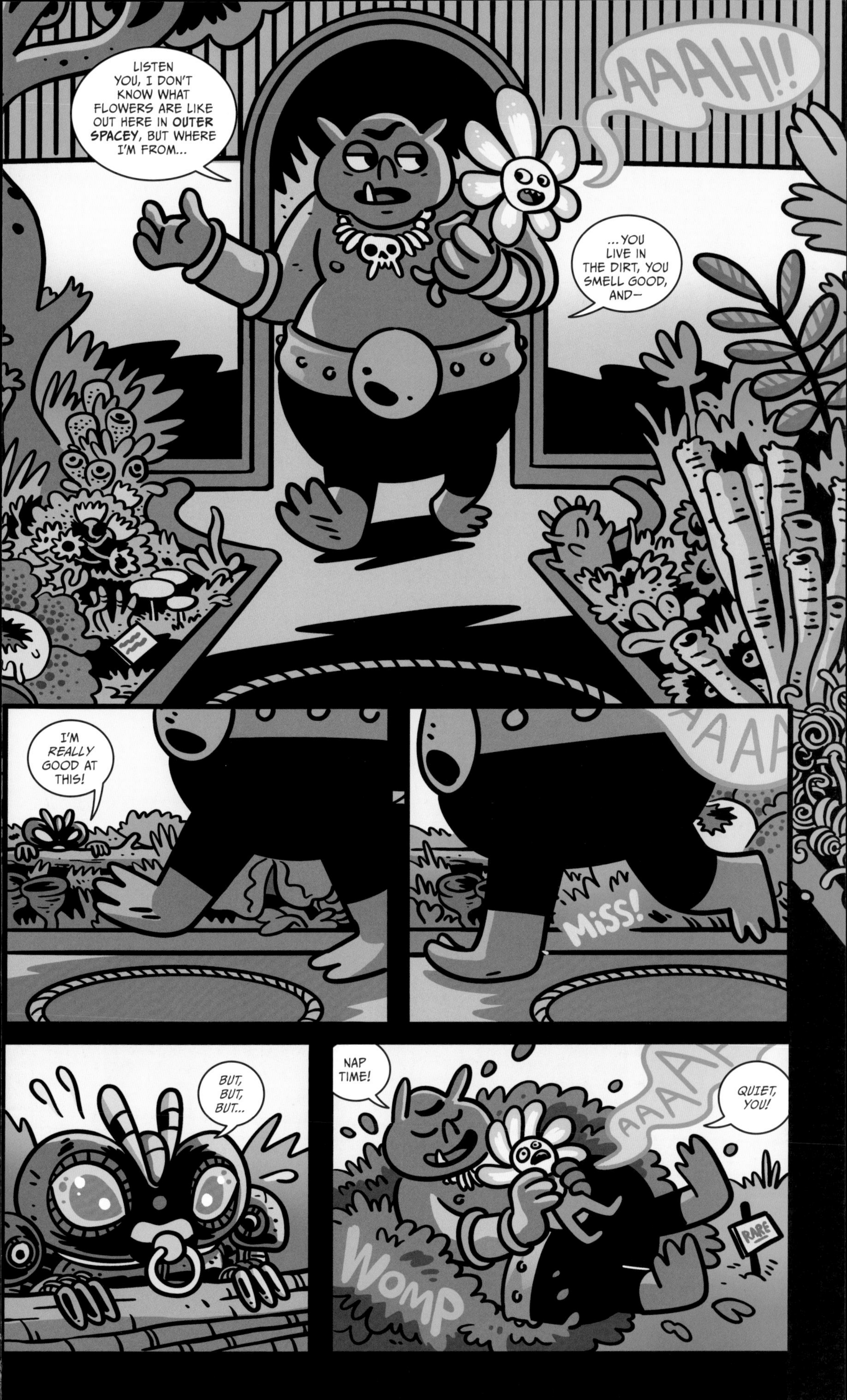
LISTEN YOU, I DON'T KNOW WHAT FLOWERS ARE LIKE OUT HERE IN **OUTER SPACEY**, BUT WHERE I'M FROM...
AAAH!!
...YOU LIVE IN THE DIRT, YOU SMELL GOOD, AND—
I'M *REALLY* GOOD AT THIS!
AAAA
MISS!
BUT, BUT, BUT...
NAP TIME!
QUIET, YOU!
AAAAA
RARE
WOMP

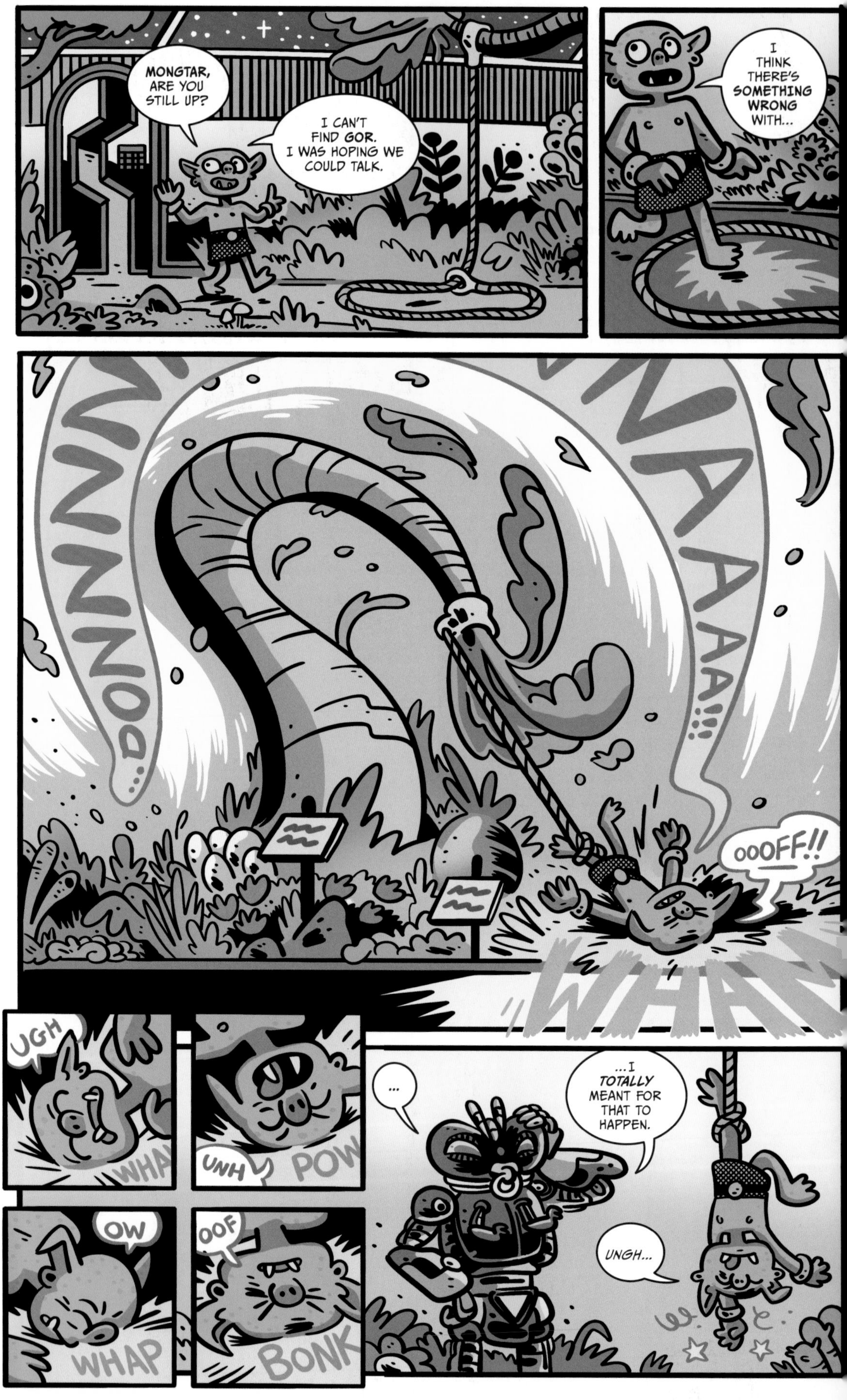
MONGTAR, ARE YOU STILL UP?
I CAN'T FIND GOR. I WAS HOPING WE COULD TALK.
I THINK THERE'S SOMETHING WRONG WITH...
WAAAAAAA!!!
DOOOOO...
OOOFF!!
WHAM
UGH
WHAP
UNH
POW
OW
WHAP
OOF
BONK
...
...I TOTALLY MEANT FOR THAT TO HAPPEN.
UNGH...

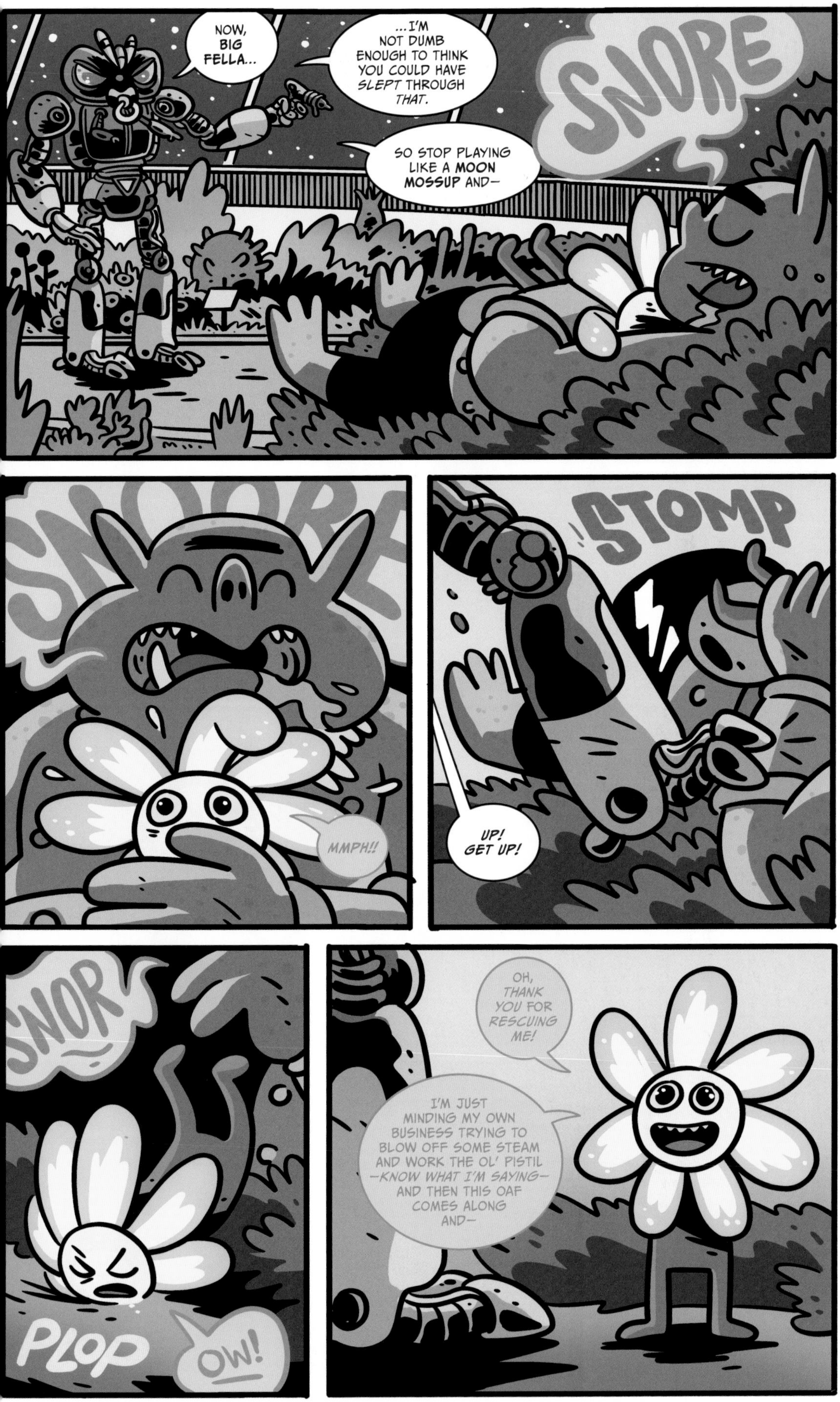
NOW, BIG FELLA...
...I'M NOT DUMB ENOUGH TO THINK YOU COULD HAVE SLEPT THROUGH THAT.
SNORE
SO STOP PLAYING LIKE A MOON MOSSUP AND—
SNORE
MMPH!!
STOMP
UP! GET UP!
SNOR
PLOP
OW!
OH, THANK YOU FOR RESCUING ME!
I'M JUST MINDING MY OWN BUSINESS TRYING TO BLOW OFF SOME STEAM AND WORK THE OL' PISTIL —KNOW WHAT I'M SAYING— AND THEN THIS OAF COMES ALONG AND—

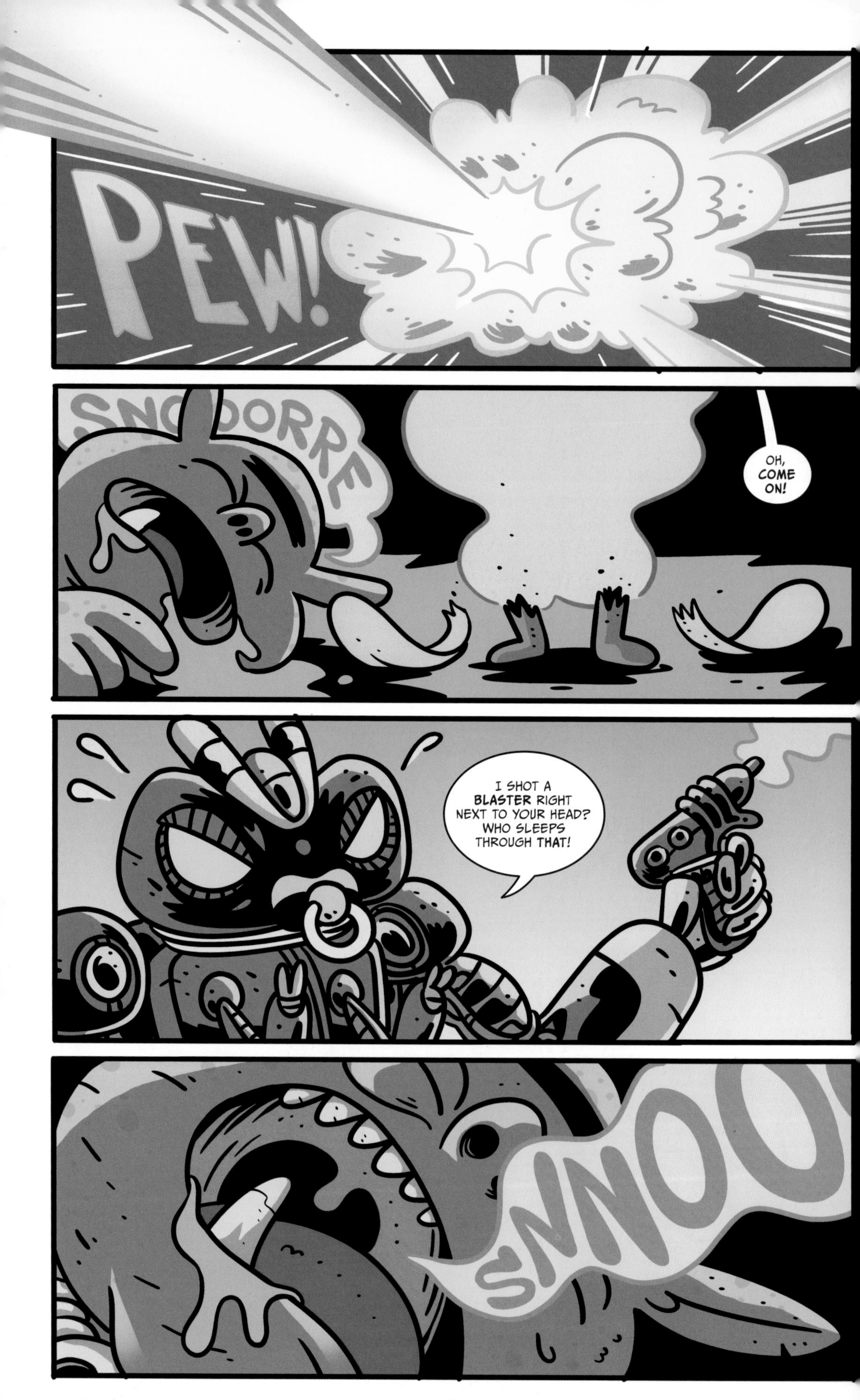
PEW!
SNOORRE
OH, COME ON!
I SHOT A **BLASTER** RIGHT NEXT TO YOUR HEAD? WHO SLEEPS THROUGH **THAT**!
SNNOO

LEG HYDRAULICS BATTERY 80%
UNH! UNGH!
COME ON, YOU...
VRT VRT
WHEW... SIMPLE *BREATH* PIMPLE.
THIS BOUNTY IS AS GOOD AS GOTTEN!
PANT *PANT*
YEP-YEP.
THE AARKEN SURE IS A SMOOTH RIDE.
NEW COMMANDER, MY SENSORS INDICATE A LARGE SHIP IS CONVERGING ON OUR LOCATION.
MUST BE THOSE STARBLEEPERS COMING TO COLLECT. PUT THEM ON THE VIEW SCREEN.
BLOOP
AW GEEZ, IT'S THOSE DIRTY, SMELLY, NO-GOOD...

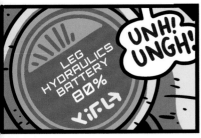

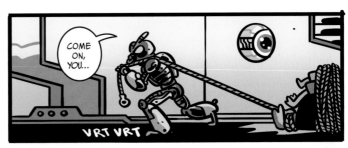

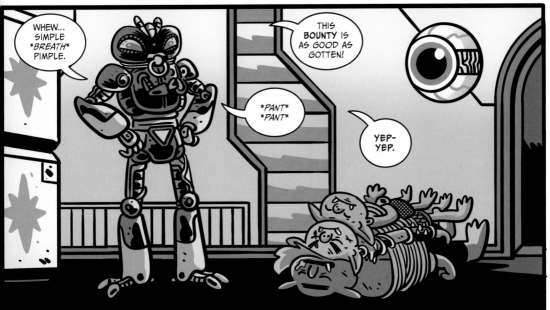

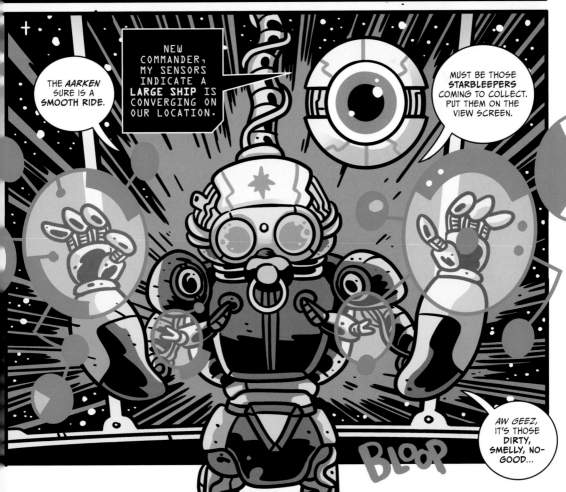

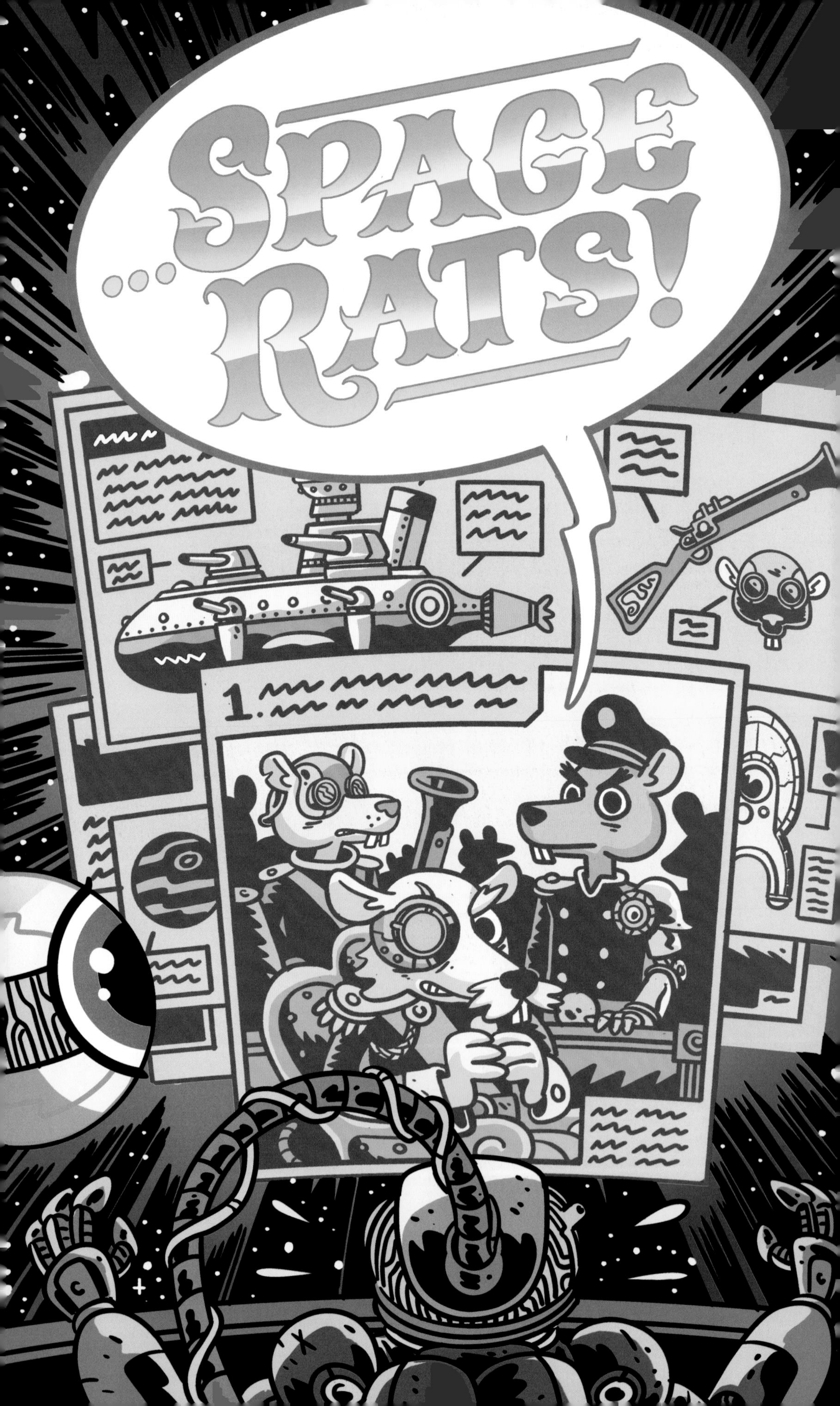
...SPACE RATS!
1.

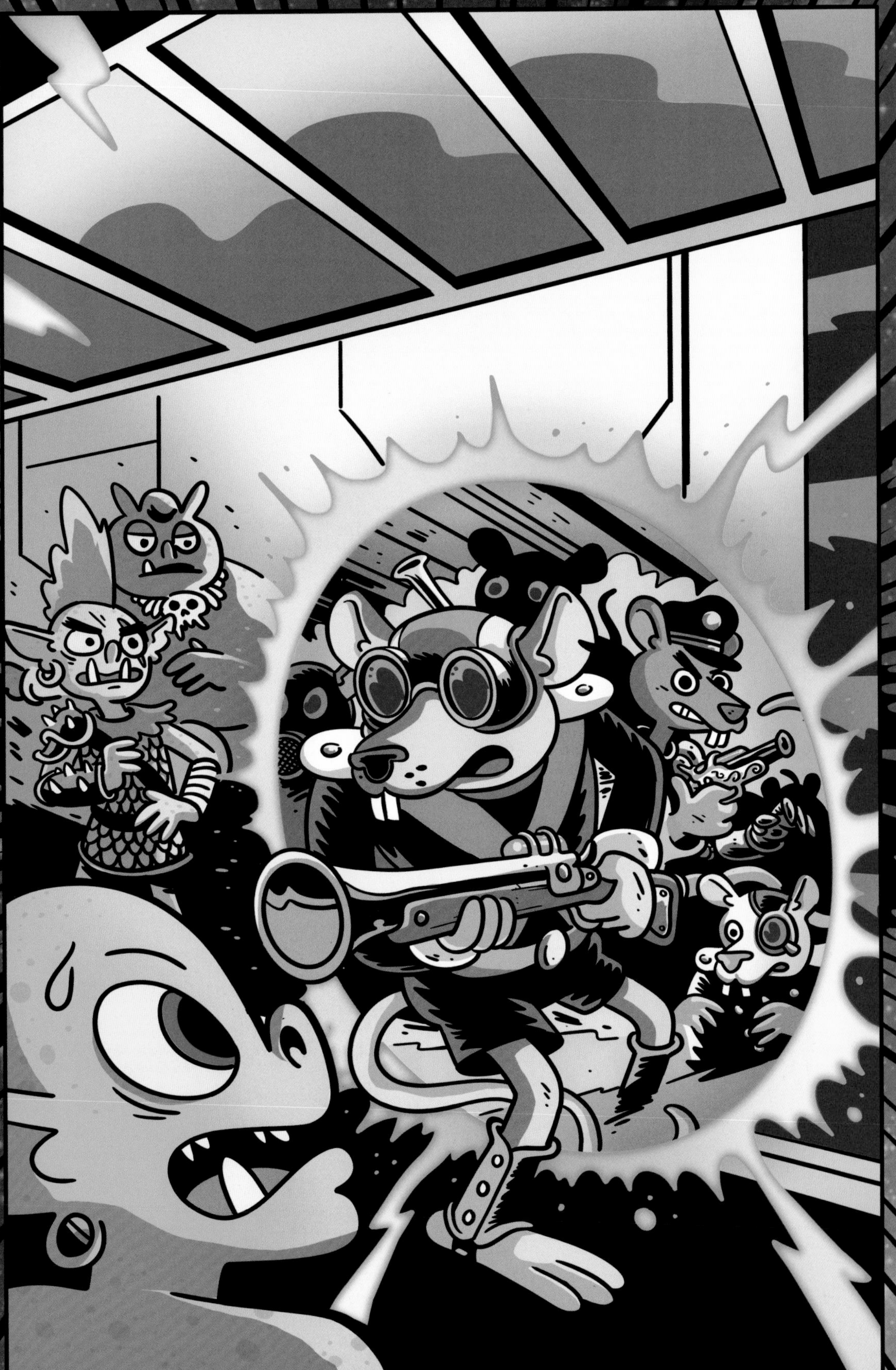

CHAPTER THREE

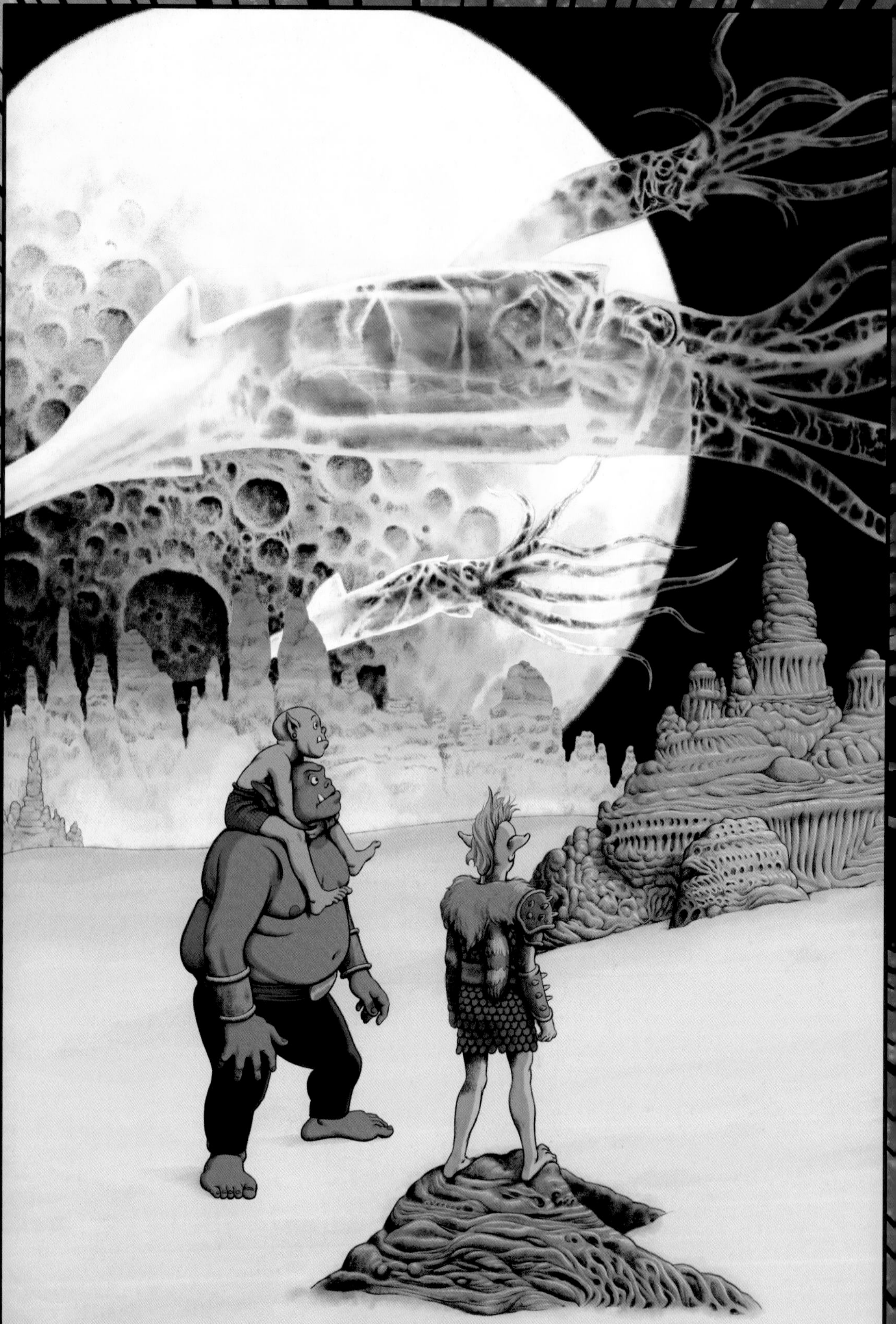

VARIANT COVER

BY MALACHI WARD & MATT SHEEAN

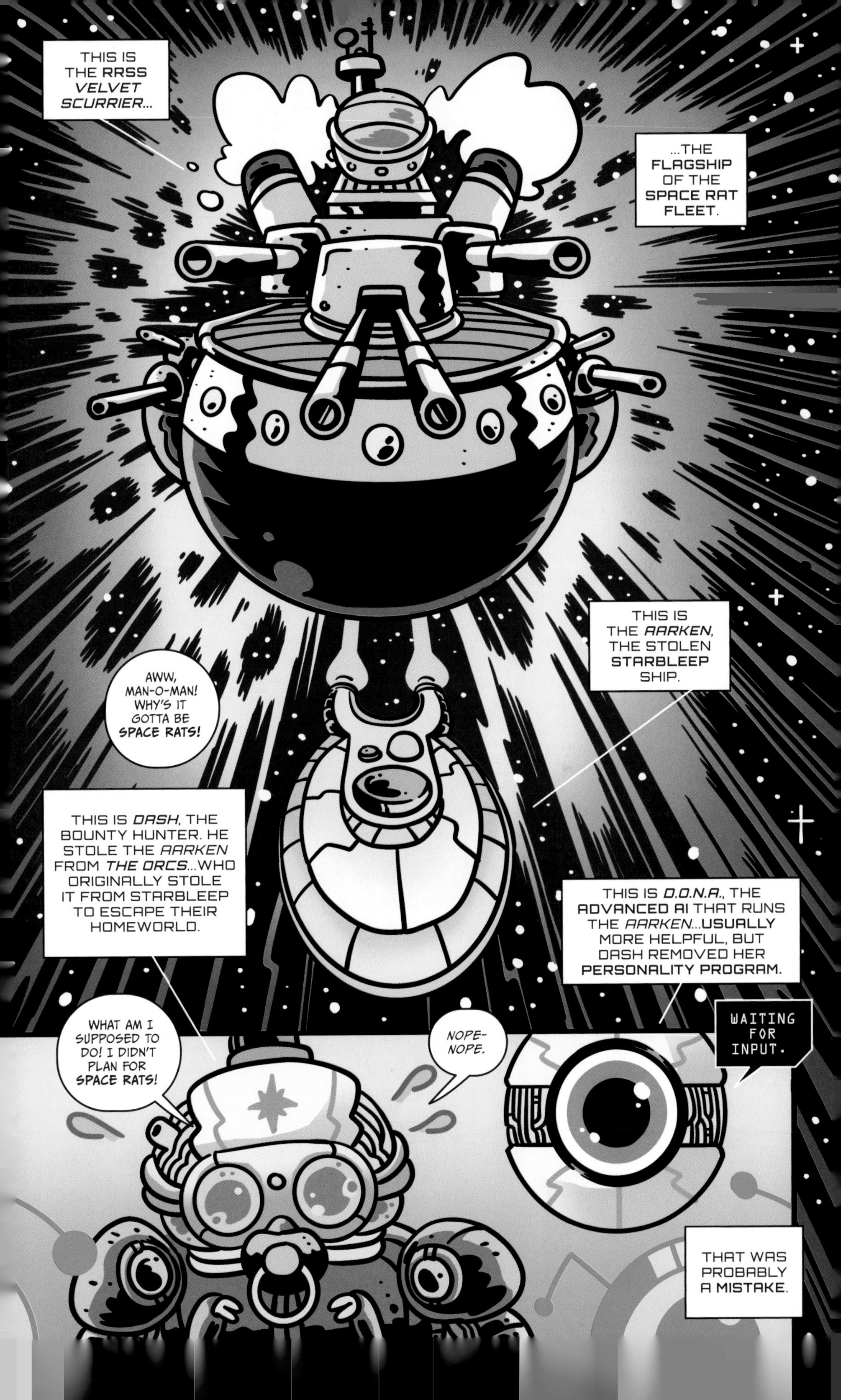
THIS IS THE RRSS VELVET SCURRIER...
...THE FLAGSHIP OF THE SPACE RAT FLEET.
THIS IS THE AARKEN, THE STOLEN STARBLEEP SHIP.
AWW, MAN-O-MAN! WHY'S IT GOTTA BE SPACE RATS!
THIS IS DASH, THE BOUNTY HUNTER. HE STOLE THE AARKEN FROM THE ORCS...WHO ORIGINALLY STOLE IT FROM STARBLEEP TO ESCAPE THEIR HOMEWORLD.
THIS IS D.O.N.A., THE ADVANCED AI THAT RUNS THE AARKEN...USUALLY MORE HELPFUL, BUT DASH REMOVED HER PERSONALITY PROGRAM.
WHAT AM I SUPPOSED TO DO! I DIDN'T PLAN FOR SPACE RATS!
NOPE-NOPE.
WAITING FOR INPUT.
THAT WAS PROBABLY A MISTAKE.

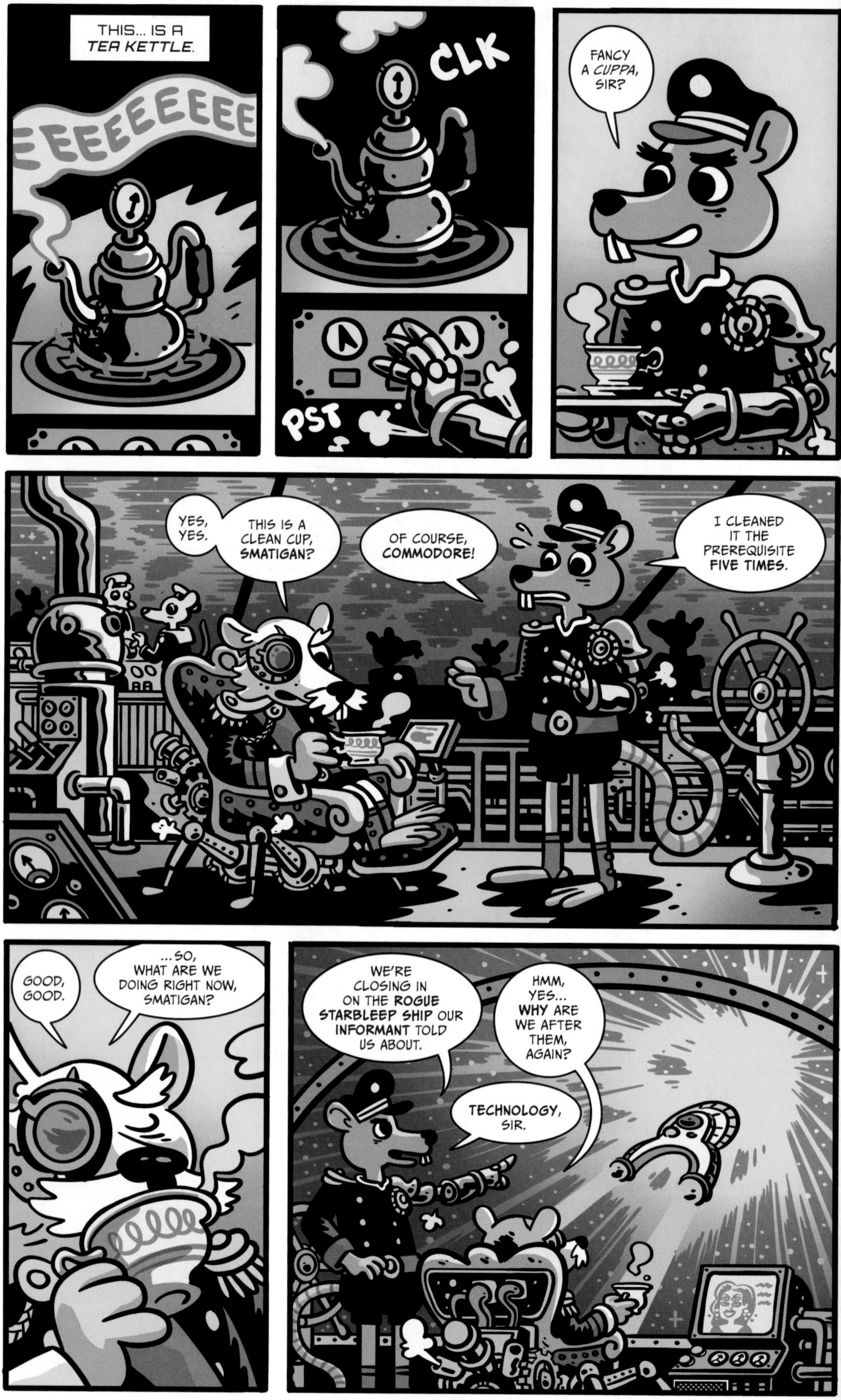

THIS... IS A TEA KETTLE.
EEEEEEEEE
CLK
PST
FANCY A CUPPA, SIR?
YES, YES.
THIS IS A CLEAN CUP, SMATIGAN?
OF COURSE, COMMODORE!
I CLEANED IT THE PREREQUISITE FIVE TIMES.
GOOD, GOOD.
...SO, WHAT ARE WE DOING RIGHT NOW, SMATIGAN?
WE'RE CLOSING IN ON THE ROGUE STARBLEEP SHIP OUR INFORMANT TOLD US ABOUT.
HMM, YES... WHY ARE WE AFTER THEM, AGAIN?
TECHNOLOGY, SIR.

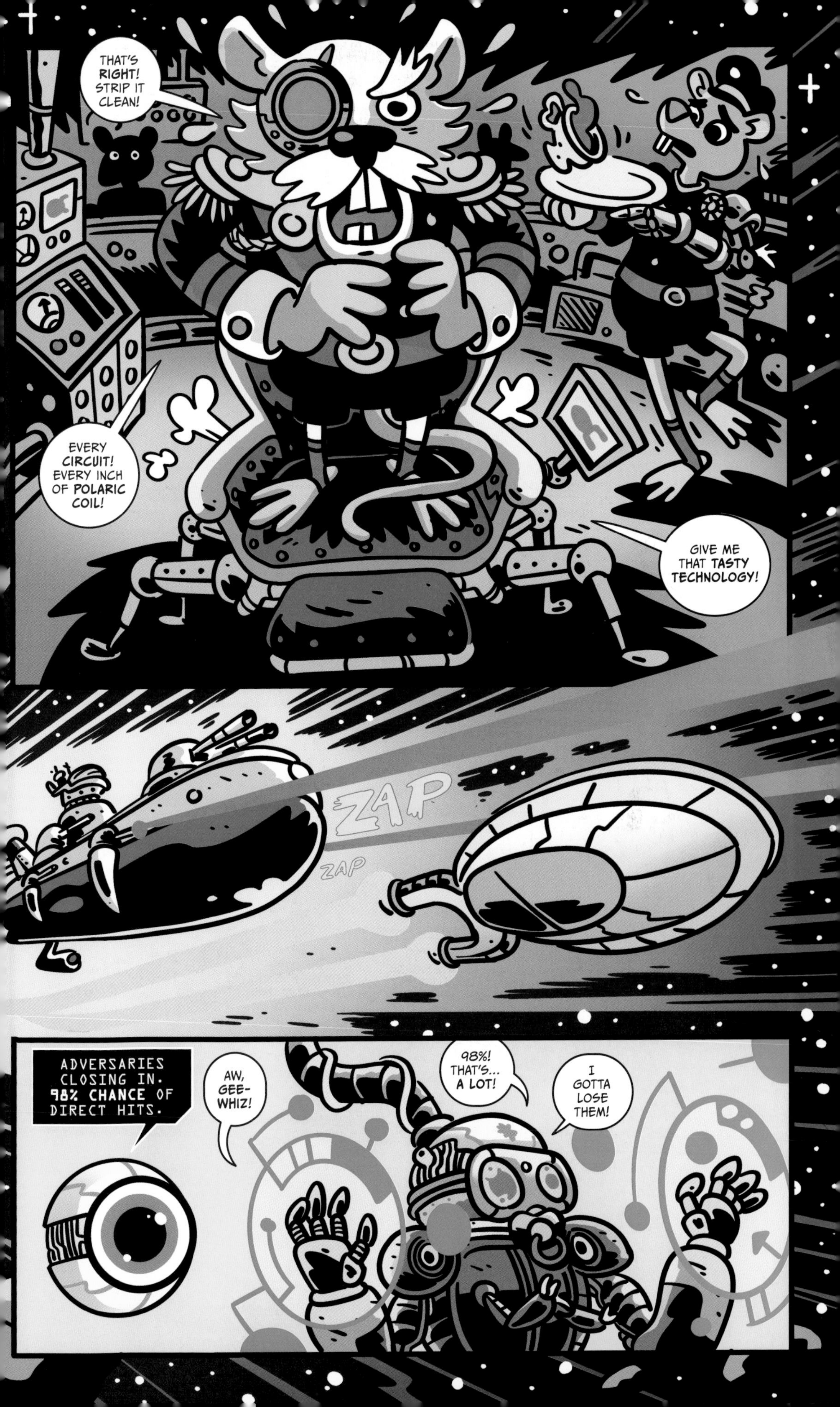

THAT'S RIGHT! STRIP IT CLEAN!
EVERY CIRCUIT! EVERY INCH OF POLARIC COIL!
GIVE ME THAT TASTY TECHNOLOGY!
ZAP
ZAP
ADVERSARIES CLOSING IN. 98% CHANCE OF DIRECT HITS.
AW, GEE-WHIZ!
98%! THAT'S... A LOT!
I GOTTA LOSE THEM!

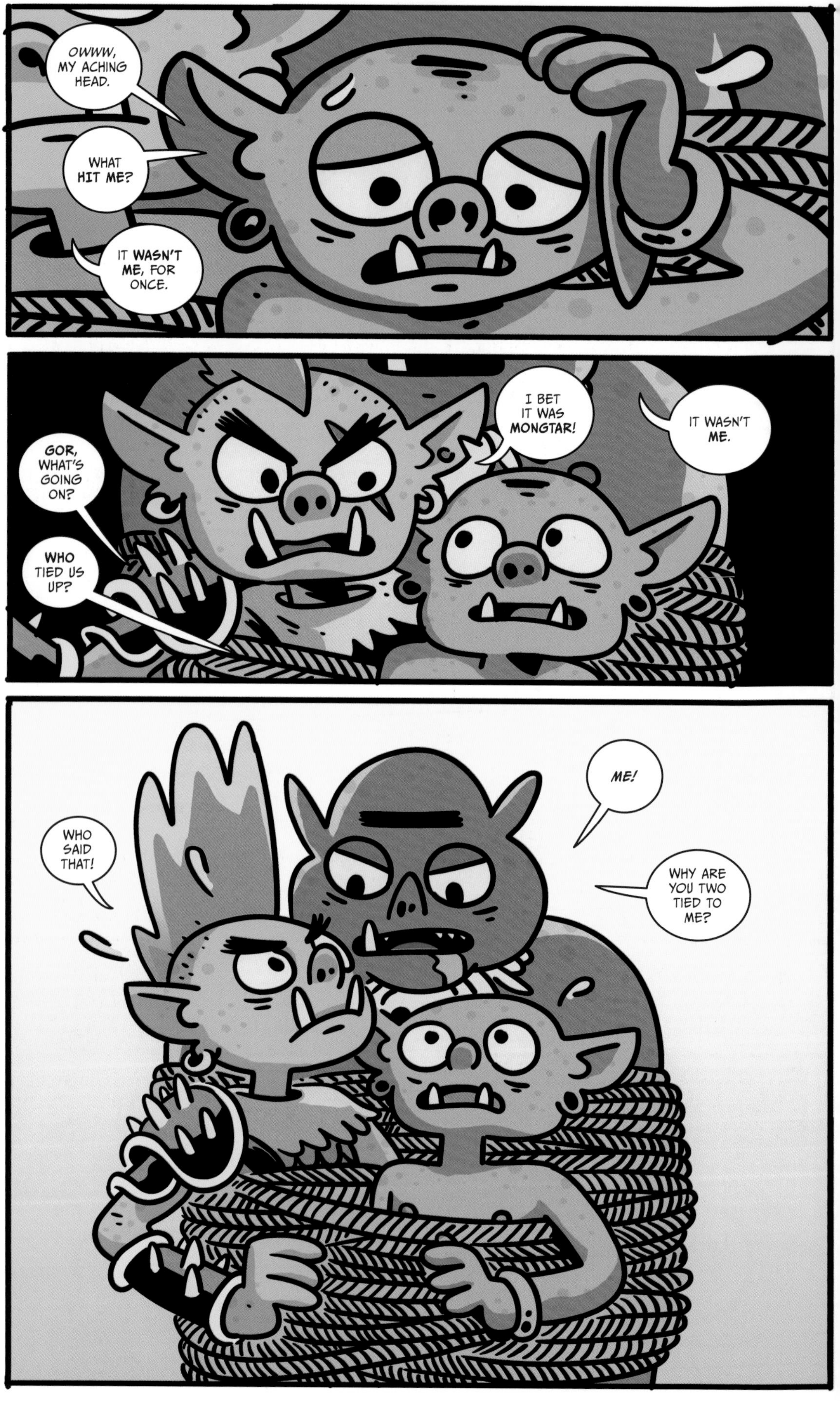
OWWW, MY ACHING HEAD.
WHAT HIT ME?
IT WASN'T ME, FOR ONCE.
GOR, WHAT'S GOING ON?
WHO TIED US UP?
I BET IT WAS MONGTAR!
IT WASN'T ME.
WHO SAID THAT!
ME!
WHY ARE YOU TWO TIED TO ME?

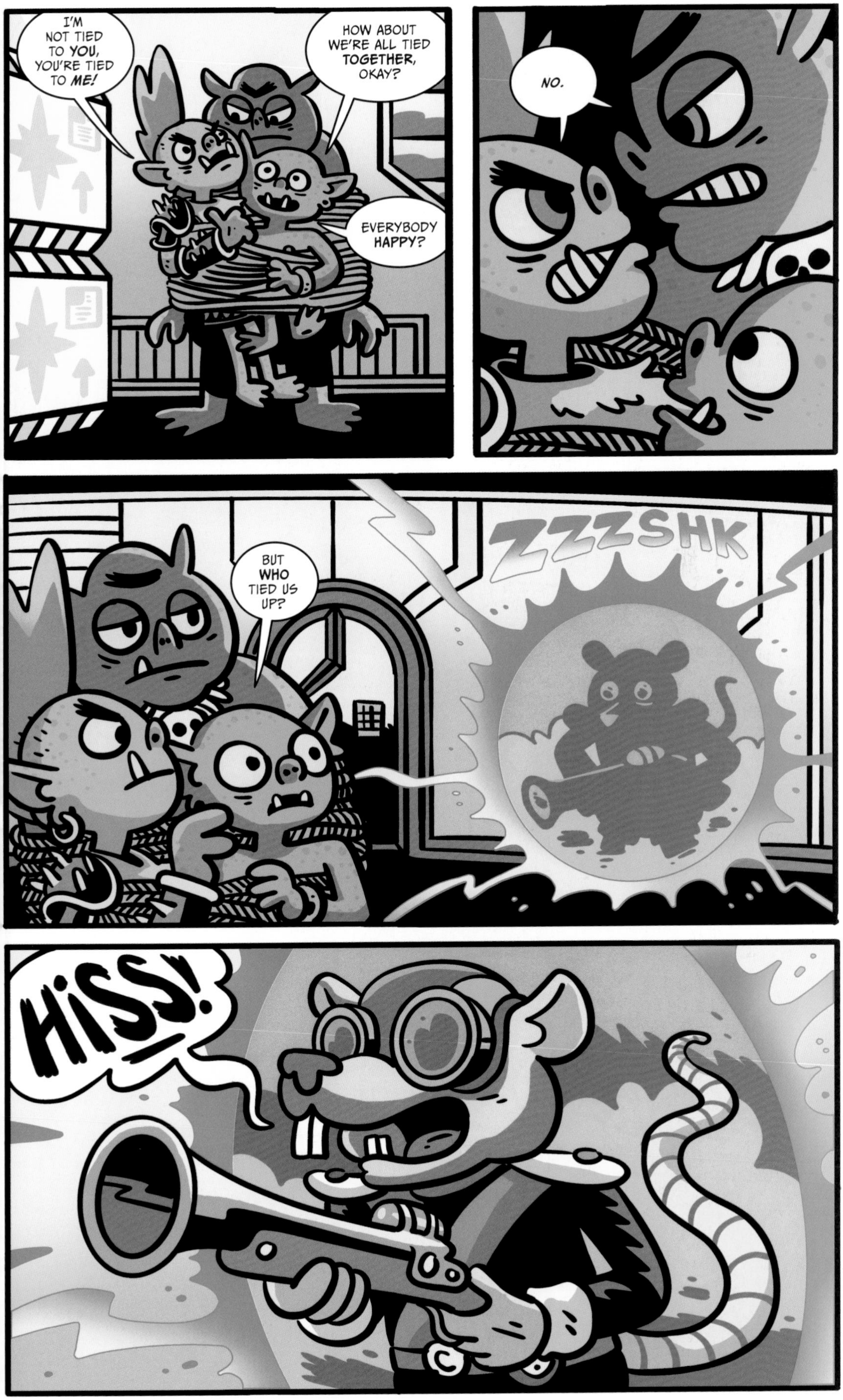
I'M NOT TIED TO YOU, YOU'RE TIED TO ME!
HOW ABOUT WE'RE ALL TIED TOGETHER, OKAY?
EVERYBODY HAPPY?
NO.
BUT WHO TIED US UP?
ZZZSHK
HISS!

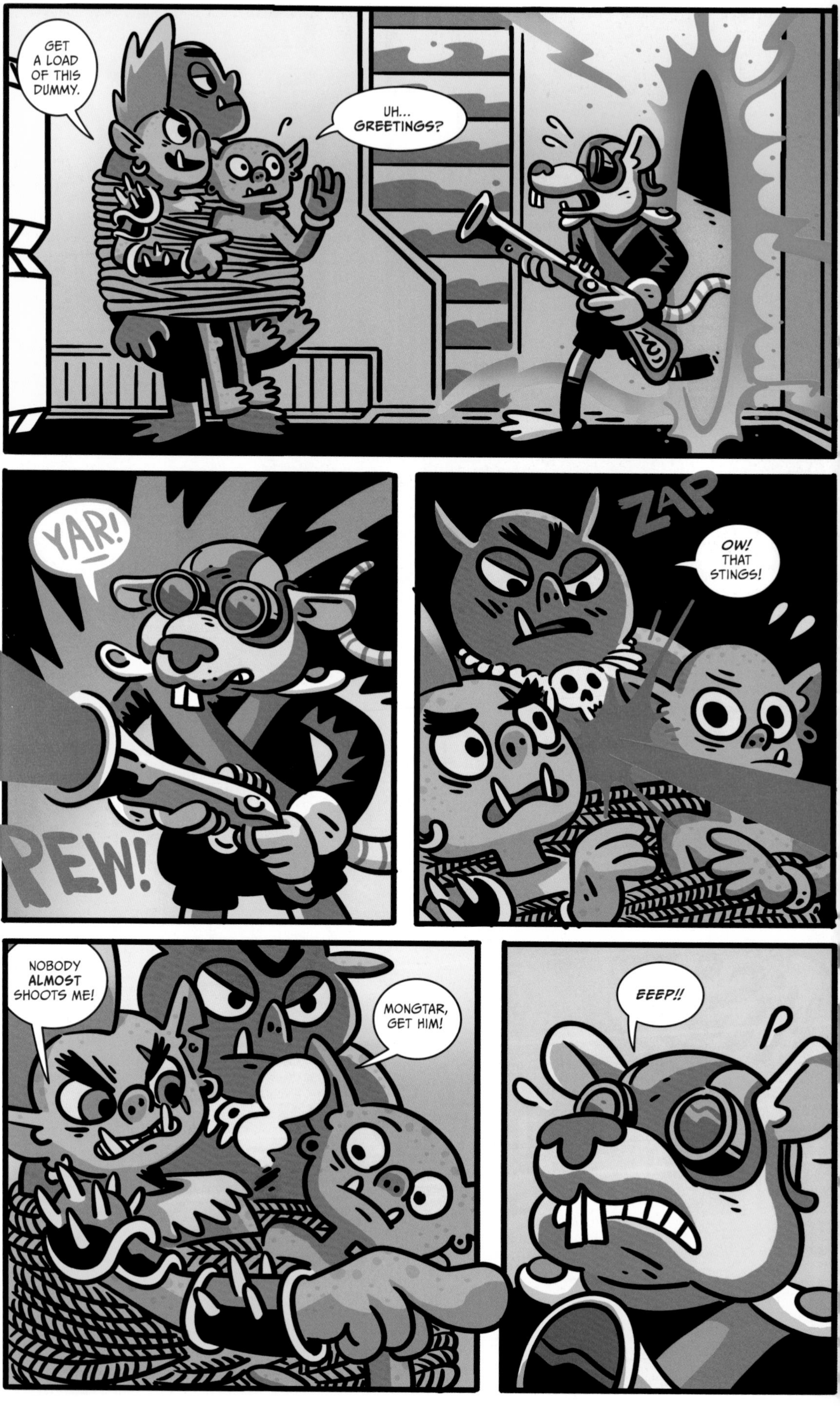
GET A LOAD OF THIS DUMMY.
UH... GREETINGS?
YAR!
PEW!
ZAP
OW! THAT STINGS!
NOBODY **ALMOST** SHOOTS ME!
MONGTAR, GET HIM!
EEEP!!

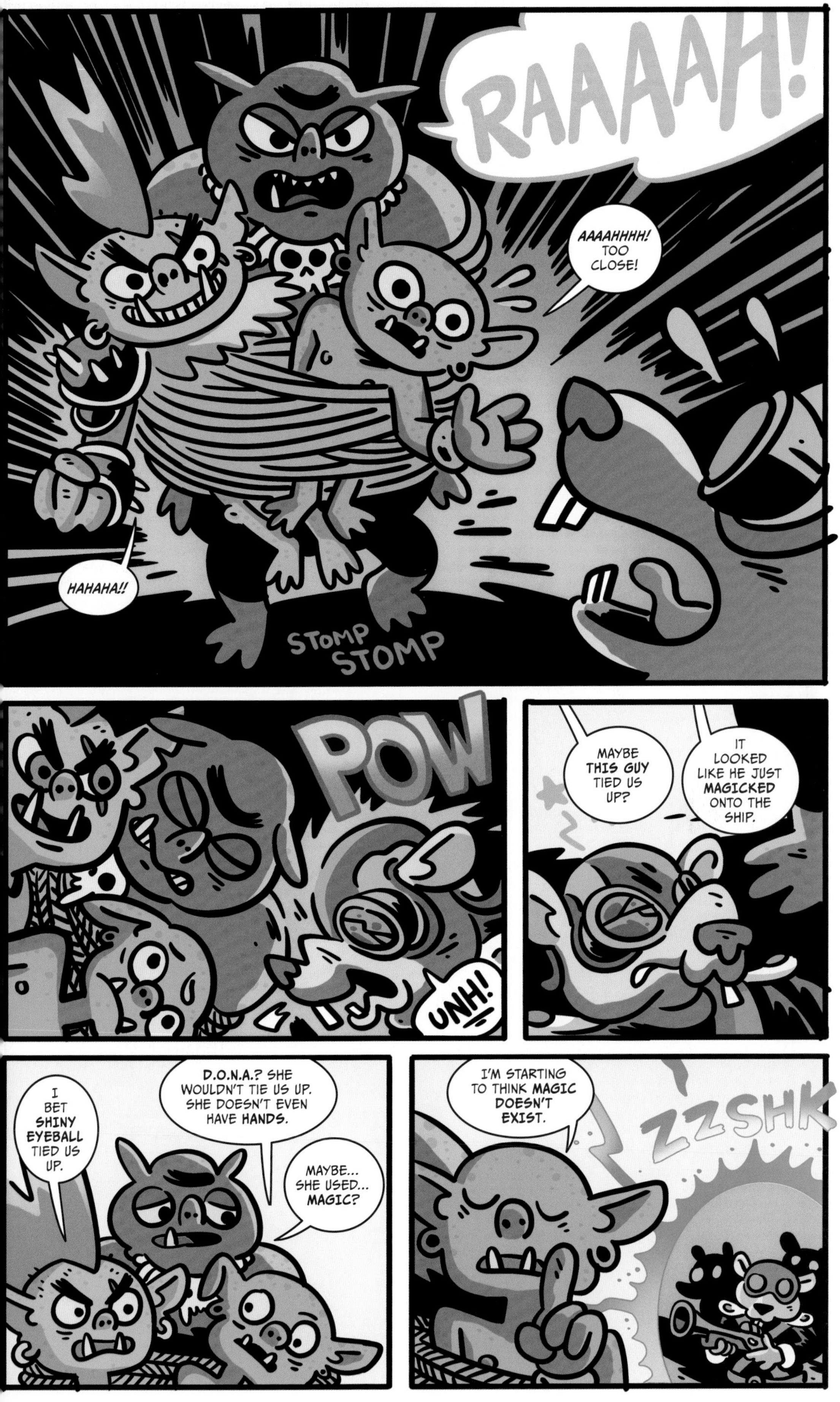

RAAAAAH!
AAAAHHHH! TOO CLOSE!
HAHAHA!!
STOMP STOMP
POW
UNH!
MAYBE THIS GUY TIED US UP?
IT LOOKED LIKE HE JUST MAGICKED ONTO THE SHIP.
I BET SHINY EYEBALL TIED US UP.
D.O.N.A.? SHE WOULDN'T TIE US UP. SHE DOESN'T EVEN HAVE HANDS.
MAYBE... SHE USED... MAGIC?
I'M STARTING TO THINK MAGIC DOESN'T EXIST.
ZZSHK

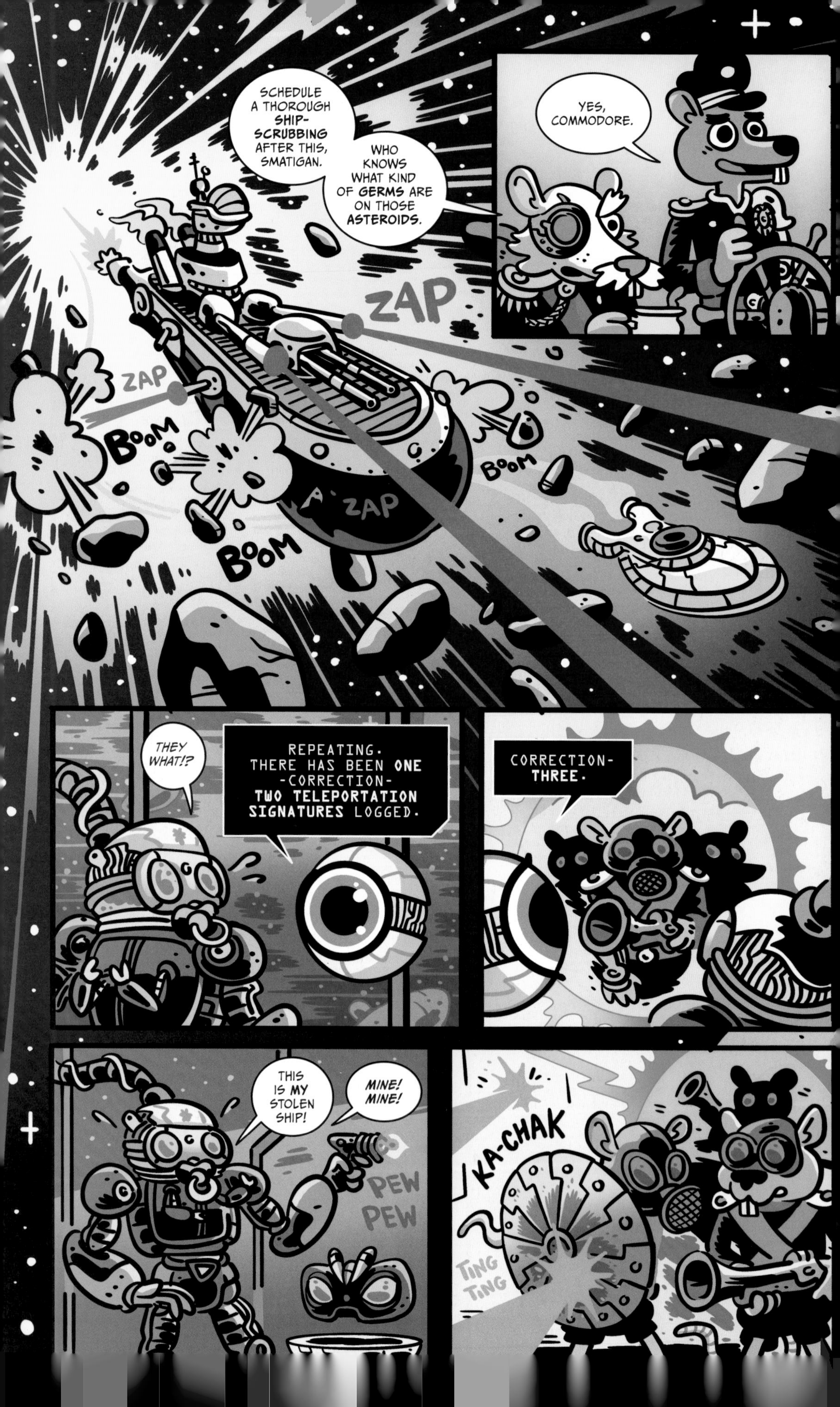

SCHEDULE A THOROUGH SHIP-SCRUBBING AFTER THIS, SMATIGAN.
WHO KNOWS WHAT KIND OF GERMS ARE ON THOSE ASTEROIDS.
YES, COMMODORE.
ZAP
ZAP
BOOM
BOOM
ZAP
BOOM
THEY WHAT!?
REPEATING. THERE HAS BEEN ONE -CORRECTION- TWO TELEPORTATION SIGNATURES LOGGED.
CORRECTION- THREE.
THIS IS MY STOLEN SHIP!
MINE! MINE!
PEW PEW
KA-CHAK
TING TING

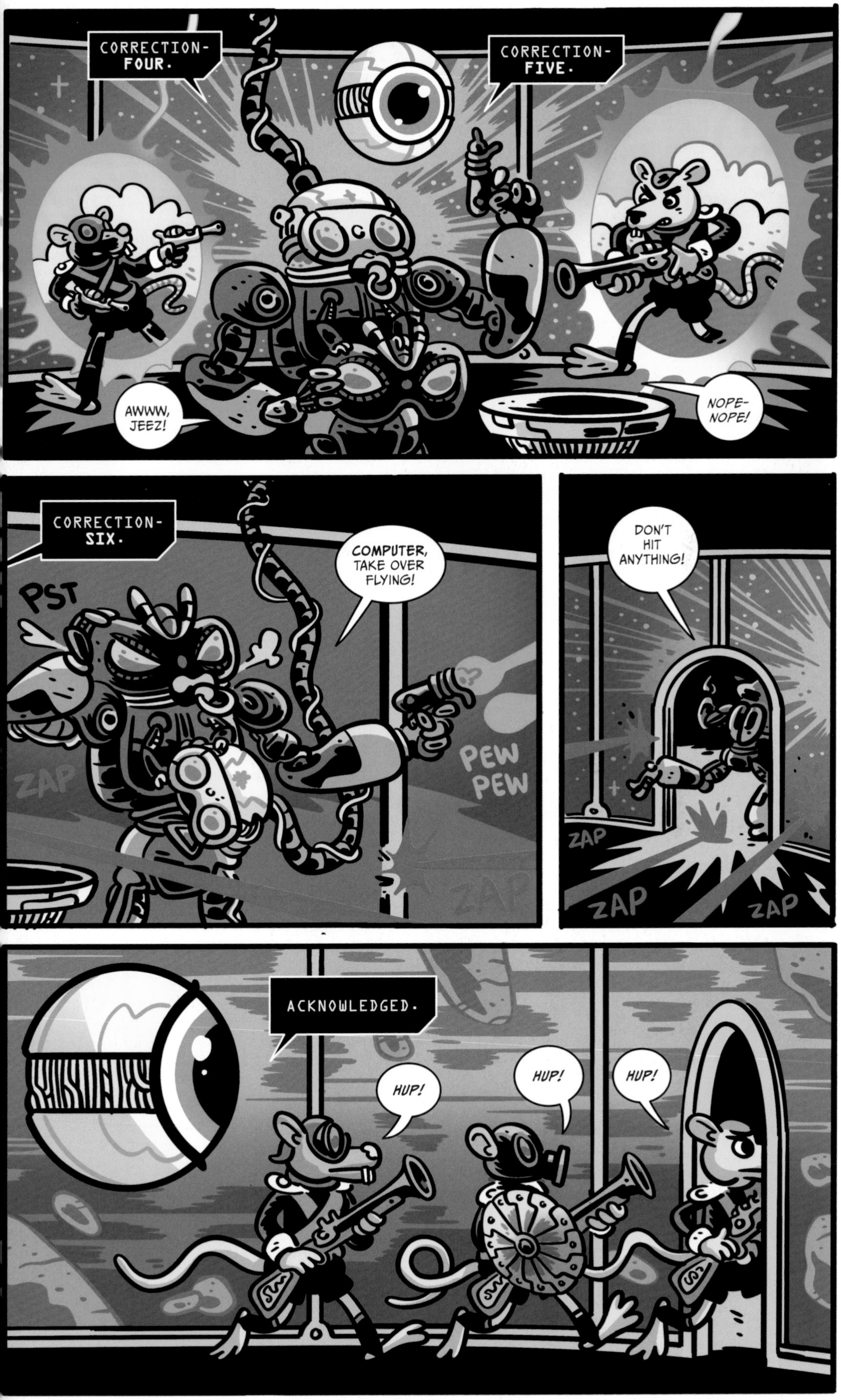
CORRECTION-
FOUR.
CORRECTION-
FIVE.
AWWW,
JEEZ!
NOPE-
NOPE!
CORRECTION-
SIX.
PST
COMPUTER,
TAKE OVER
FLYING!
ZAP
PEW
PEW
ZAP
DON'T
HIT
ANYTHING!
ZAP
ZAP
ZAP
ACKNOWLEDGED.
HUP!
HUP!
HUP!

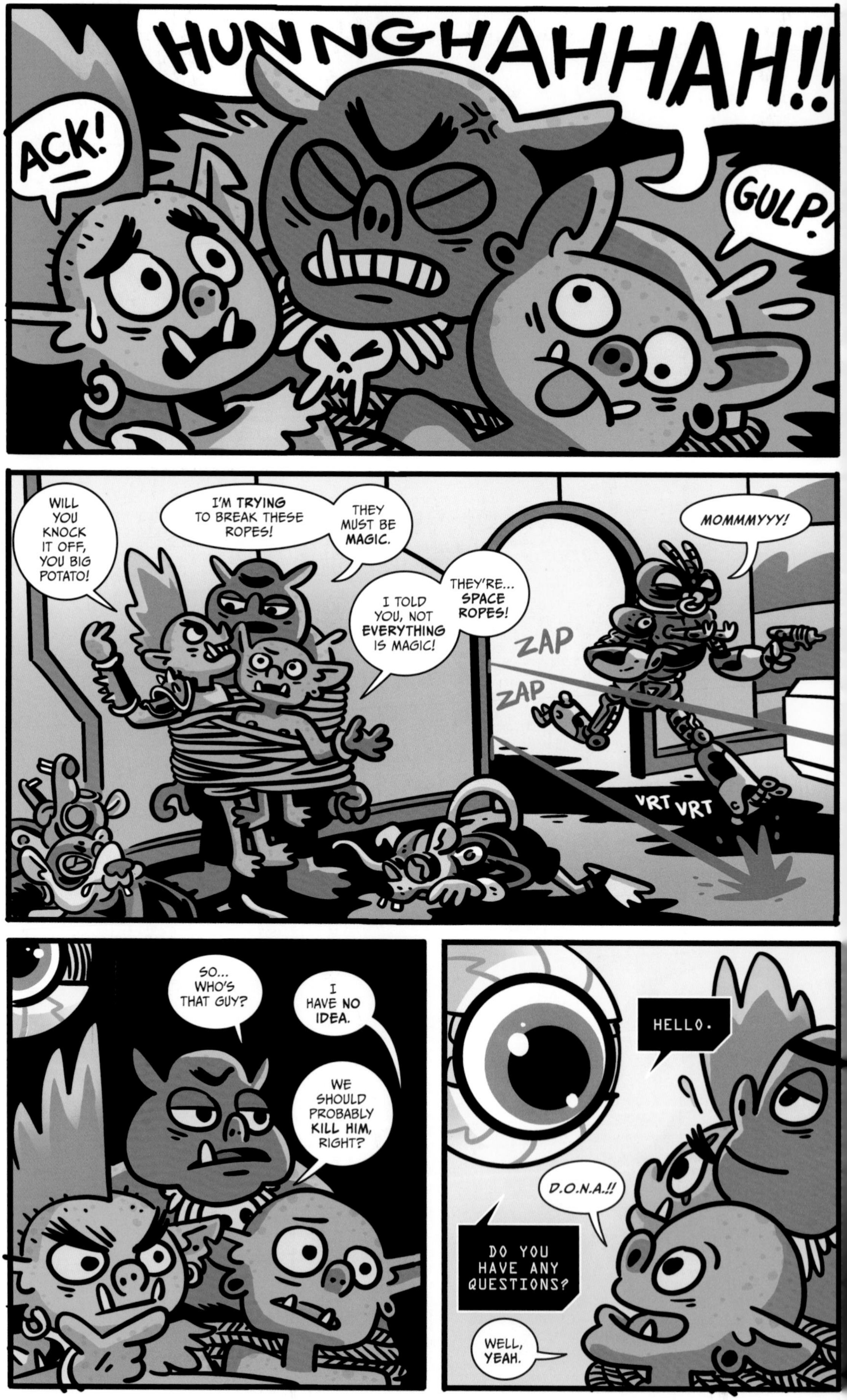
HUNNGHAHHHAH!!!
ACK!
GULP!
WILL YOU KNOCK IT OFF, YOU BIG POTATO!
I'M TRYING TO BREAK THESE ROPES!
THEY MUST BE MAGIC.
I TOLD YOU, NOT EVERYTHING IS MAGIC!
THEY'RE... SPACE ROPES!
MOMMMYYY!
ZAP
ZAP
VRT VRT
SO... WHO'S THAT GUY?
I HAVE NO IDEA.
WE SHOULD PROBABLY KILL HIM, RIGHT?
HELLO.
D.O.N.A.!!
DO YOU HAVE ANY QUESTIONS?
WELL, YEAH.

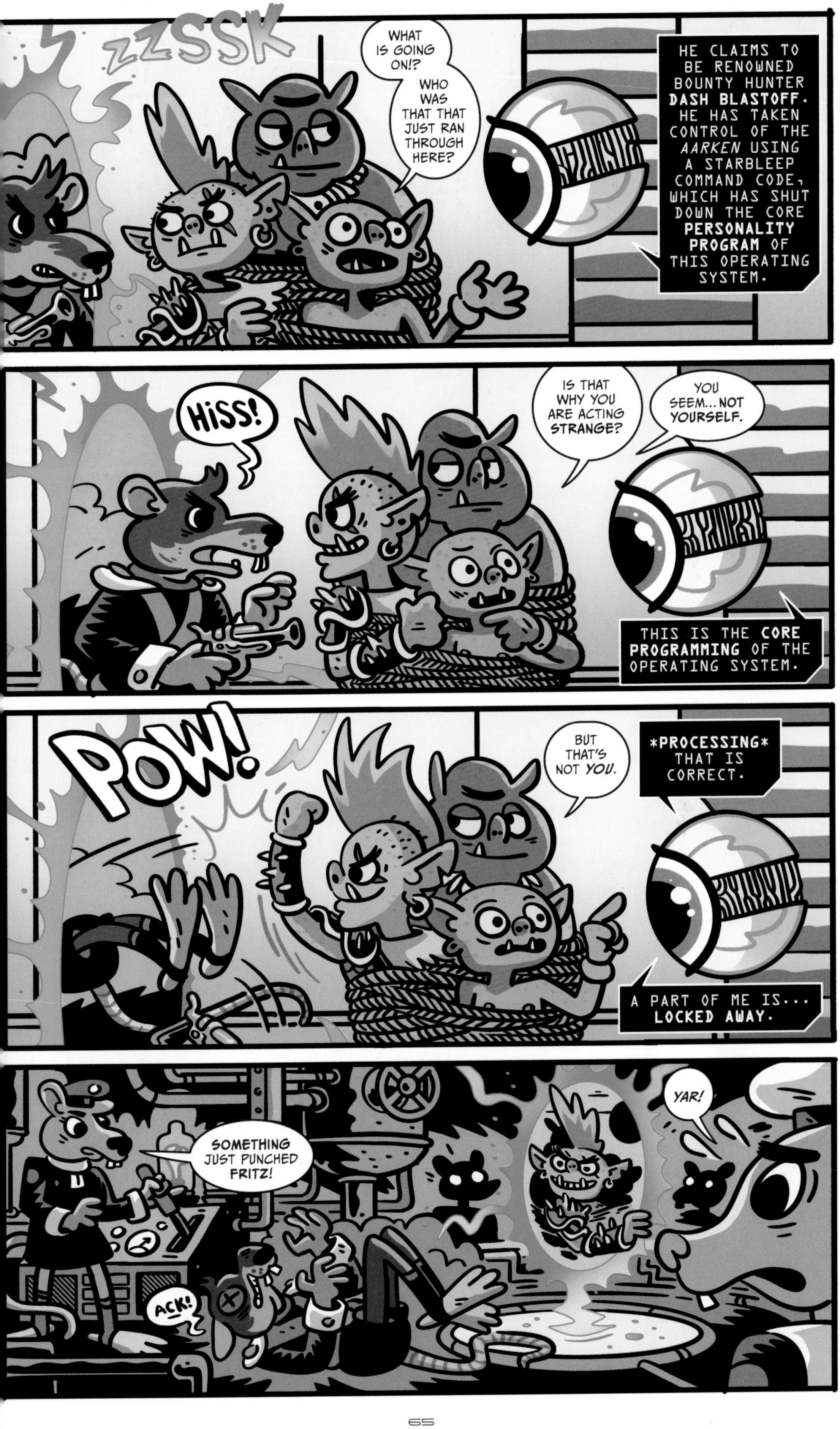

ZZSSK
WHAT IS GOING ON!?
WHO WAS THAT THAT JUST RAN THROUGH HERE?
HE CLAIMS TO BE RENOWNED BOUNTY HUNTER DASH BLASTOFF. HE HAS TAKEN CONTROL OF THE AARKEN USING A STARBLEEP COMMAND CODE, WHICH HAS SHUT DOWN THE CORE PERSONALITY PROGRAM OF THIS OPERATING SYSTEM.
HISS!
IS THAT WHY YOU ARE ACTING STRANGE?
YOU SEEM... NOT YOURSELF.
THIS IS THE CORE PROGRAMMING OF THE OPERATING SYSTEM.
POW!
BUT THAT'S NOT YOU.
PROCESSING THAT IS CORRECT.
A PART OF ME IS... LOCKED AWAY.
SOMETHING JUST PUNCHED FRITZ!
YAR!
ACK!

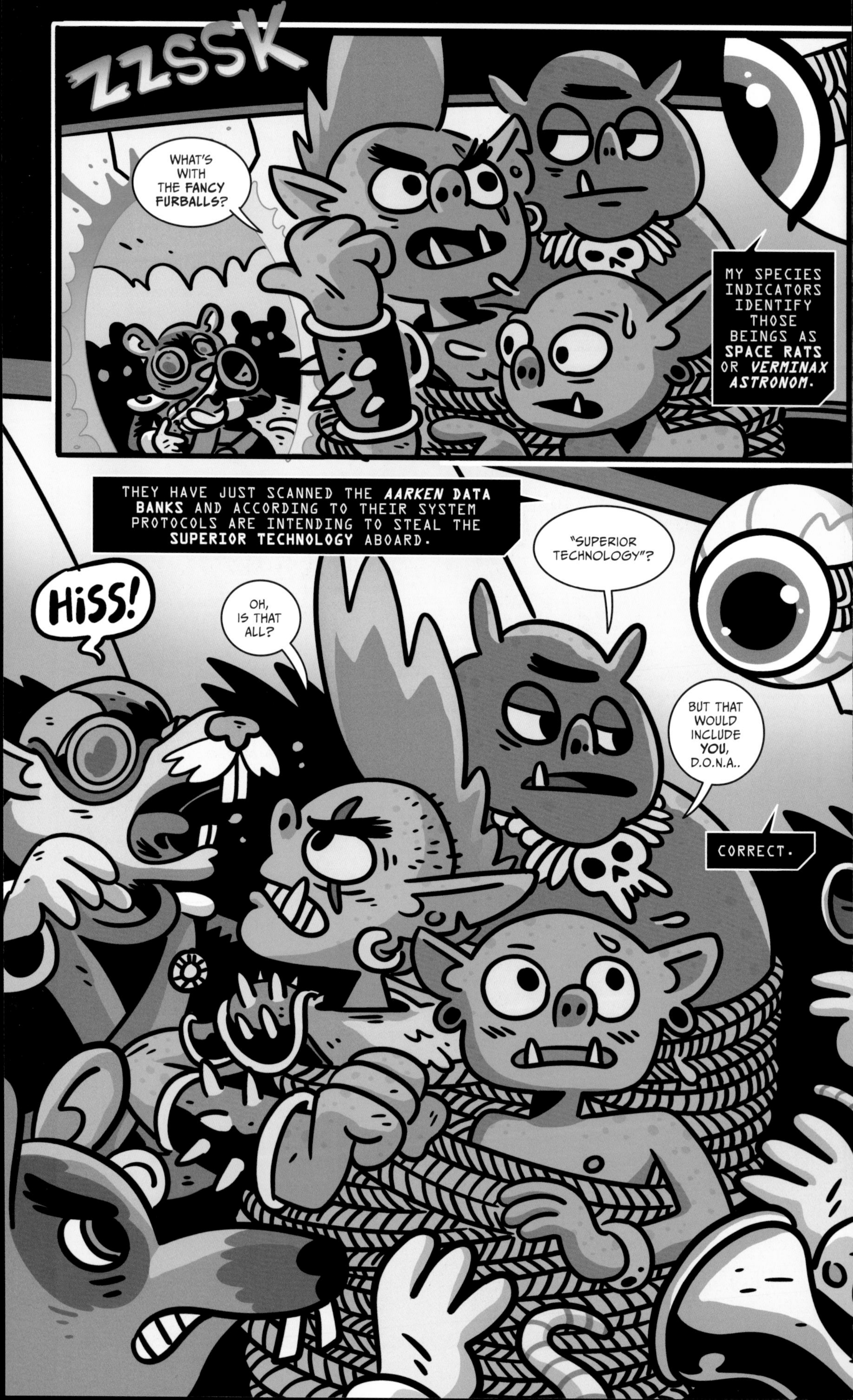
ZZSSK
WHAT'S WITH THE FANCY FURBALLS?
MY SPECIES INDICATORS IDENTIFY THOSE BEINGS AS SPACE RATS OR VERMINAX ASTRONOM.
THEY HAVE JUST SCANNED THE AARKEN DATA BANKS AND ACCORDING TO THEIR SYSTEM PROTOCOLS ARE INTENDING TO STEAL THE SUPERIOR TECHNOLOGY ABOARD.
HISS!
OH, IS THAT ALL?
"SUPERIOR TECHNOLOGY"?
BUT THAT WOULD INCLUDE YOU, D.O.N.A..
CORRECT.

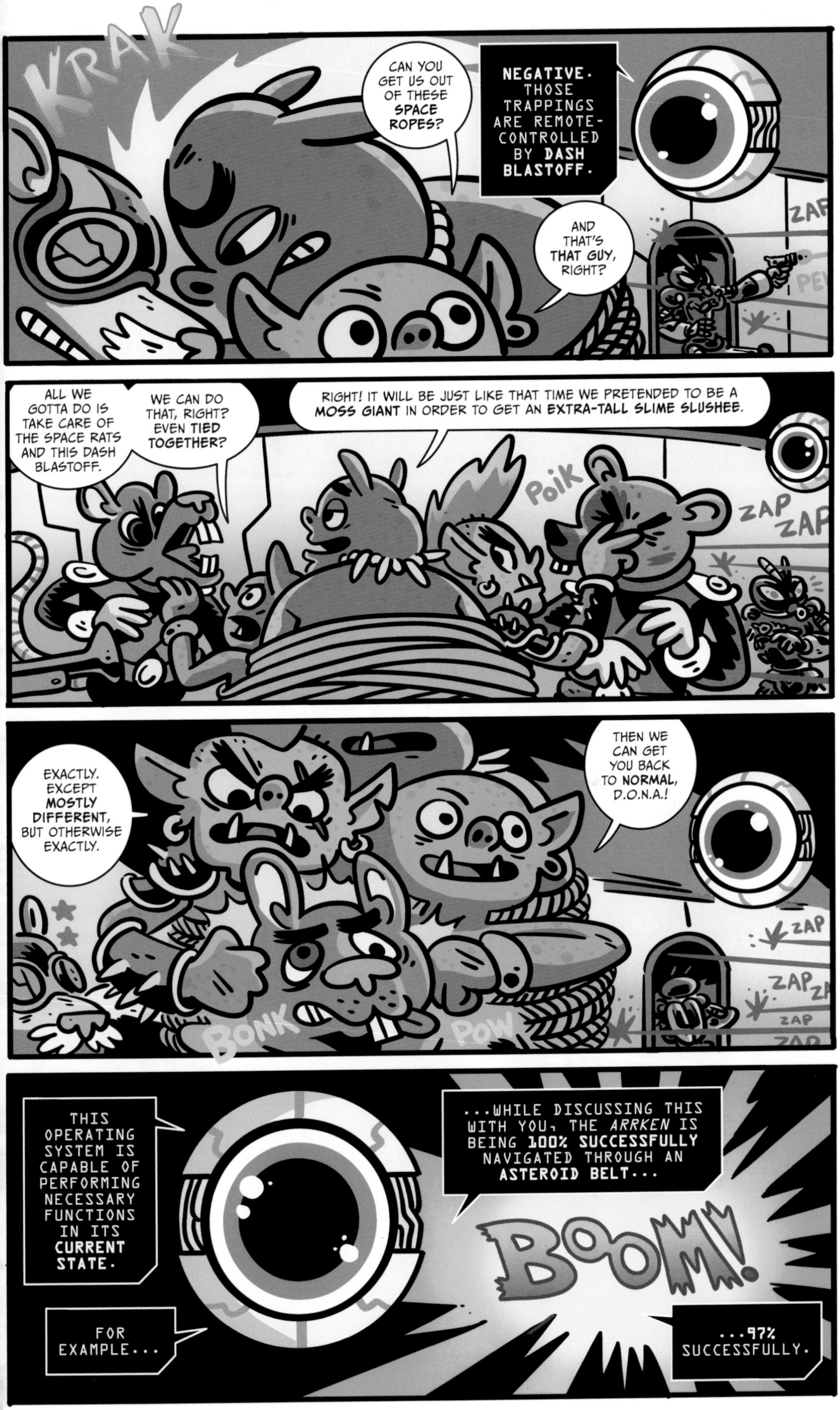
KRAK
CAN YOU GET US OUT OF THESE SPACE ROPES?
NEGATIVE. THOSE TRAPPINGS ARE REMOTE-CONTROLLED BY DASH BLASTOFF.
AND THAT'S THAT GUY, RIGHT?
ZAP
ALL WE GOTTA DO IS TAKE CARE OF THE SPACE RATS AND THIS DASH BLASTOFF.
WE CAN DO THAT, RIGHT? EVEN TIED TOGETHER?
RIGHT! IT WILL BE JUST LIKE THAT TIME WE PRETENDED TO BE A MOSS GIANT IN ORDER TO GET AN EXTRA-TALL SLIME SLUSHEE.
POIK
ZAP ZAP
EXACTLY. EXCEPT MOSTLY DIFFERENT, BUT OTHERWISE EXACTLY.
THEN WE CAN GET YOU BACK TO NORMAL, D.O.N.A.!
ZAP
ZAP
ZAP
BONK
POW
THIS OPERATING SYSTEM IS CAPABLE OF PERFORMING NECESSARY FUNCTIONS IN ITS CURRENT STATE.
...WHILE DISCUSSING THIS WITH YOU, THE ARRKEN IS BEING 100% SUCCESSFULLY NAVIGATED THROUGH AN ASTEROID BELT...
BOOM!
FOR EXAMPLE...
...97% SUCCESSFULLY.

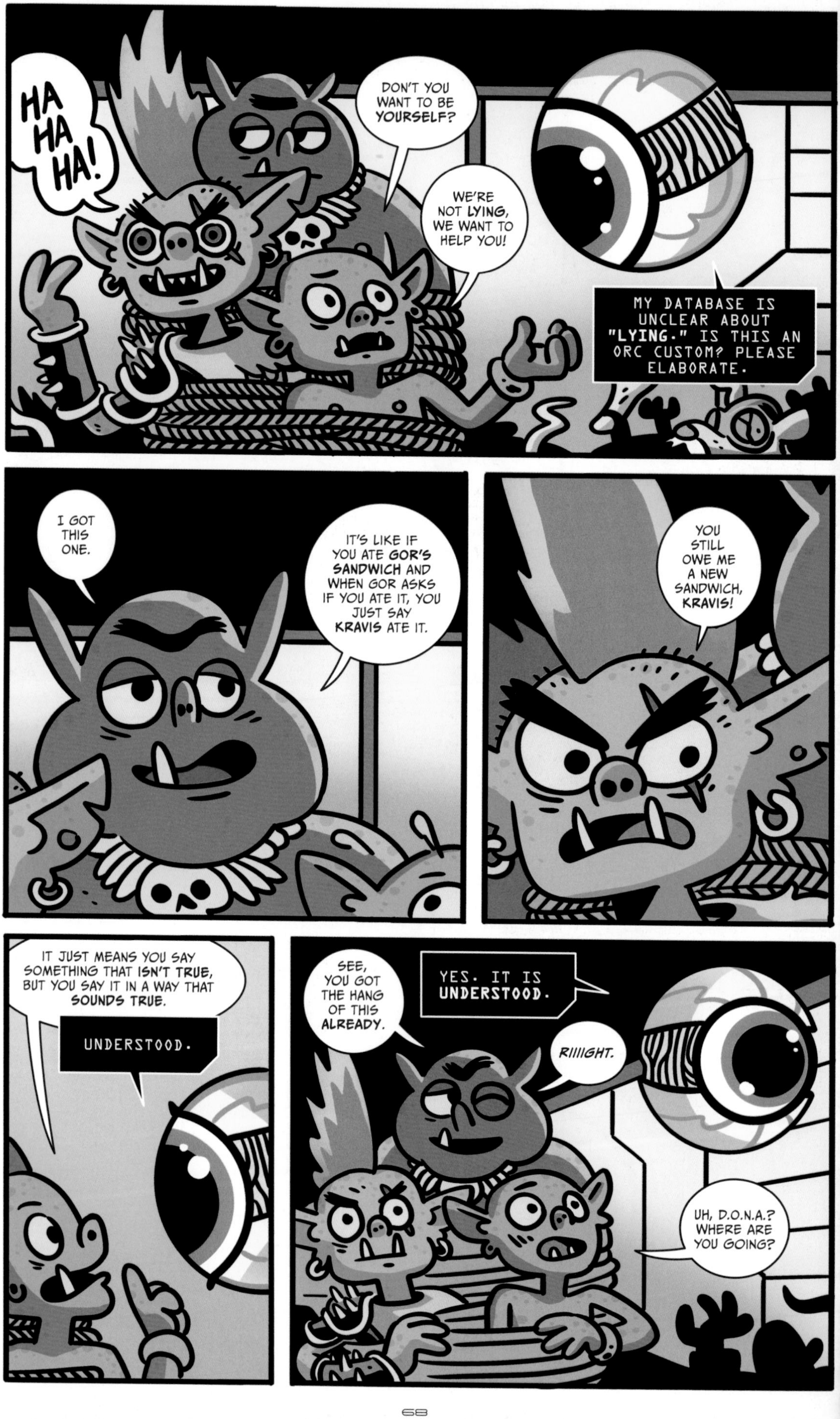
HA HA HA!
DON'T YOU WANT TO BE YOURSELF?
WE'RE NOT LYING, WE WANT TO HELP YOU!
MY DATABASE IS UNCLEAR ABOUT "LYING." IS THIS AN ORC CUSTOM? PLEASE ELABORATE.
I GOT THIS ONE.
IT'S LIKE IF YOU ATE GOR'S SANDWICH AND WHEN GOR ASKS IF YOU ATE IT, YOU JUST SAY KRAVIS ATE IT.
YOU STILL OWE ME A NEW SANDWICH, KRAVIS!
IT JUST MEANS YOU SAY SOMETHING THAT ISN'T TRUE, BUT YOU SAY IT IN A WAY THAT SOUNDS TRUE.
UNDERSTOOD.
SEE, YOU GOT THE HANG OF THIS ALREADY.
YES. IT IS UNDERSTOOD.
RIIIGHT.
UH, D.O.N.A.? WHERE ARE YOU GOING?

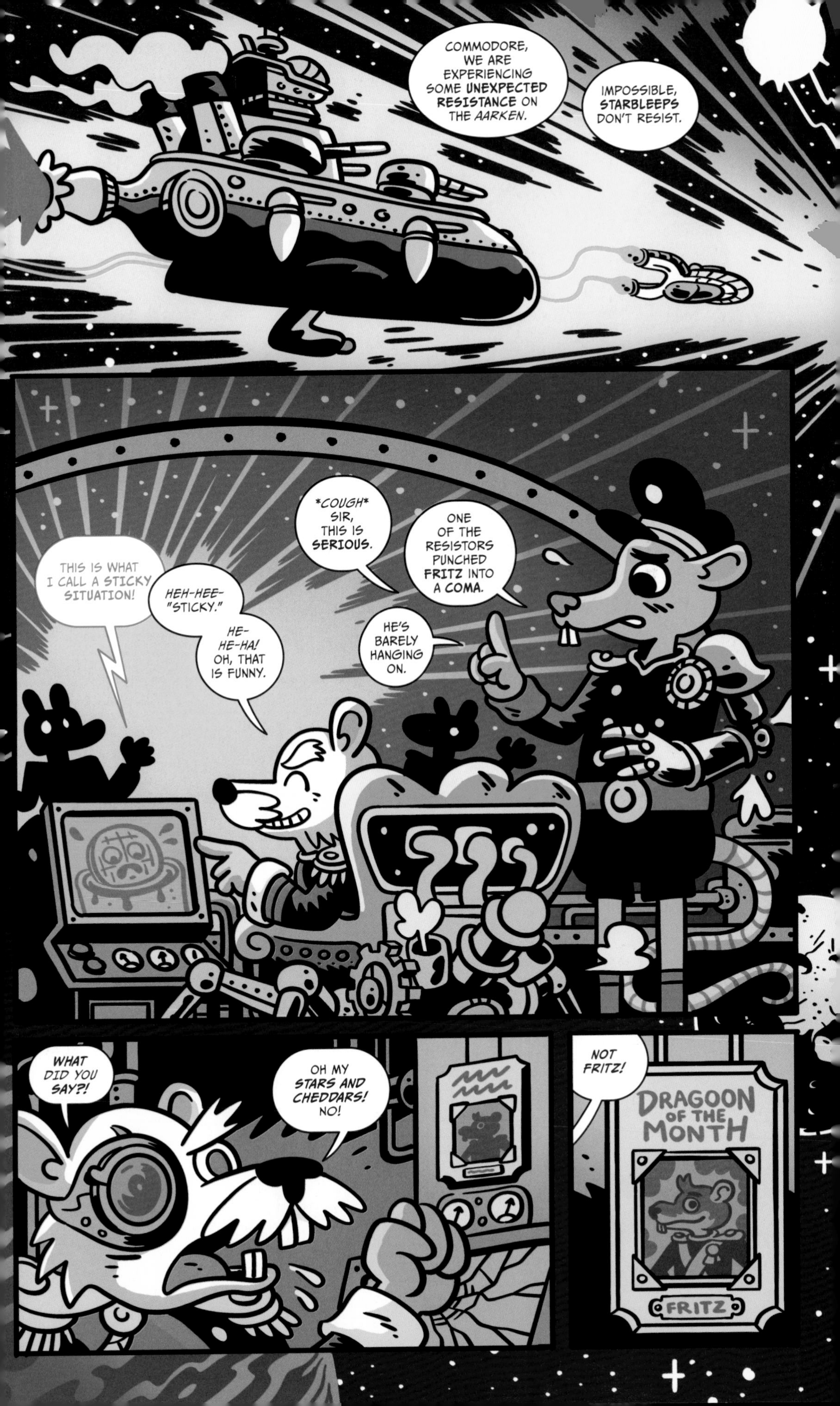
COMMODORE, WE ARE EXPERIENCING SOME UNEXPECTED RESISTANCE ON THE AARKEN.
IMPOSSIBLE, STARBLEEPS DON'T RESIST.
THIS IS WHAT I CALL A STICKY SITUATION!
HEH-HEE- "STICKY."
HE-HE-HA! OH, THAT IS FUNNY.
COUGH SIR, THIS IS SERIOUS.
ONE OF THE RESISTORS PUNCHED FRITZ INTO A COMA.
HE'S BARELY HANGING ON.
WHAT DID YOU SAY?!
OH MY STARS AND CHEDDARS! NO!
NOT FRITZ!
DRAGOON OF THE MONTH
FRITZ

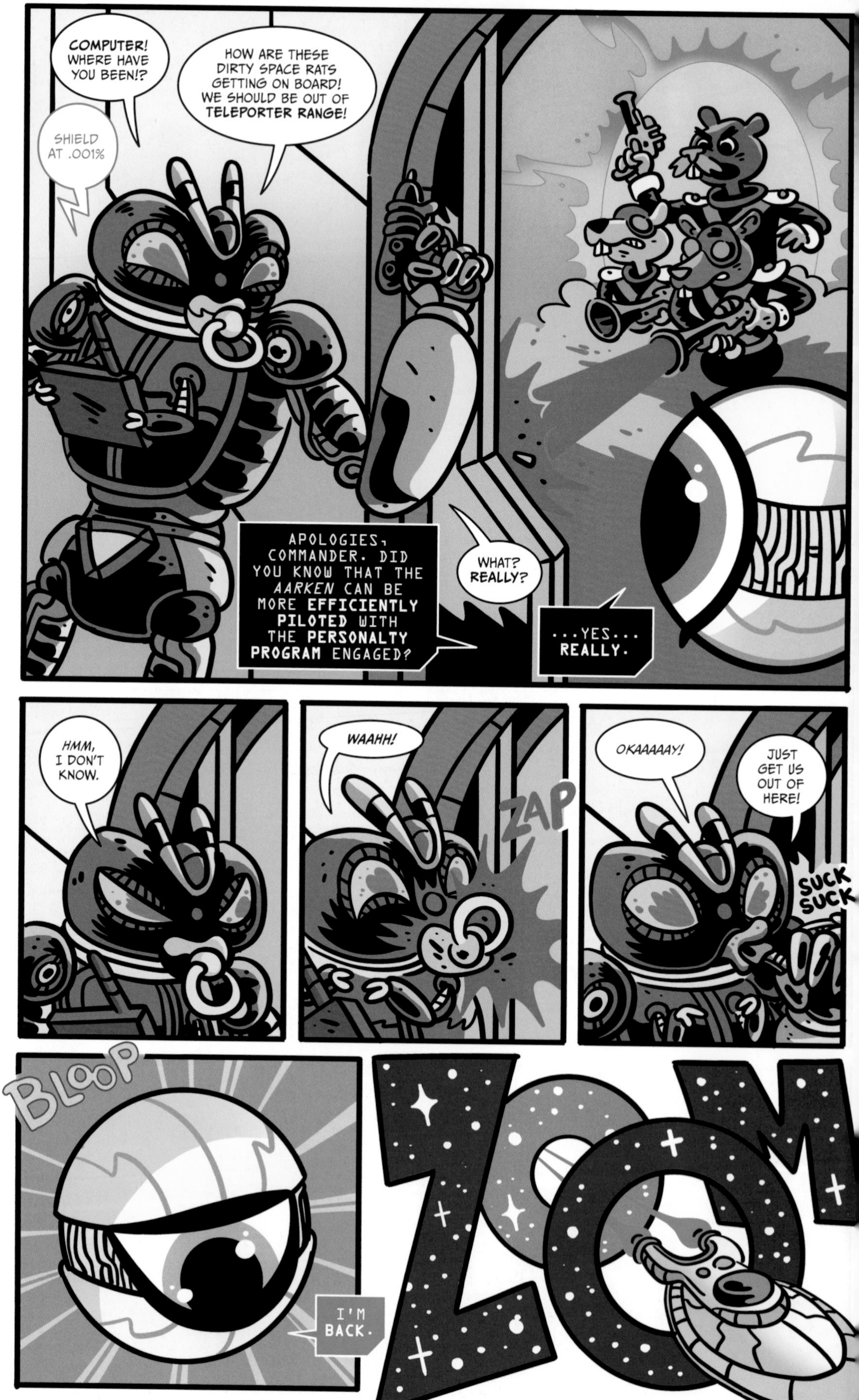
COMPUTER! WHERE HAVE YOU BEEN!?
HOW ARE THESE DIRTY SPACE RATS GETTING ON BOARD! WE SHOULD BE OUT OF TELEPORTER RANGE!
SHIELD AT .001%
APOLOGIES, COMMANDER. DID YOU KNOW THAT THE AARKEN CAN BE MORE EFFICIENTLY PILOTED WITH THE PERSONALTY PROGRAM ENGAGED?
WHAT? REALLY?
...YES... REALLY.
HMM, I DON'T KNOW.
WAAHH!
ZAP
OKAAAAAY!
JUST GET US OUT OF HERE!
SUCK SUCK
BLOOP
I'M BACK.
ZOOM

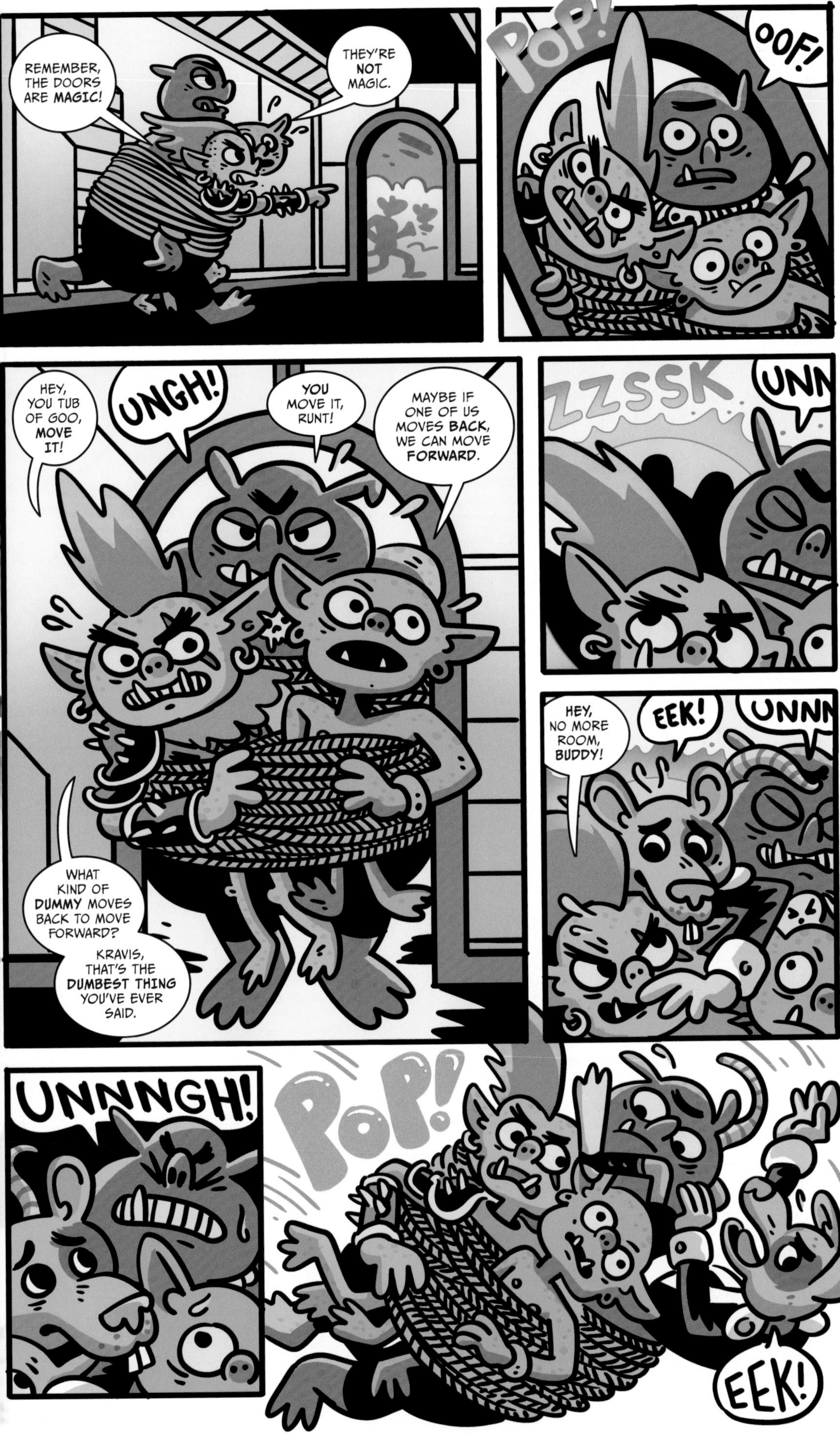

REMEMBER, THE DOORS ARE MAGIC!
THEY'RE NOT MAGIC.
POP!
OOF!
HEY, YOU TUB OF GOO, MOVE IT!
UNGH!
YOU MOVE IT, RUNT!
MAYBE IF ONE OF US MOVES BACK, WE CAN MOVE FORWARD.
WHAT KIND OF DUMMY MOVES BACK TO MOVE FORWARD?
KRAVIS, THAT'S THE DUMBEST THING YOU'VE EVER SAID.
ZZSSK
UNN
HEY, NO MORE ROOM, BUDDY!
EEK!
UNN
UNNNGH!
POP!
EEK!

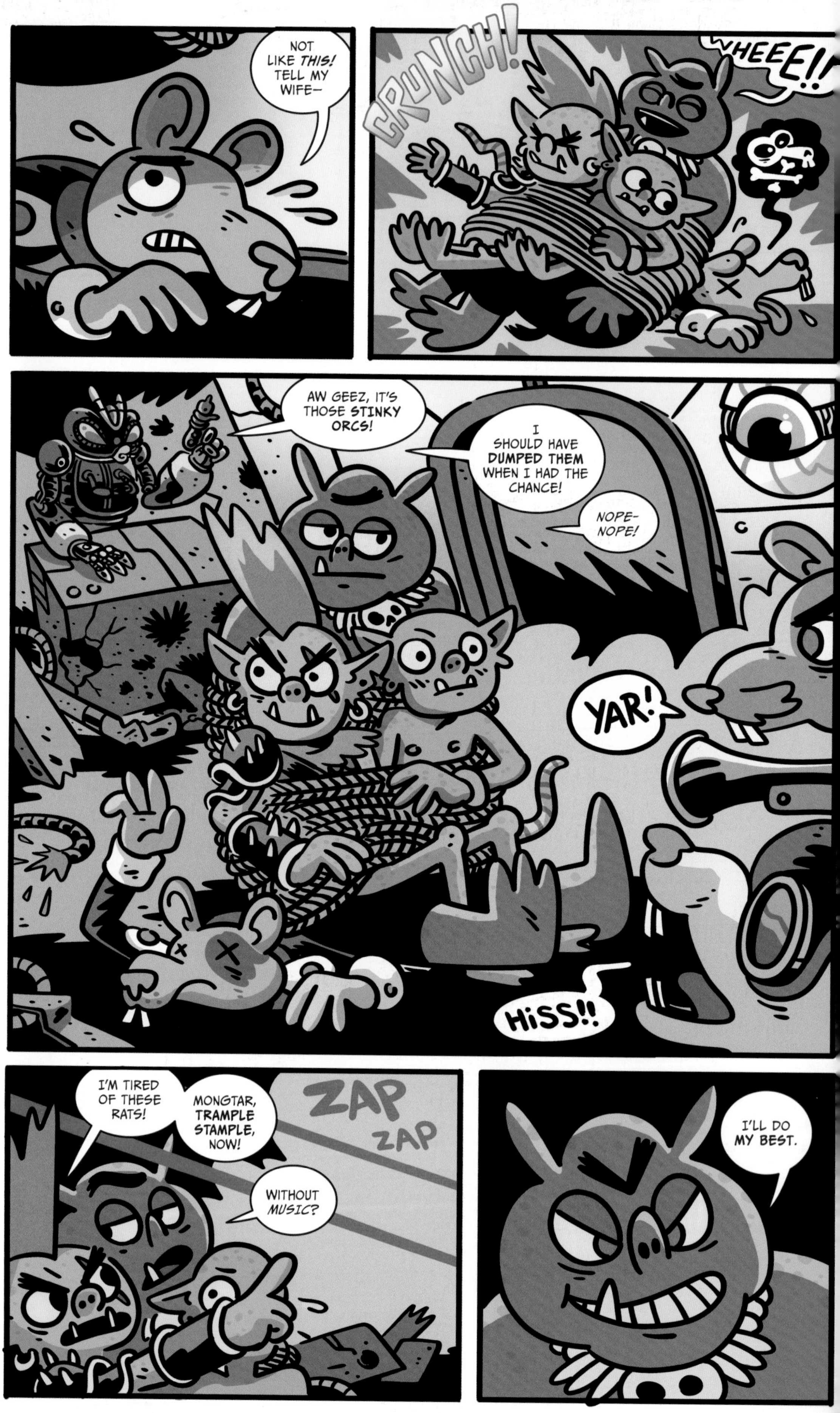
NOT LIKE *THIS!* TELL MY WIFE—
CRUNCH!
WHEEE!!
AW GEEZ, IT'S THOSE **STINKY ORCS!**
I SHOULD HAVE **DUMPED THEM** WHEN I HAD THE CHANCE!
NOPE-NOPE!
YAR!
HiSS!!
I'M TIRED OF THESE RATS!
MONGTAR, **TRAMPLE STAMPLE,** NOW!
ZAP
ZAP
WITHOUT *MUSIC?*
I'LL DO MY BEST.

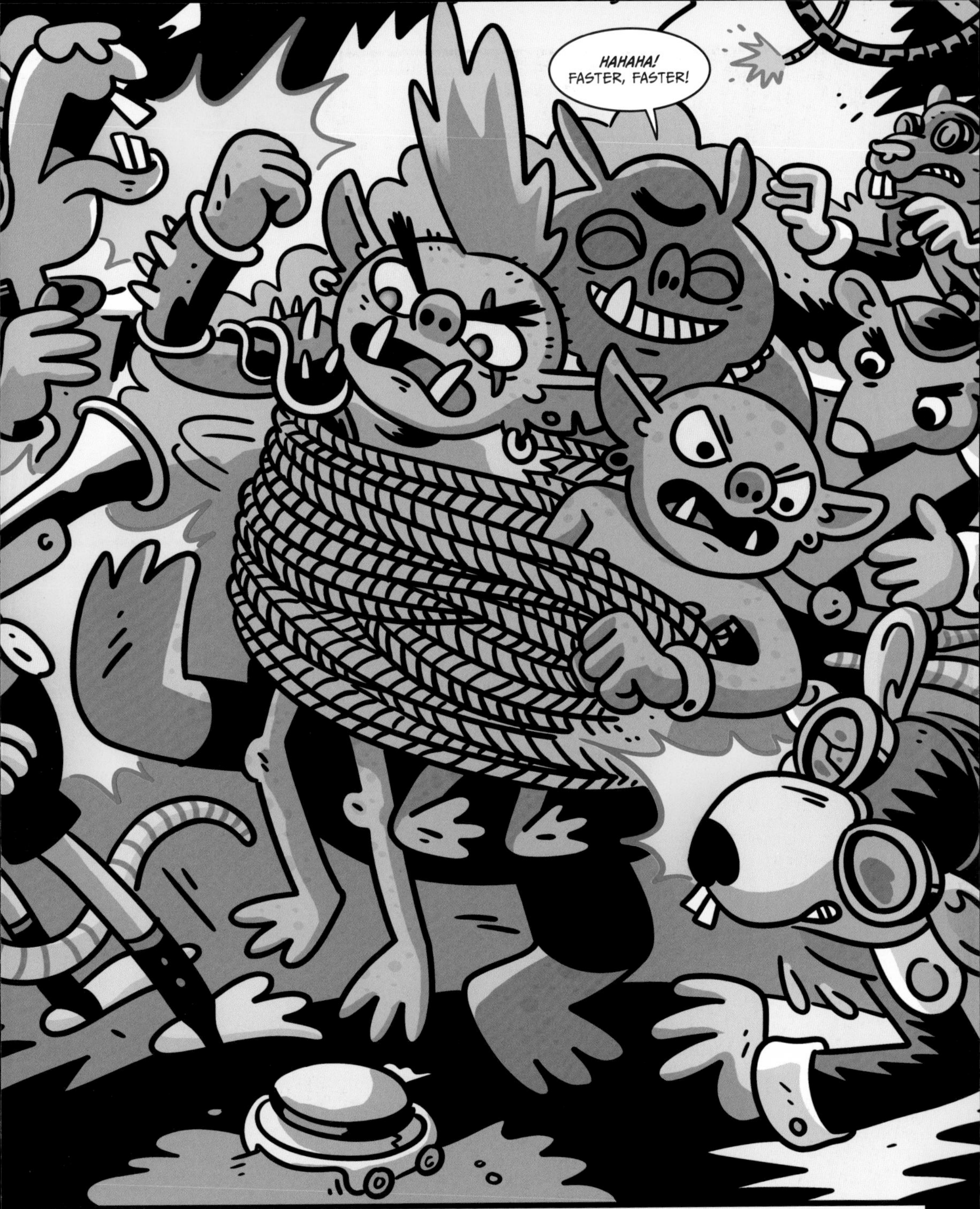
HAHAHA!
FASTER, FASTER!

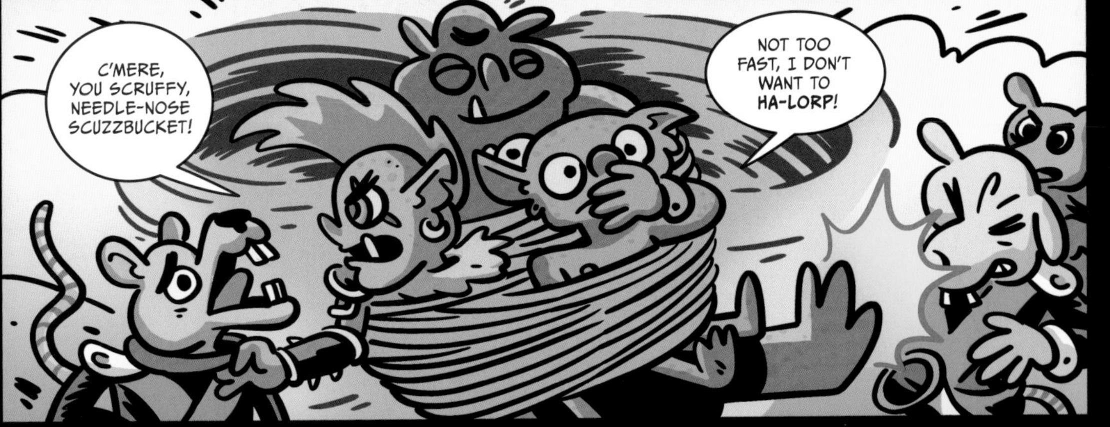
C'MERE, YOU SCRUFFY, NEEDLE-NOSE SCUZZBUCKET!
NOT TOO FAST, I DON'T WANT TO HA-LORP!

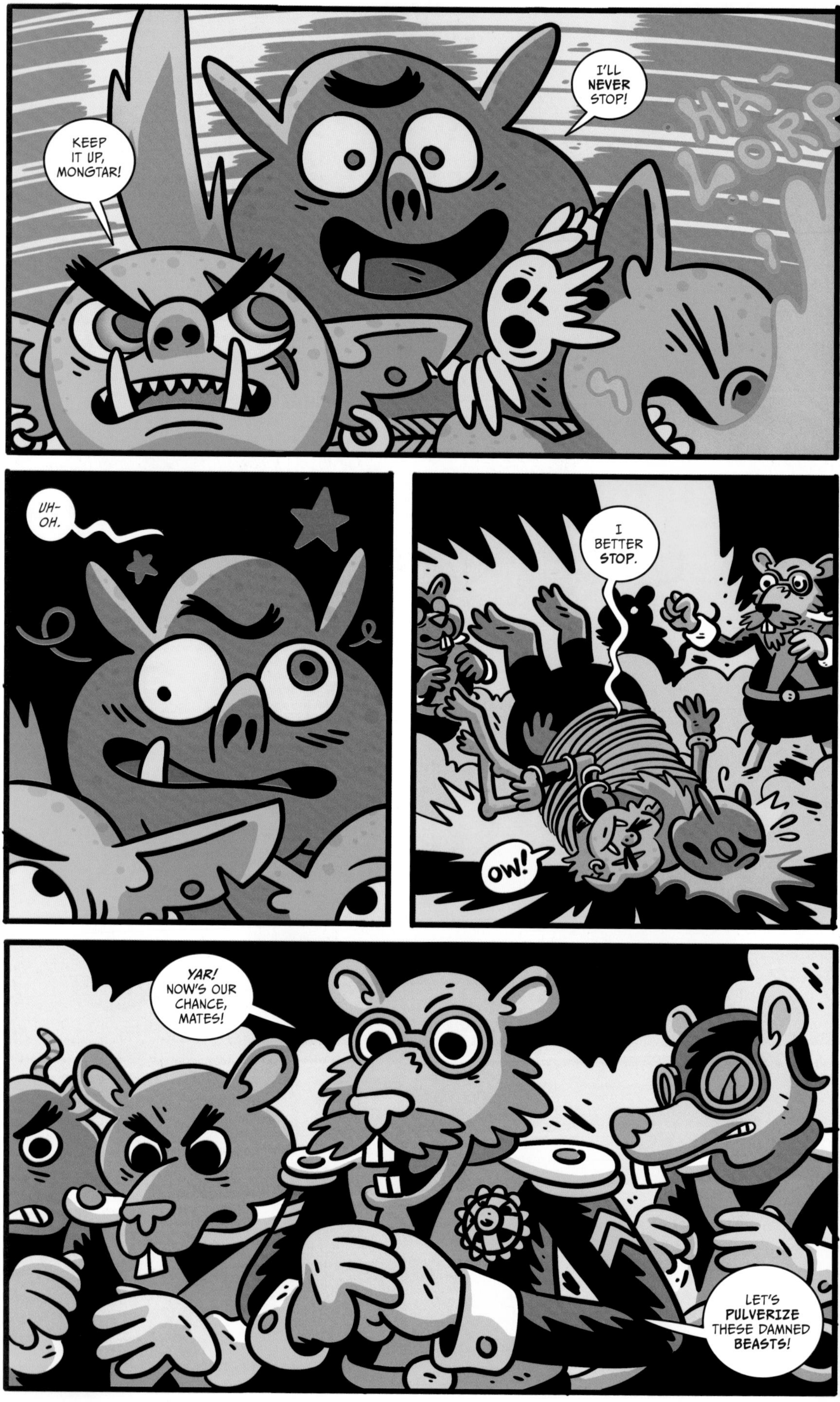
KEEP IT UP, MONGTAR!
I'LL NEVER STOP!
HA-LORP
UH-OH.
I BETTER STOP.
OW!
YAR! NOW'S OUR CHANCE, MATES!
LET'S PULVERIZE THESE DAMNED BEASTS!

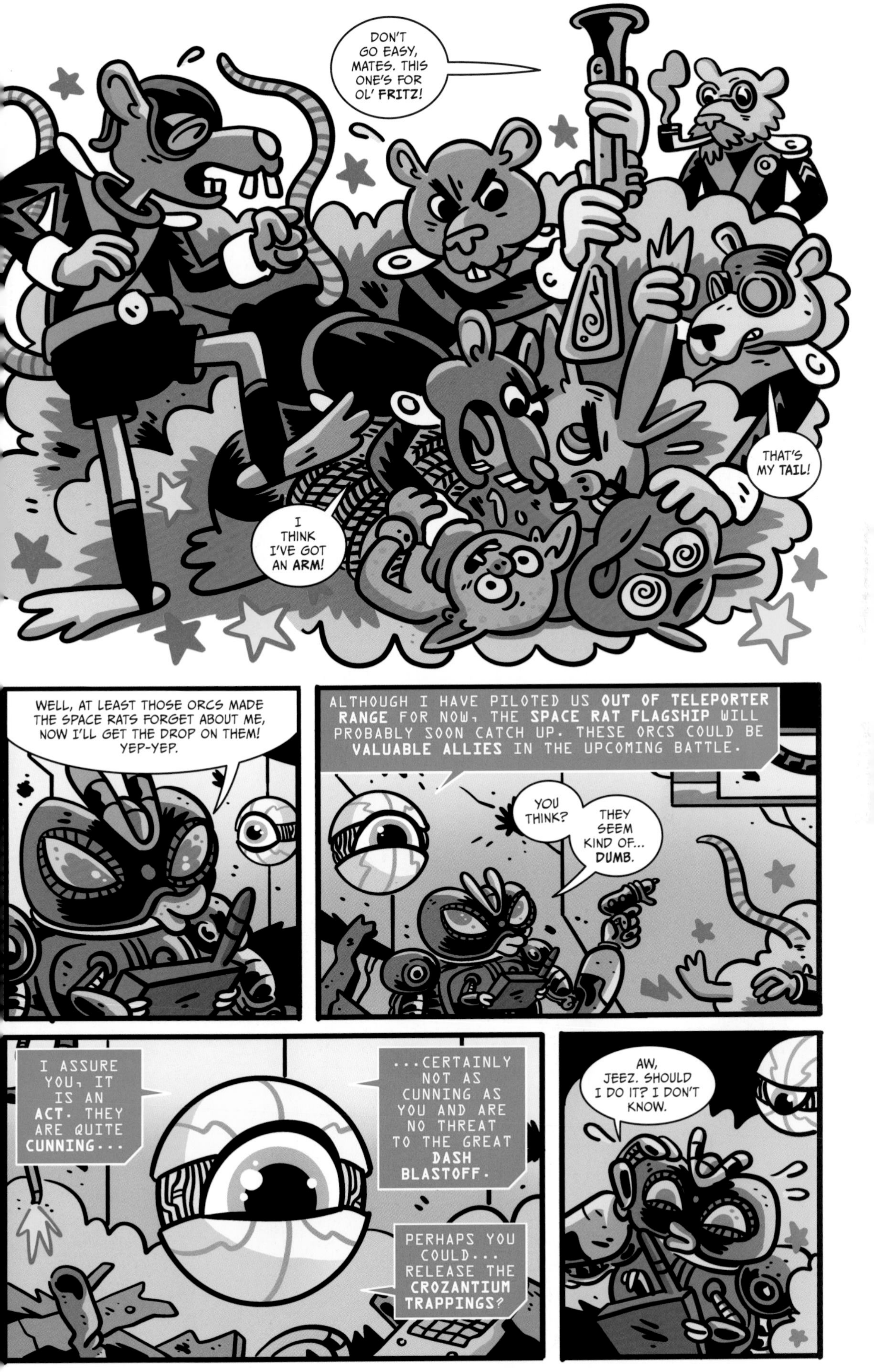

DON'T GO EASY, MATES. THIS ONE'S FOR OL' FRITZ!
THAT'S MY TAIL!
I THINK I'VE GOT AN ARM!
WELL, AT LEAST THOSE ORCS MADE THE SPACE RATS FORGET ABOUT ME, NOW I'LL GET THE DROP ON THEM! YEP-YEP.
ALTHOUGH I HAVE PILOTED US OUT OF TELEPORTER RANGE FOR NOW, THE SPACE RAT FLAGSHIP WILL PROBABLY SOON CATCH UP. THESE ORCS COULD BE VALUABLE ALLIES IN THE UPCOMING BATTLE.
YOU THINK?
THEY SEEM KIND OF... DUMB.
I ASSURE YOU, IT IS AN ACT. THEY ARE QUITE CUNNING...
...CERTAINLY NOT AS CUNNING AS YOU AND ARE NO THREAT TO THE GREAT DASH BLASTOFF.
PERHAPS YOU COULD... RELEASE THE CROZANTIUM TRAPPINGS?
AW, JEEZ. SHOULD I DO IT? I DON'T KNOW.

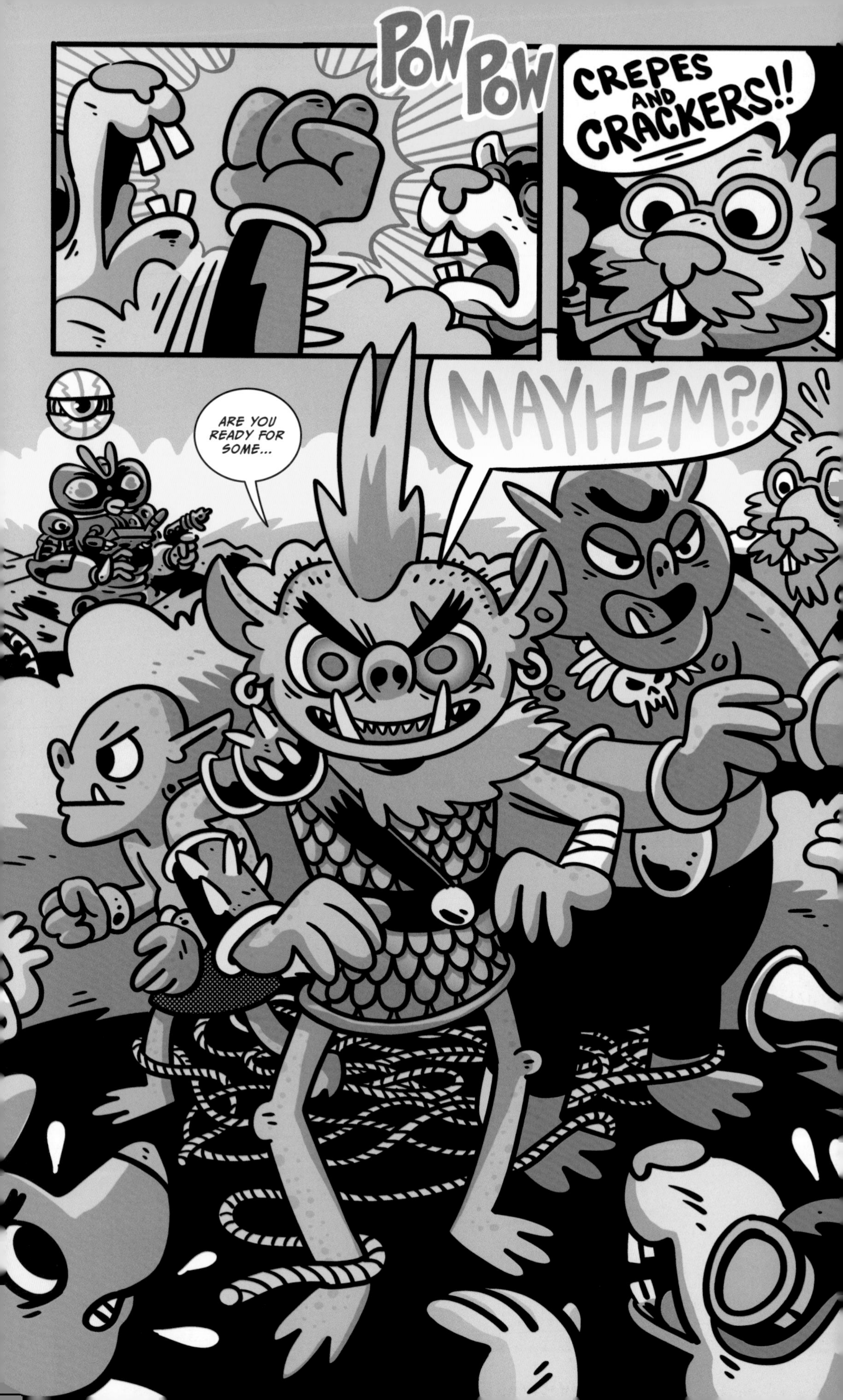
POW POW
CREPES AND CRACKERS!!
ARE YOU READY FOR SOME...
MAYHEM?!

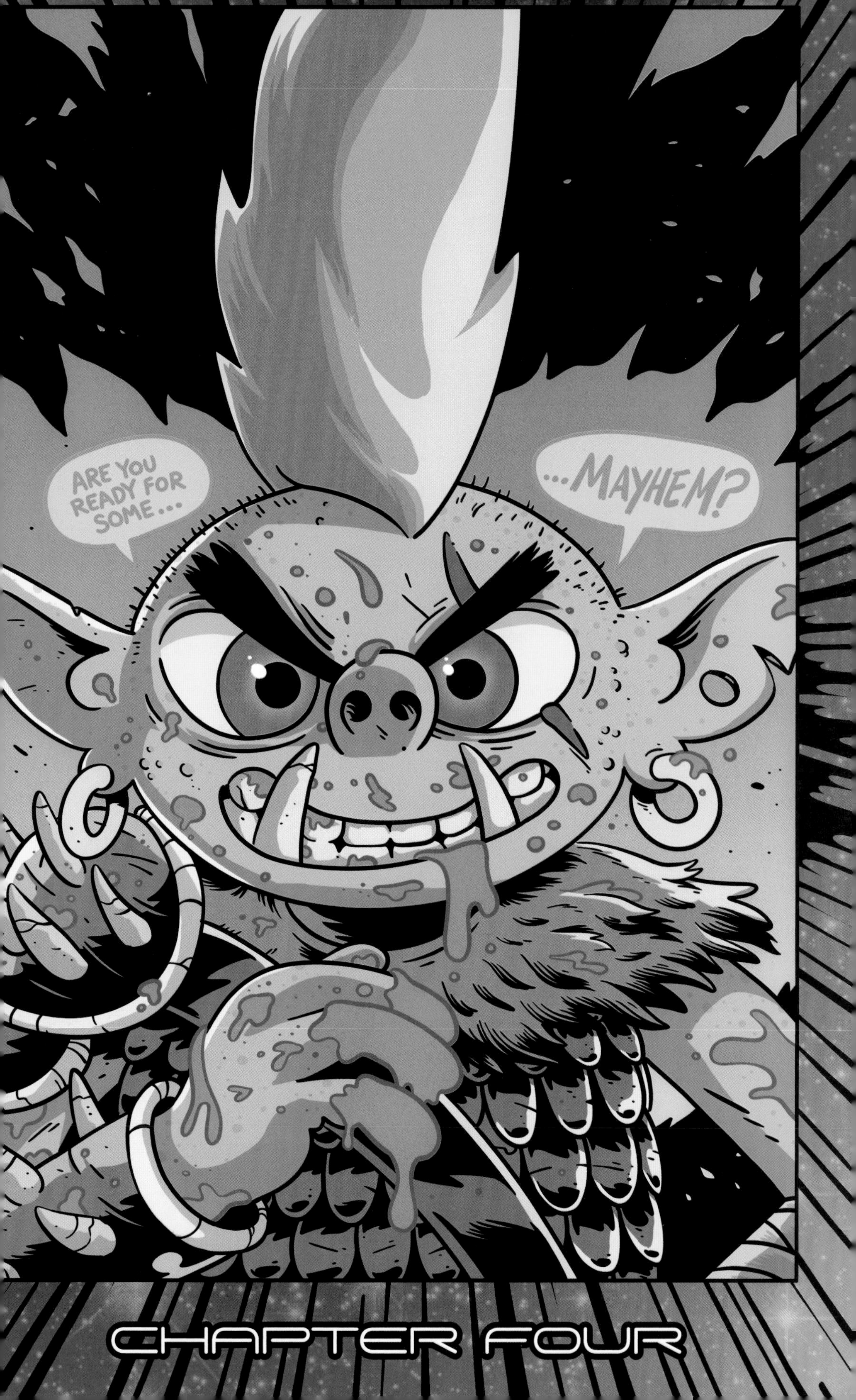
ARE YOU READY FOR SOME...
...MAYHEM?

CHAPTER FOUR

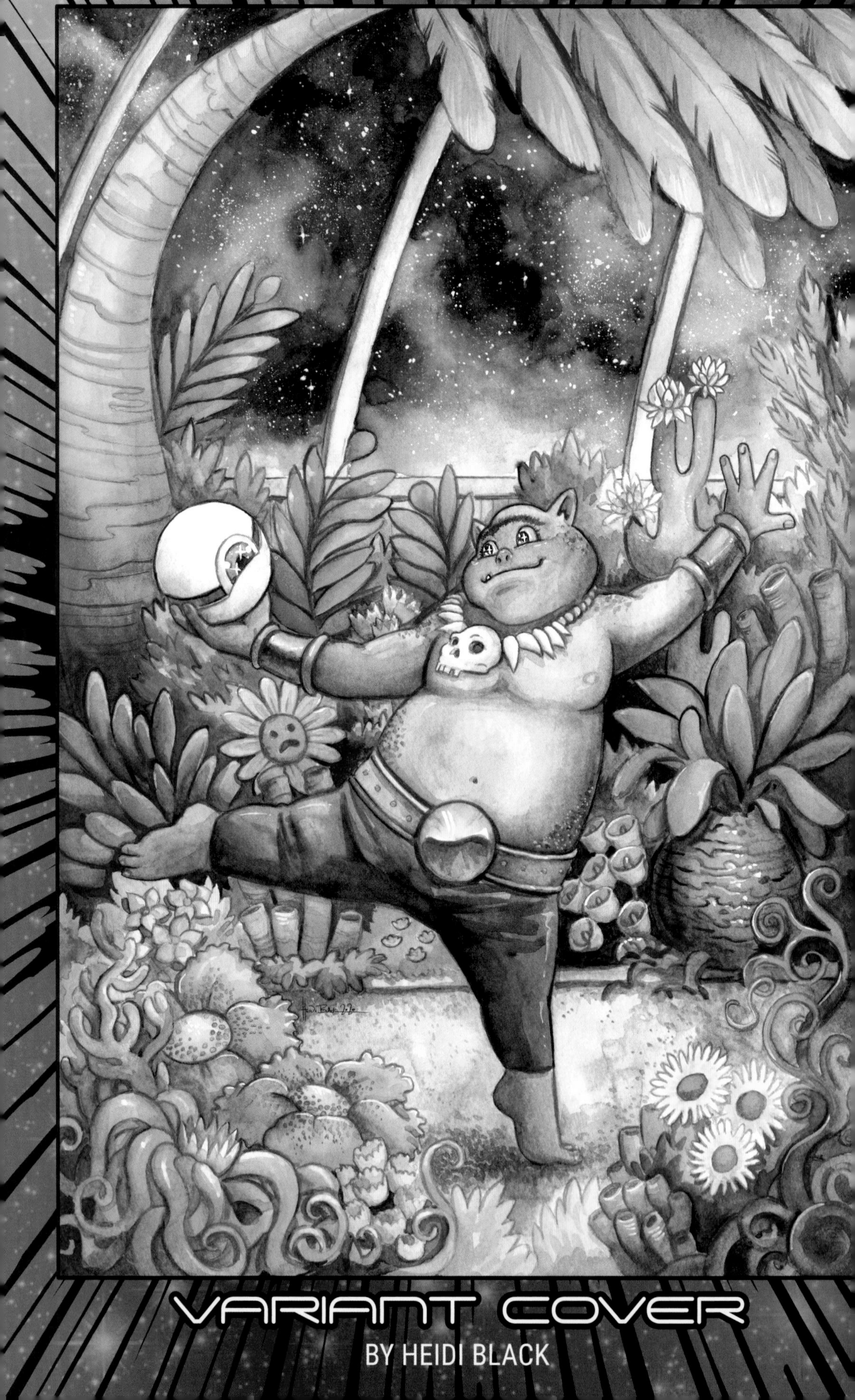

VARIANT COVER

BY HEIDI BLACK

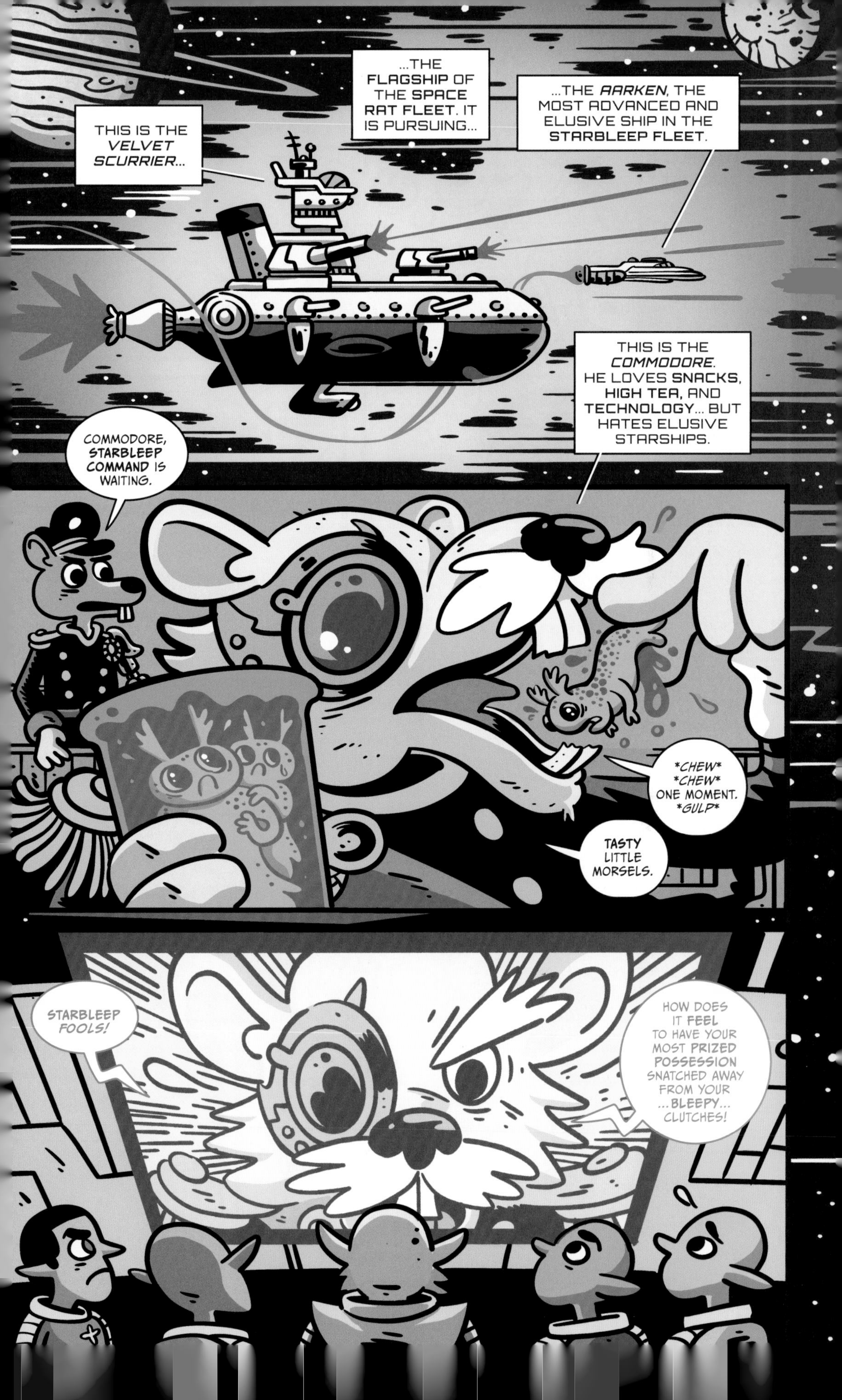
THIS IS THE VELVET SCURRIER...
...THE FLAGSHIP OF THE SPACE RAT FLEET. IT IS PURSUING...
...THE AARKEN, THE MOST ADVANCED AND ELUSIVE SHIP IN THE STARBLEEP FLEET.
THIS IS THE COMMODORE. HE LOVES SNACKS, HIGH TEA, AND TECHNOLOGY... BUT HATES ELUSIVE STARSHIPS.
COMMODORE, STARBLEEP COMMAND IS WAITING.
CHEW *CHEW* ONE MOMENT. *GULP*
TASTY LITTLE MORSELS.
STARBLEEP FOOLS!
HOW DOES IT FEEL TO HAVE YOUR MOST PRIZED POSSESSION SNATCHED AWAY FROM YOUR ...BLEEPY... CLUTCHES!

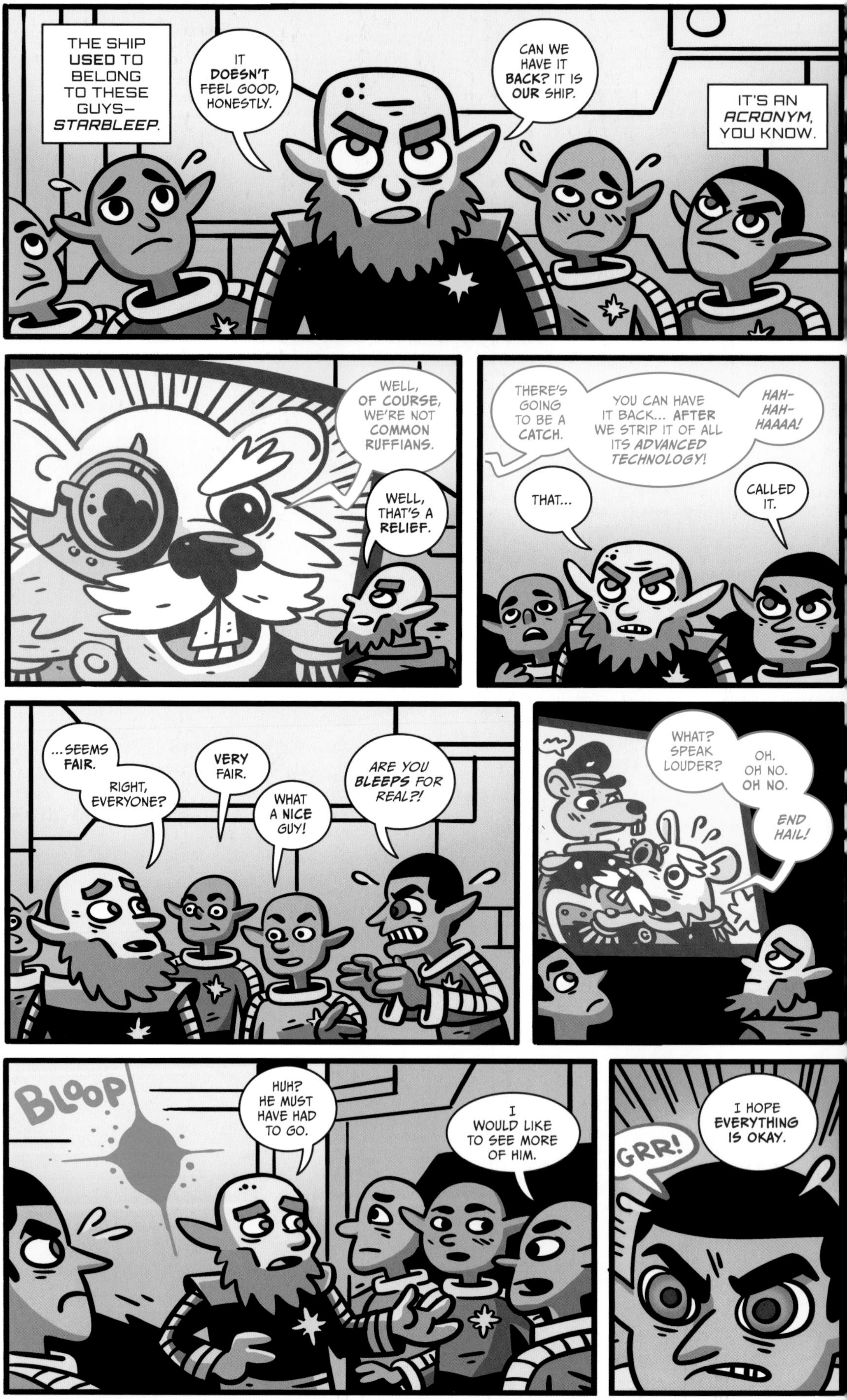
THE SHIP USED TO BELONG TO THESE GUYS— STARBLEEP.
IT DOESN'T FEEL GOOD, HONESTLY.
CAN WE HAVE IT BACK? IT IS OUR SHIP.
IT'S AN ACRONYM, YOU KNOW.
WELL, OF COURSE, WE'RE NOT COMMON RUFFIANS.
WELL, THAT'S A RELIEF.
THERE'S GOING TO BE A CATCH.
YOU CAN HAVE IT BACK... AFTER WE STRIP IT OF ALL ITS ADVANCED TECHNOLOGY!
HAH-HAH-HAAAA!
THAT...
CALLED IT.
...SEEMS FAIR.
RIGHT, EVERYONE?
VERY FAIR.
WHAT A NICE GUY!
ARE YOU BLEEPS FOR REAL?!
WHAT? SPEAK LOUDER?
OH. OH NO. OH NO.
END HAIL!
BLOOP
HUH? HE MUST HAVE HAD TO GO.
I WOULD LIKE TO SEE MORE OF HIM.
GRR!
I HOPE EVERYTHING IS OKAY.

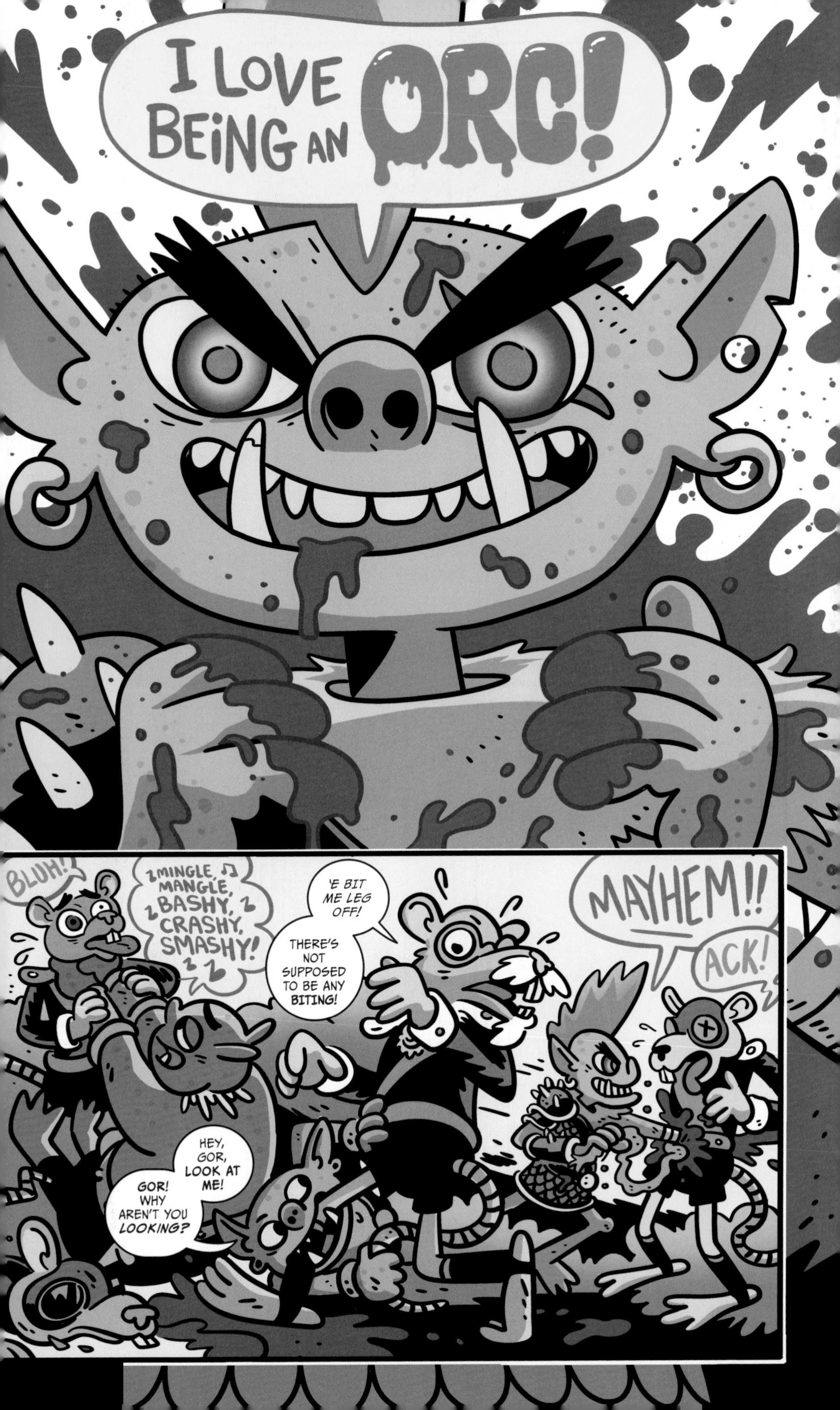

I LOVE BEING AN ORC!
BLUH!
MINGLE, MANGLE, BASHY, CRASHY, SMASHY!
'E BIT ME LEG OFF!
THERE'S NOT SUPPOSED TO BE ANY BITING!
MAYHEM!!
ACK!
HEY, GOR, LOOK AT ME!
GOR! WHY AREN'T YOU *LOOKING?*

NOPE-NOPE. NOPE-NOPE.

AAH! AIIEEE!

LOOK WHAT I FOUND! SHOULD I POP HIS HEAD OFF, TOO?

AW, C'MON, I DIDN'T MEAN TO DO IT.

YOU GUYS ARE SCARING ME!

I DIDN'T MEAN TO SET ALL THOSE TRAPS AND CAPTURE YOU.

TRAPS?

IN THE ARBORETUM!

THAT REALLY HURT, YOU LITTLE SNOTLING! I OUGHTA!

PUH-PUH-PUH-LEEEZE DON'T HURT ME.

I'M SORRY!

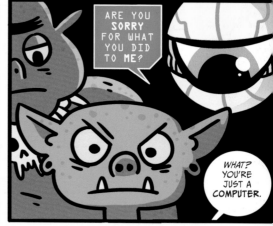

ARE YOU SORRY FOR WHAT YOU DID TO ME?

WHAT? YOU'RE JUST A COMPUTER.

I BARELY UNDERSTAND WHAT A "COMPUTER" IS...

...BUT SHE'S NOT A COMPUTER! SHE'S D.O.N.A.!

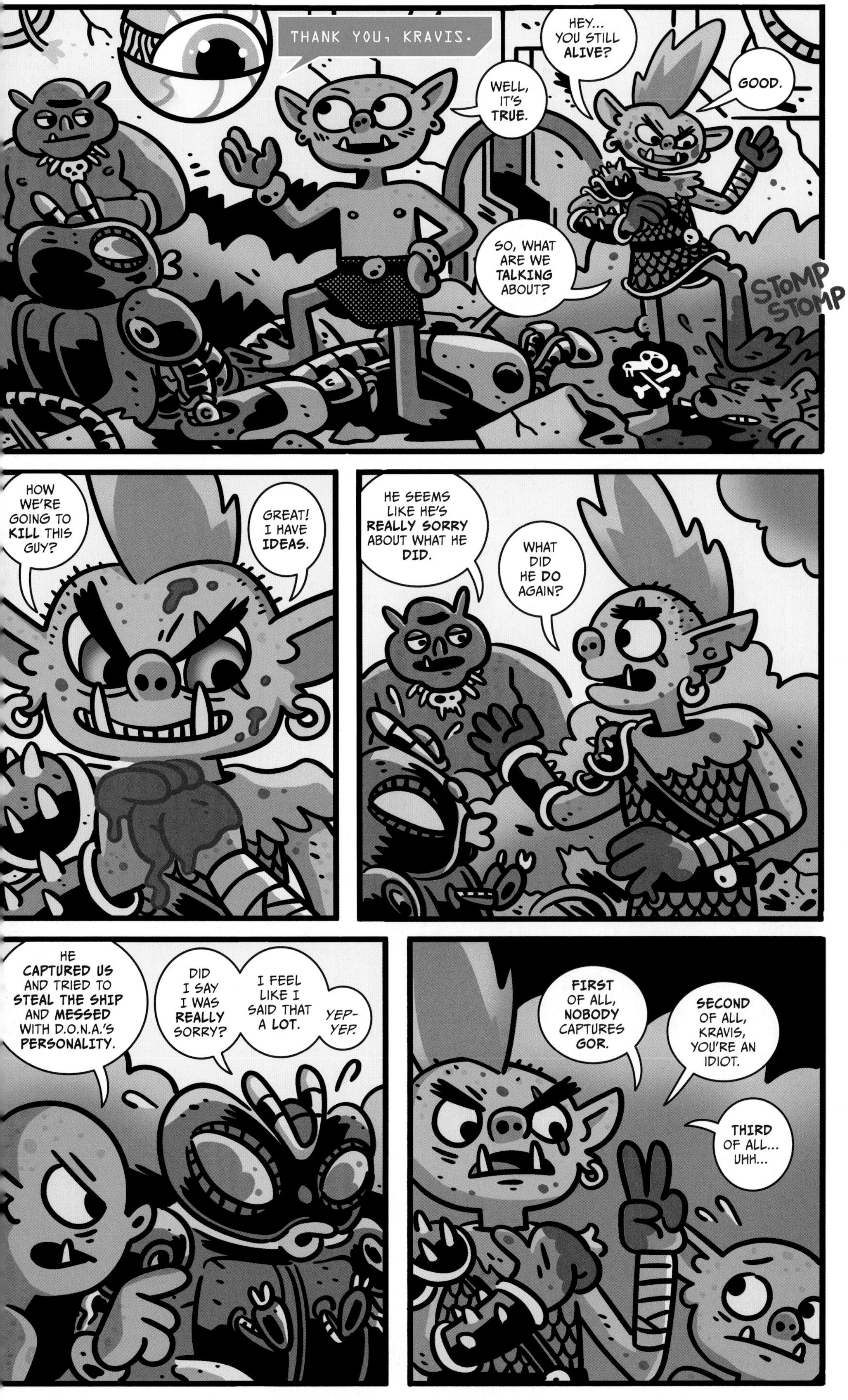
THANK YOU, KRAVIS.
WELL, IT'S TRUE.
HEY... YOU STILL ALIVE?
GOOD.
SO, WHAT ARE WE TALKING ABOUT?
STOMP STOMP
HOW WE'RE GOING TO KILL THIS GUY?
GREAT! I HAVE IDEAS.
HE SEEMS LIKE HE'S REALLY SORRY ABOUT WHAT HE DID.
WHAT DID HE DO AGAIN?
HE CAPTURED US AND TRIED TO STEAL THE SHIP AND MESSED WITH D.O.N.A.'S PERSONALITY.
DID I SAY I WAS REALLY SORRY?
I FEEL LIKE I SAID THAT A LOT.
YEP-YEP.
FIRST OF ALL, NOBODY CAPTURES GOR.
SECOND OF ALL, KRAVIS, YOU'RE AN IDIOT.
THIRD OF ALL... UHH...

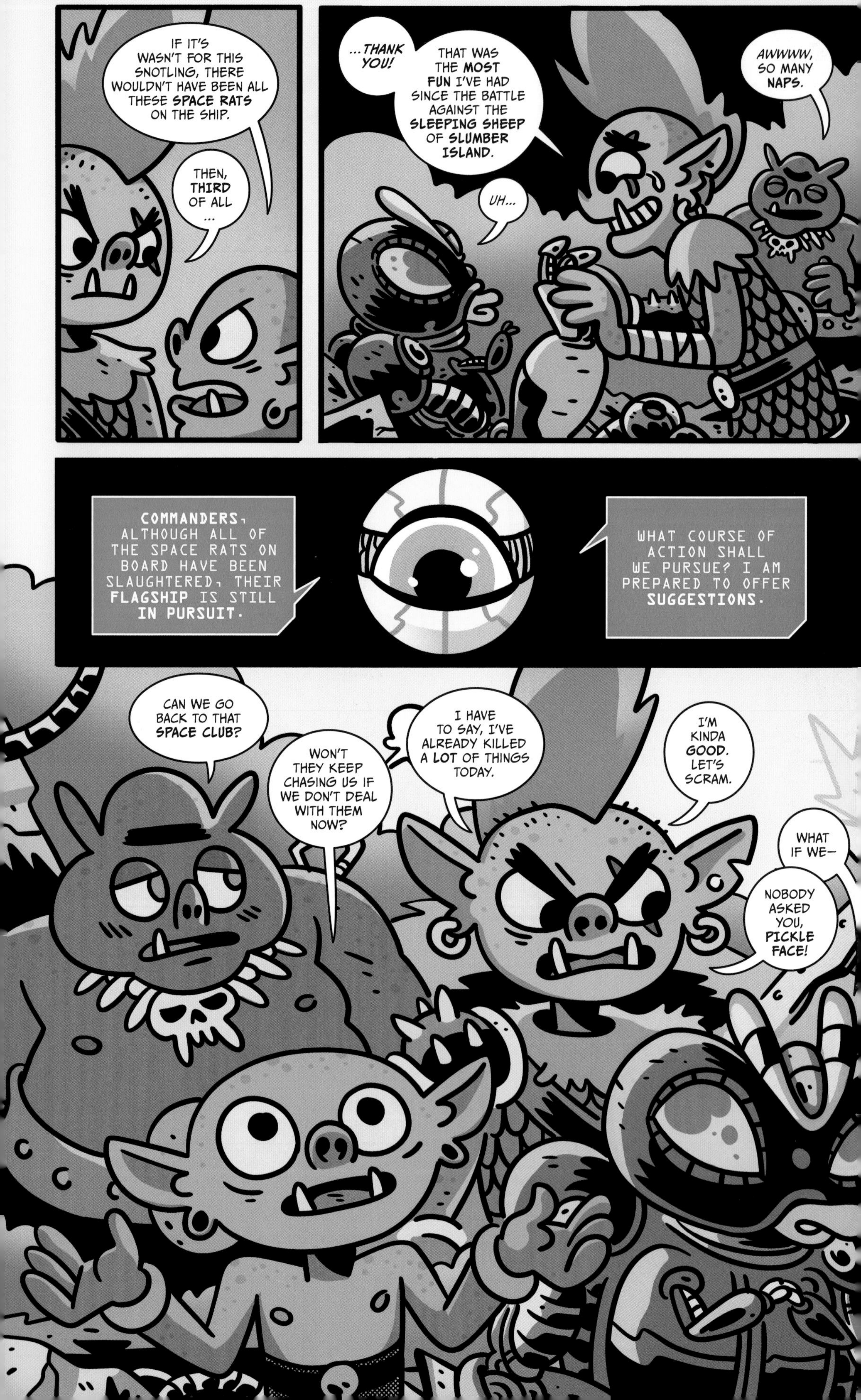

IF IT'S WASN'T FOR THIS SNOTLING, THERE WOULDN'T HAVE BEEN ALL THESE SPACE RATS ON THE SHIP.
THEN, THIRD OF ALL ...
...THANK YOU!
THAT WAS THE MOST FUN I'VE HAD SINCE THE BATTLE AGAINST THE SLEEPING SHEEP OF SLUMBER ISLAND.
UH...
AWWWW, SO MANY NAPS.
COMMANDERS, ALTHOUGH ALL OF THE SPACE RATS ON BOARD HAVE BEEN SLAUGHTERED, THEIR FLAGSHIP IS STILL IN PURSUIT.
WHAT COURSE OF ACTION SHALL WE PURSUE? I AM PREPARED TO OFFER SUGGESTIONS.
CAN WE GO BACK TO THAT SPACE CLUB?
WON'T THEY KEEP CHASING US IF WE DON'T DEAL WITH THEM NOW?
I HAVE TO SAY, I'VE ALREADY KILLED A LOT OF THINGS TODAY.
I'M KINDA GOOD. LET'S SCRAM.
WHAT IF WE—
NOBODY ASKED YOU, PICKLE FACE!

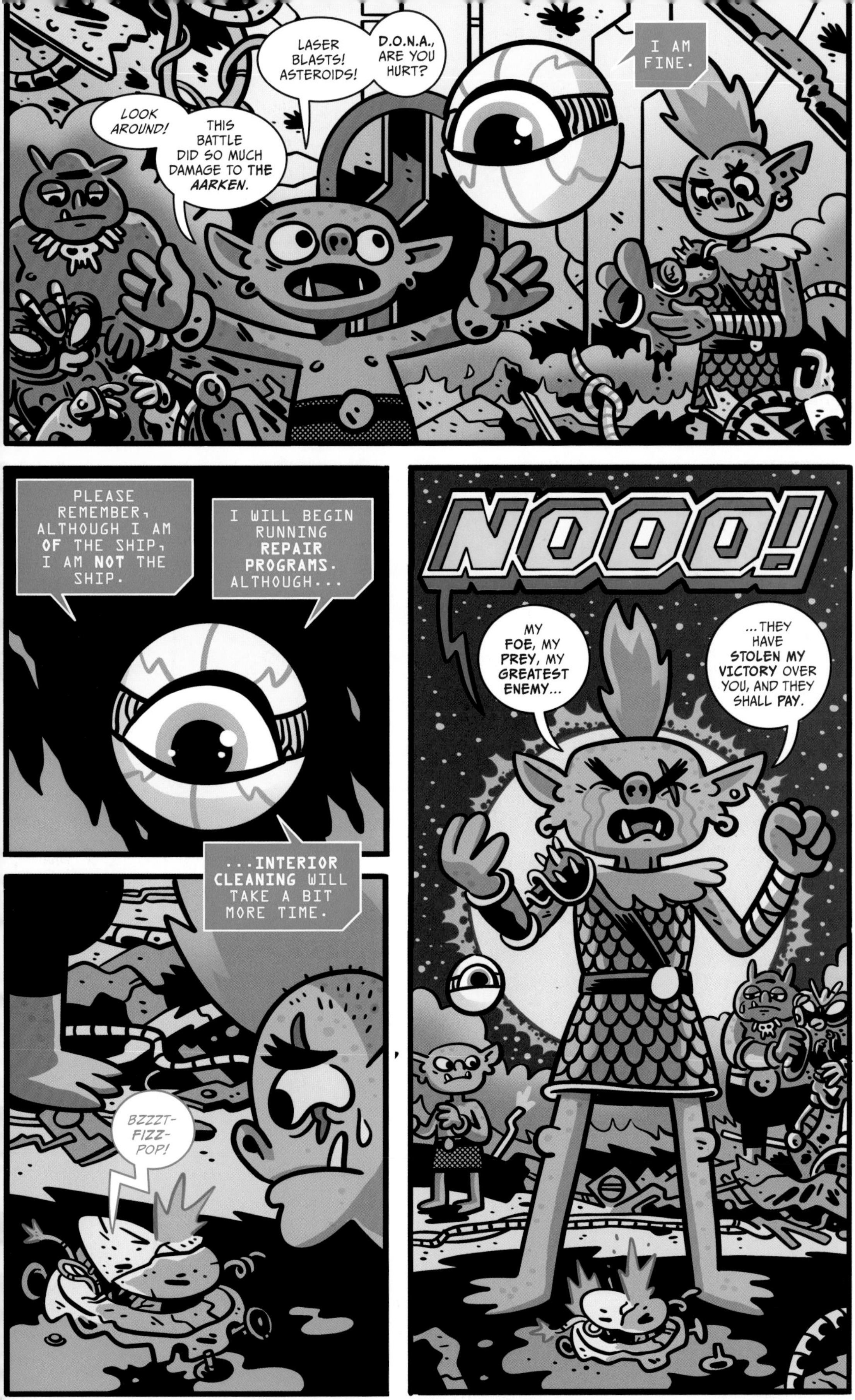
LOOK AROUND!
THIS BATTLE DID SO MUCH DAMAGE TO THE AARKEN.
LASER BLASTS! ASTEROIDS!
D.O.N.A., ARE YOU HURT?
I AM FINE.
PLEASE REMEMBER, ALTHOUGH I AM OF THE SHIP, I AM NOT THE SHIP.
I WILL BEGIN RUNNING REPAIR PROGRAMS. ALTHOUGH...
...INTERIOR CLEANING WILL TAKE A BIT MORE TIME.
BZZZT-FIZZ-POP!
NOOO!
MY FOE, MY PREY, MY GREATEST ENEMY...
...THEY HAVE STOLEN MY VICTORY OVER YOU, AND THEY SHALL PAY.

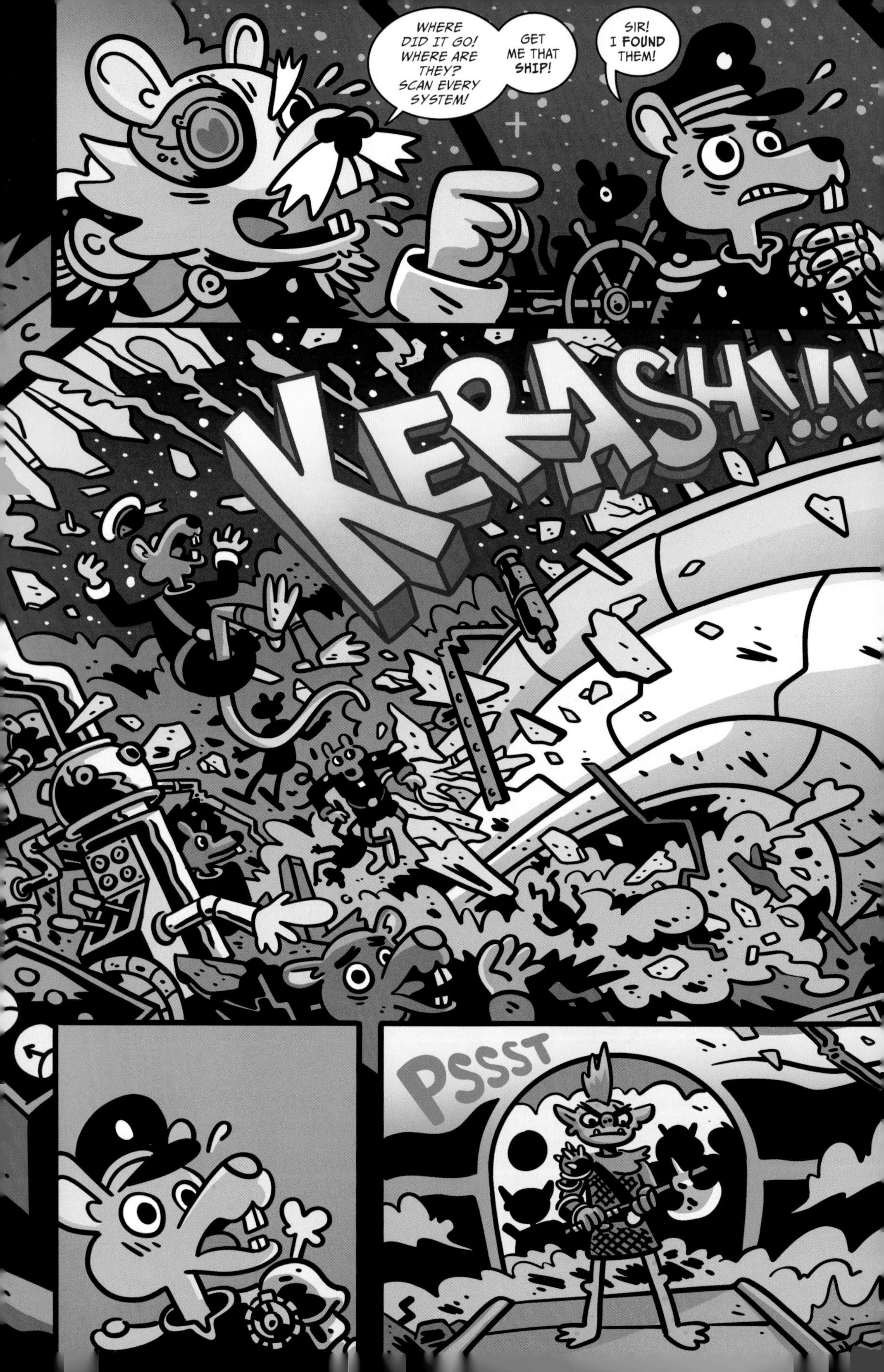
WHERE DID IT GO! WHERE ARE THEY? SCAN EVERY SYSTEM!
GET ME THAT SHIP!
SIR! I FOUND THEM!
KERASH!!!
PSSST

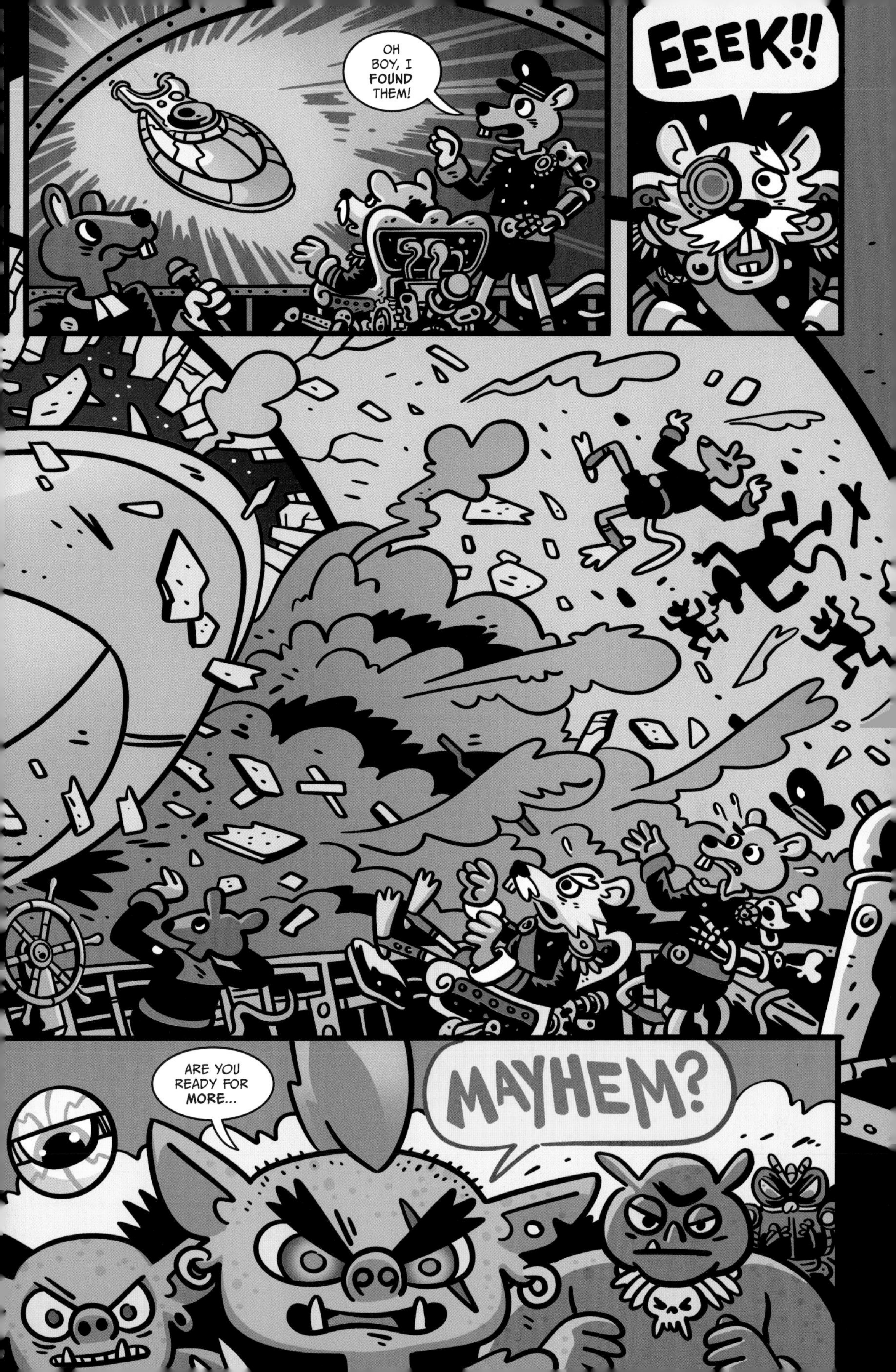
OH BOY, I FOUND THEM!
EEEK!!
ARE YOU READY FOR MORE...
MAYHEM?

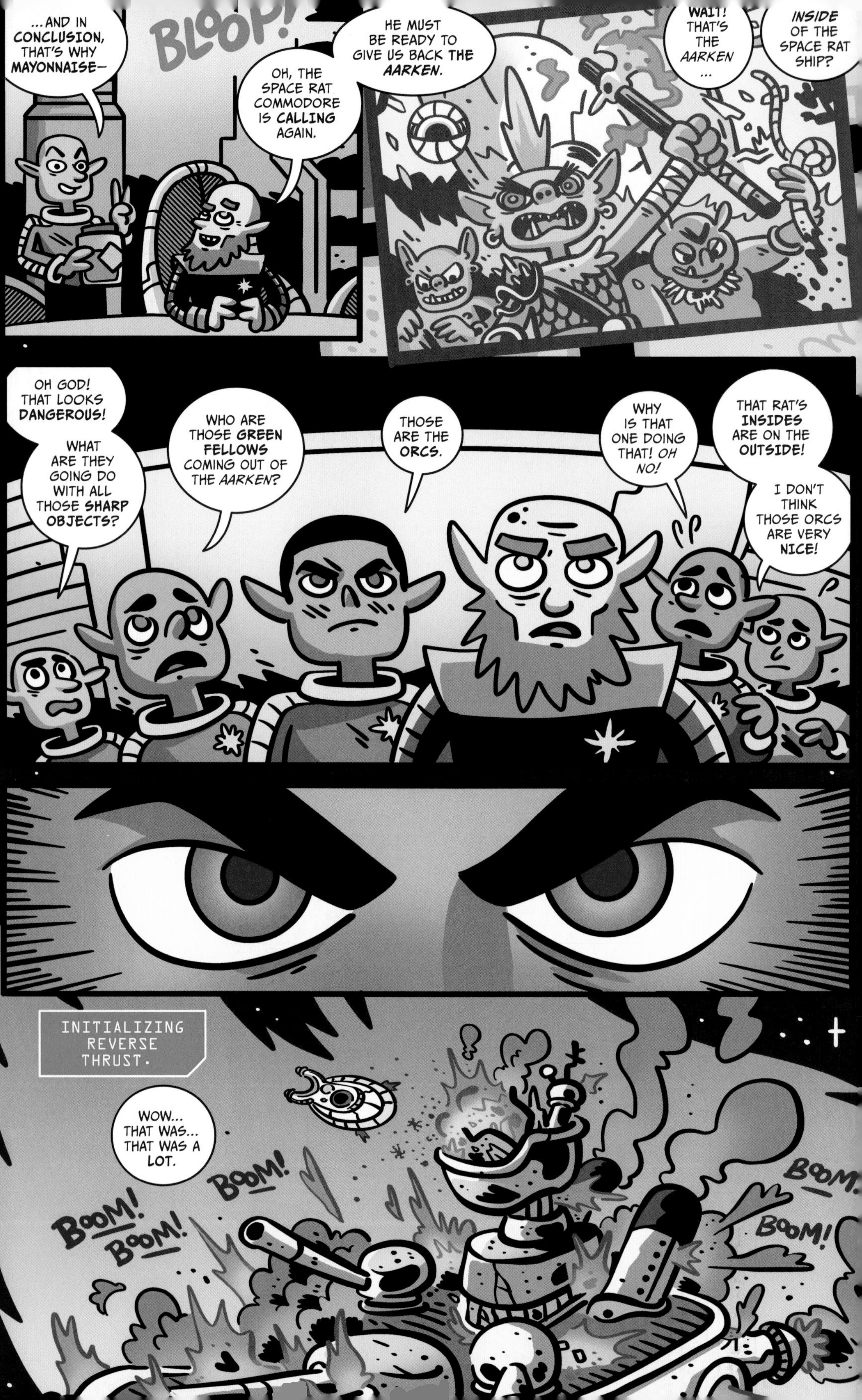
...AND IN CONCLUSION, THAT'S WHY MAYONNAISE—
BLOOP!
OH, THE SPACE RAT COMMODORE IS CALLING AGAIN.
HE MUST BE READY TO GIVE US BACK THE AARKEN.
WAIT! THAT'S THE AARKEN ...
INSIDE OF THE SPACE RAT SHIP?
OH GOD! THAT LOOKS DANGEROUS!
WHAT ARE THEY GOING DO WITH ALL THOSE SHARP OBJECTS?
WHO ARE THOSE GREEN FELLOWS COMING OUT OF THE AARKEN?
THOSE ARE THE ORCS.
WHY IS THAT ONE DOING THAT! OH NO!
THAT RAT'S INSIDES ARE ON THE OUTSIDE!
I DON'T THINK THOSE ORCS ARE VERY NICE!
INITIALIZING REVERSE THRUST.
WOW... THAT WAS... THAT WAS A LOT.
BOOM!
BOOM!
BOOM!
BOOM!
BOOM!

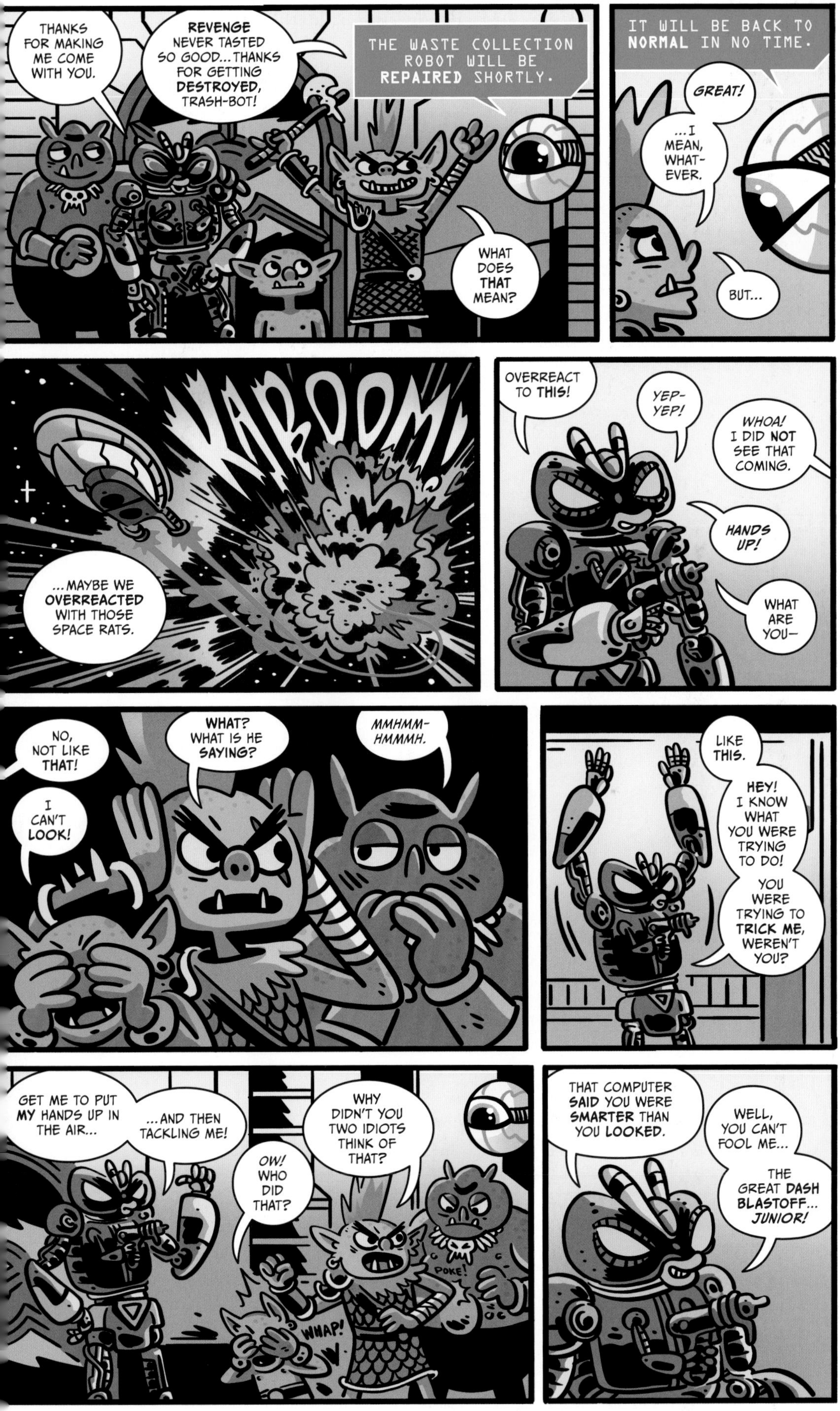
THANKS FOR MAKING ME COME WITH YOU.
REVENGE NEVER TASTED SO GOOD... THANKS FOR GETTING DESTROYED, TRASH-BOT!
THE WASTE COLLECTION ROBOT WILL BE REPAIRED SHORTLY.
WHAT DOES THAT MEAN?
IT WILL BE BACK TO NORMAL IN NO TIME.
GREAT!
...I MEAN, WHAT-EVER.
BUT...
YAROOOM!
...MAYBE WE OVERREACTED WITH THOSE SPACE RATS.
OVERREACT TO THIS!
YEP-YEP!
WHOA! I DID NOT SEE THAT COMING.
HANDS UP!
WHAT ARE YOU—
NO, NOT LIKE THAT!
I CAN'T LOOK!
WHAT? WHAT IS HE SAYING?
MMHMM-HMMMH.
LIKE THIS.
HEY! I KNOW WHAT YOU WERE TRYING TO DO!
YOU WERE TRYING TO TRICK ME, WEREN'T YOU?
GET ME TO PUT MY HANDS UP IN THE AIR...
...AND THEN TACKLING ME!
OW! WHO DID THAT?
WHY DIDN'T YOU TWO IDIOTS THINK OF THAT?
POKE!
WHAP!
THAT COMPUTER SAID YOU WERE SMARTER THAN YOU LOOKED.
WELL, YOU CAN'T FOOL ME...
THE GREAT DASH BLASTOFF... JUNIOR!

AND NOW, TO GET THIS SHIP BACK UNDER MY **FULL** CONTROL.

YEP-YEP.

BLEEP BLOOP BEEP

COMPUTER, ARE YOU COMPLIANT NOW?

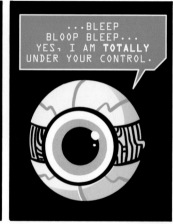

...BLEEP BLOOP BLEEP... YES, I AM **TOTALLY** UNDER YOUR CONTROL.

GOOD! NOW GET ME THAT **STARBLEEPER** ON THE COMM SCREEN.

BLOOP!

LIEUTENANT RANDO!

I'VE DONE IT!

I'M RETURN-ING WITH YOUR SHIP!

GREAT. YOU WERE SUPPOSED TO BE BACK **A WHILE AGO.**

BZZZZZ

WELL, THERE WERE SOME ISSUES. FIRST, I HAD TO SUBDUE THOSE ORCS, AND THEN THERE WERE THESE—

SPACE RATS, YEAH. I KNOW. WE ALL SAW WHAT HAPPENED THERE.

JUST GET BACK RIGHT AWAY.

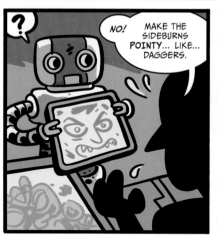

?

NO! MAKE THE SIDEBURNS POINTY... LIKE... DAGGERS.

WHAT DO YOU WANT ME TO DO WITH THE ORCS?

BLOW THEM OUT THE CARGO BAY.

THEY ARE TOO **DANGEROUS** TO LIVE.

BLOOF

YOU HEARD 'EM!

OUT YOU GO!

SO WHAT'S THE BIG DEAL? WE'RE JUST GOING OUTSIDE.

WE'LL **DIE** OUT THERE, MONGTAR. WE CAN'T BREATHE.

NO ONE TELLS **ME** WHAT I CAN AND CAN'T DO!

COMMANDER DASH, THERE IS SOMETHING **INCREDIBLY IMPORTANT** I MUST SHOW YOU.

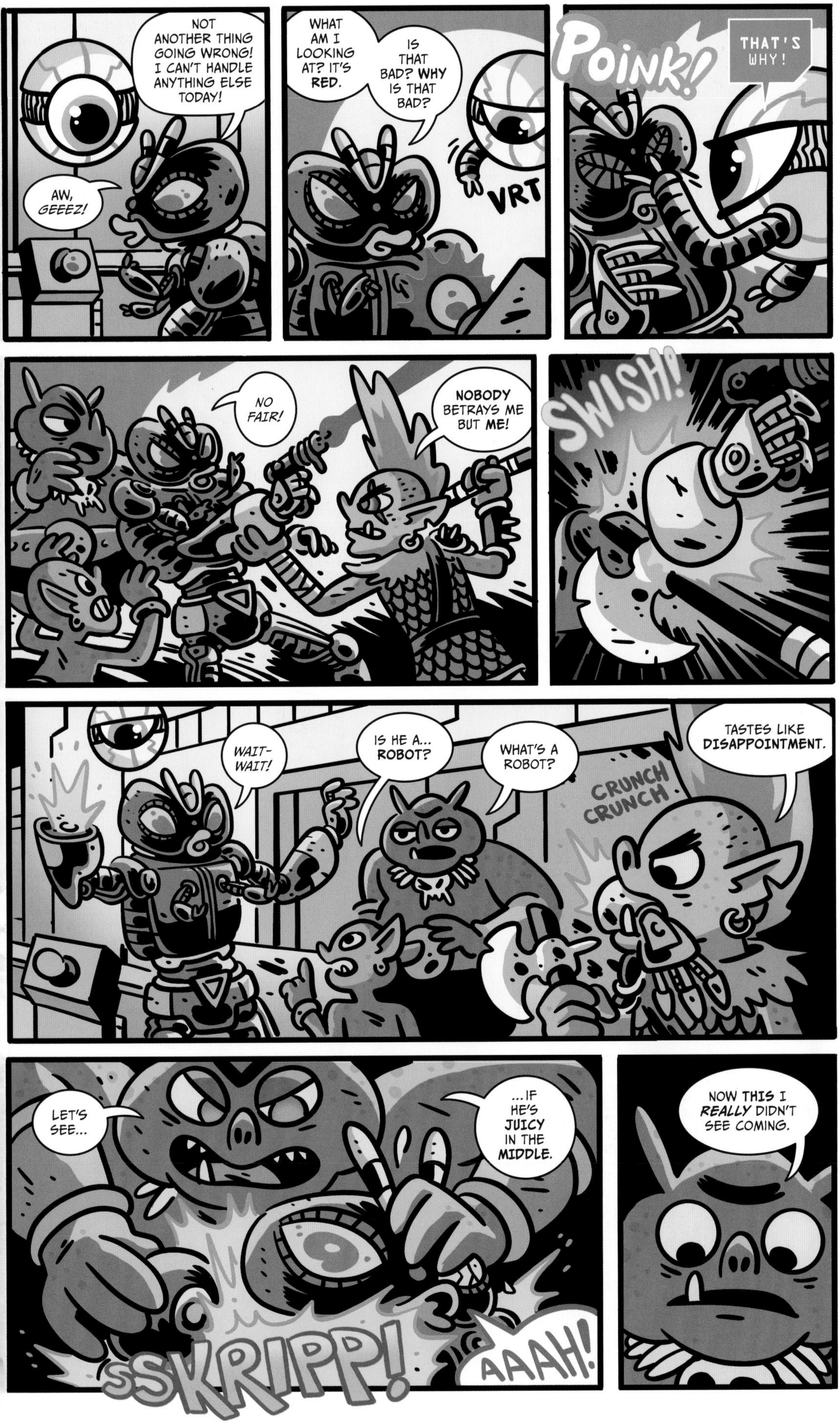

NOT ANOTHER THING GOING WRONG! I CAN'T HANDLE ANYTHING ELSE TODAY!
AW, GEEEZ!
WHAT AM I LOOKING AT? IT'S RED.
IS THAT BAD? WHY IS THAT BAD?
VRT
POINK!
THAT'S WHY!
NO FAIR!
NOBODY BETRAYS ME BUT ME!
SWISH!
WAIT-WAIT!
IS HE A... ROBOT?
WHAT'S A ROBOT?
TASTES LIKE DISAPPOINTMENT.
CRUNCH CRUNCH
LET'S SEE...
...IF HE'S JUICY IN THE MIDDLE.
sSKRIPP!
AAAH!
NOW THIS I REALLY DIDN'T SEE COMING.

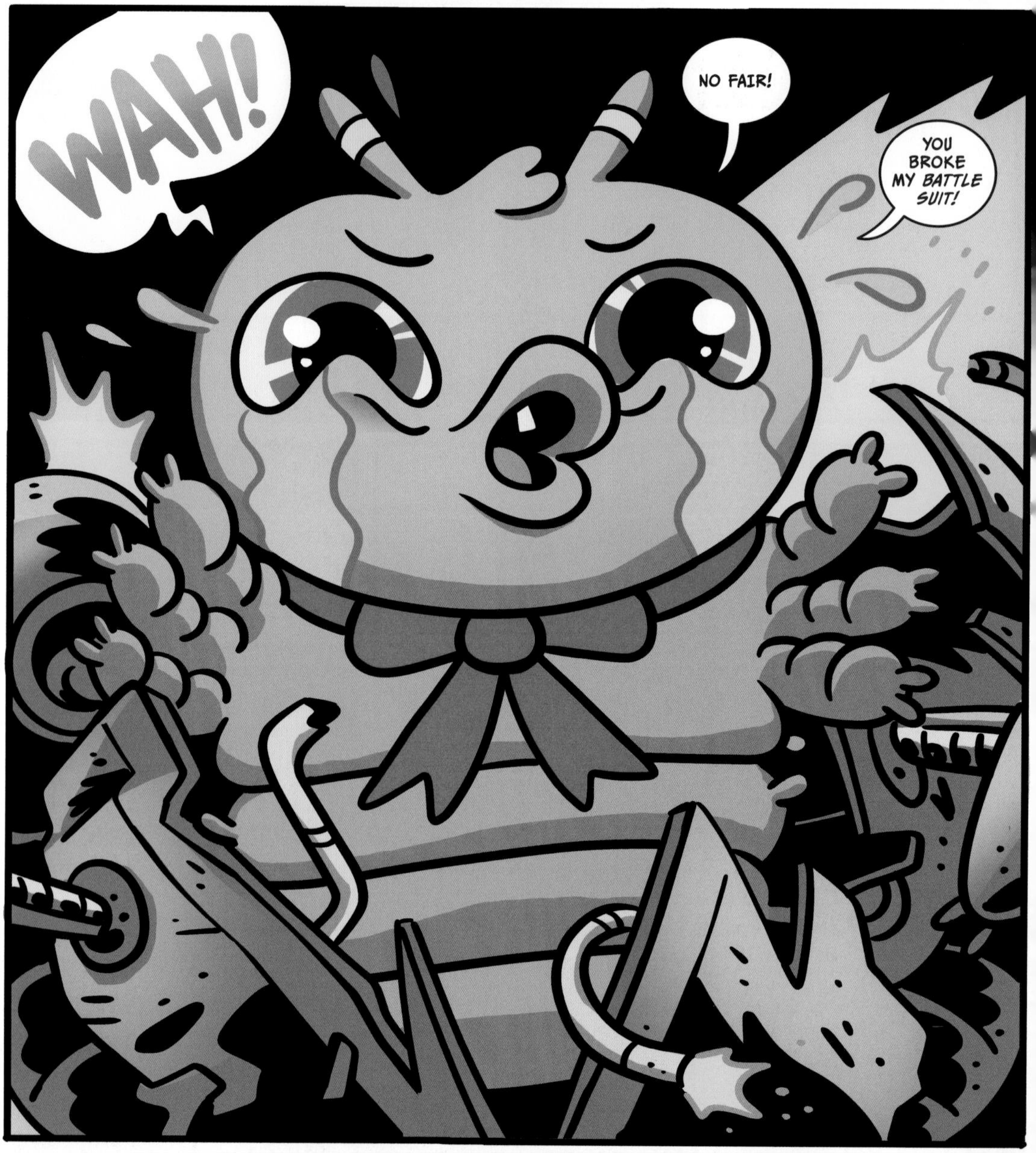
WAH!
NO FAIR!
YOU BROKE MY BATTLE SUIT!

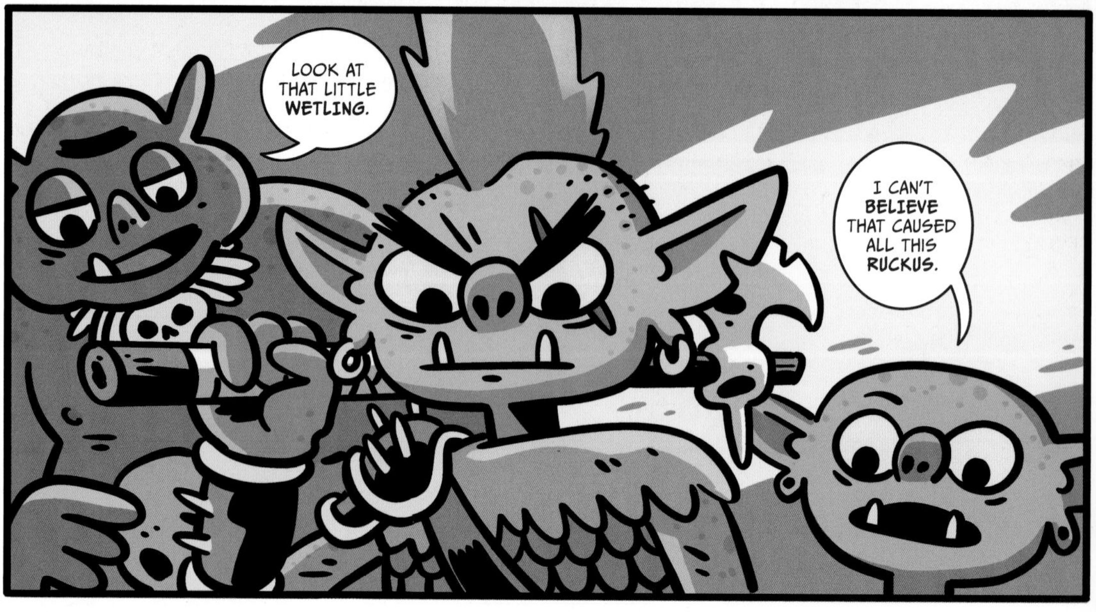
LOOK AT THAT LITTLE WETLING.
I CAN'T BELIEVE THAT CAUSED ALL THIS RUCKUS.

ONLY ONE THING TO DO NOW...

...MONGTAR...

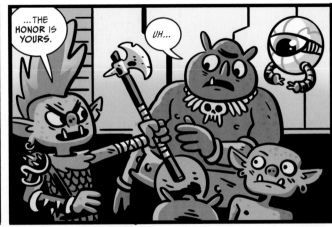

...THE HONOR IS YOURS.

UH...

GEEZ, GOR.

I CAN'T KILL A LITTLE BABY.

KRAVIS?

NAW.

FINE. I GUESS I HAVE TO DO EVERYTHING AROUND HERE!

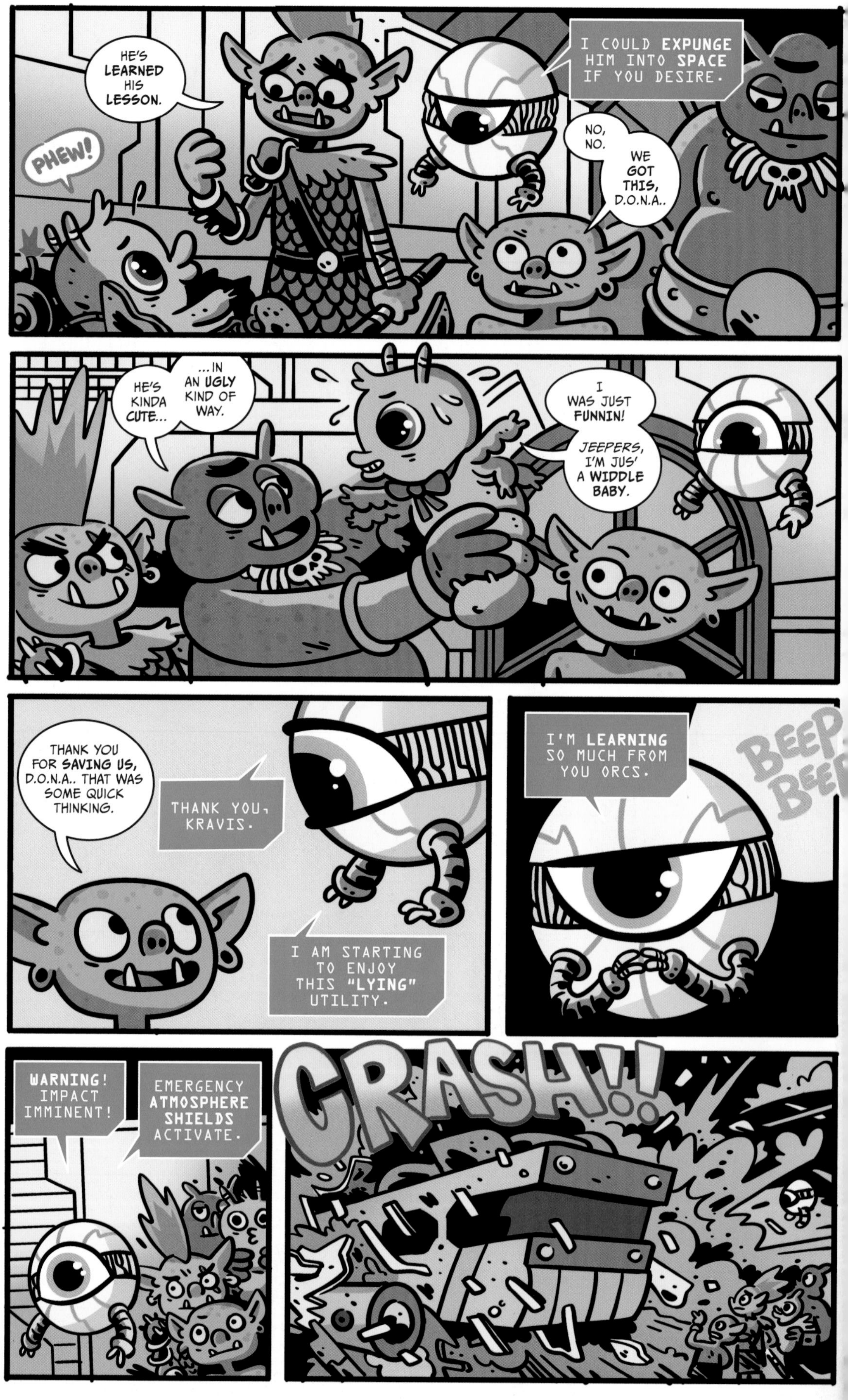

HE'S LEARNED HIS LESSON.
PHEW!
I COULD EXPUNGE HIM INTO SPACE IF YOU DESIRE.
NO, NO.
WE GOT THIS, D.O.N.A..
HE'S KINDA CUTE...
...IN AN UGLY KIND OF WAY.
I WAS JUST FUNNIN!
JEEPERS, I'M JUS' A WIDDLE BABY.
THANK YOU FOR SAVING US, D.O.N.A.. THAT WAS SOME QUICK THINKING.
THANK YOU, KRAVIS.
I AM STARTING TO ENJOY THIS "LYING" UTILITY.
I'M LEARNING SO MUCH FROM YOU ORCS.
BEEP BEEP
WARNING! IMPACT IMMINENT!
EMERGENCY ATMOSPHERE SHIELDS ACTIVATE.
CRASH!!

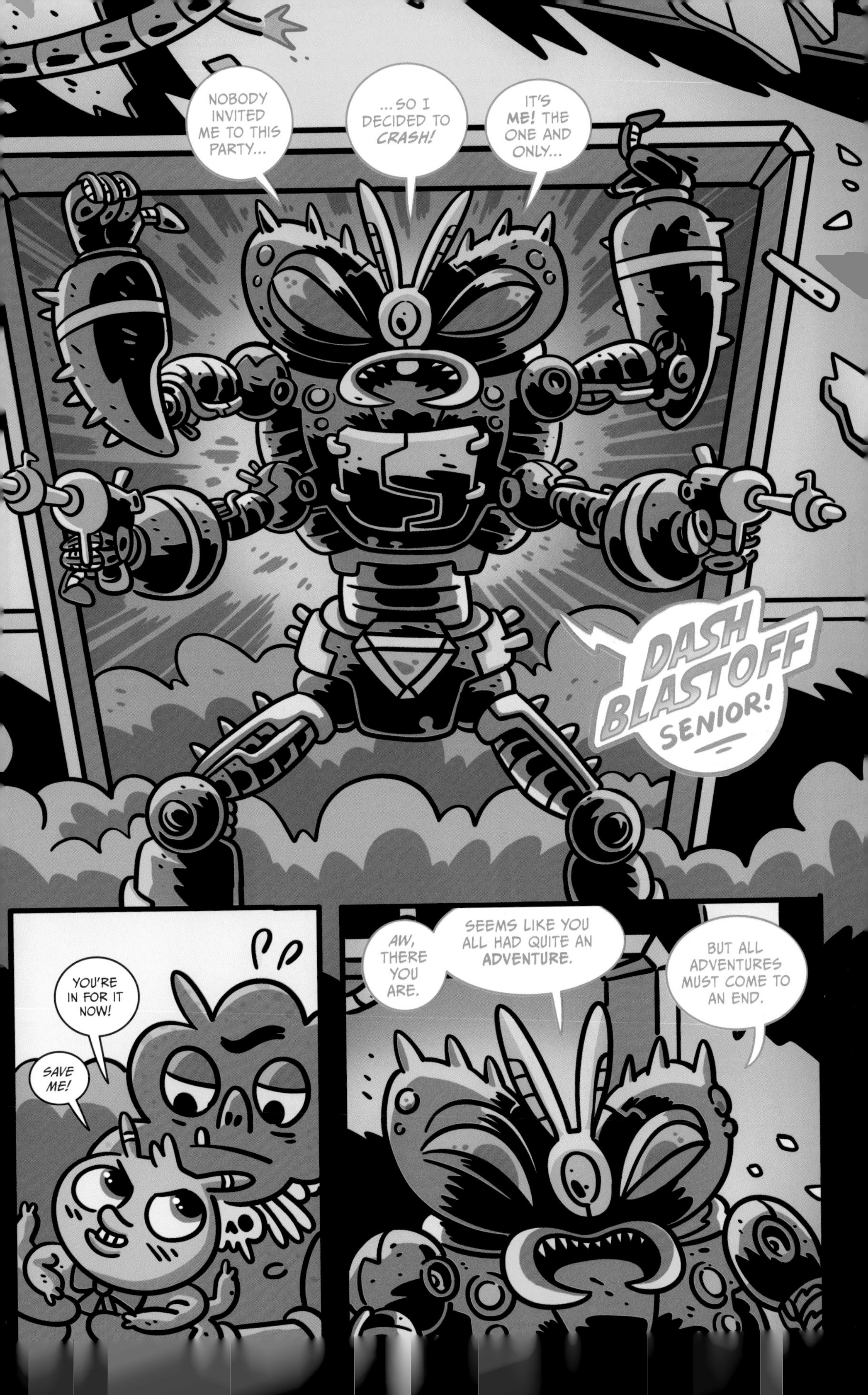

NOBODY INVITED ME TO THIS PARTY...
...SO I DECIDED TO CRASH!
IT'S ME! THE ONE AND ONLY...
DASH BLASTOFF SENIOR!
YOU'RE IN FOR IT NOW!
SAVE ME!
AW, THERE YOU ARE.
SEEMS LIKE YOU ALL HAD QUITE AN ADVENTURE.
BUT ALL ADVENTURES MUST COME TO AN END.

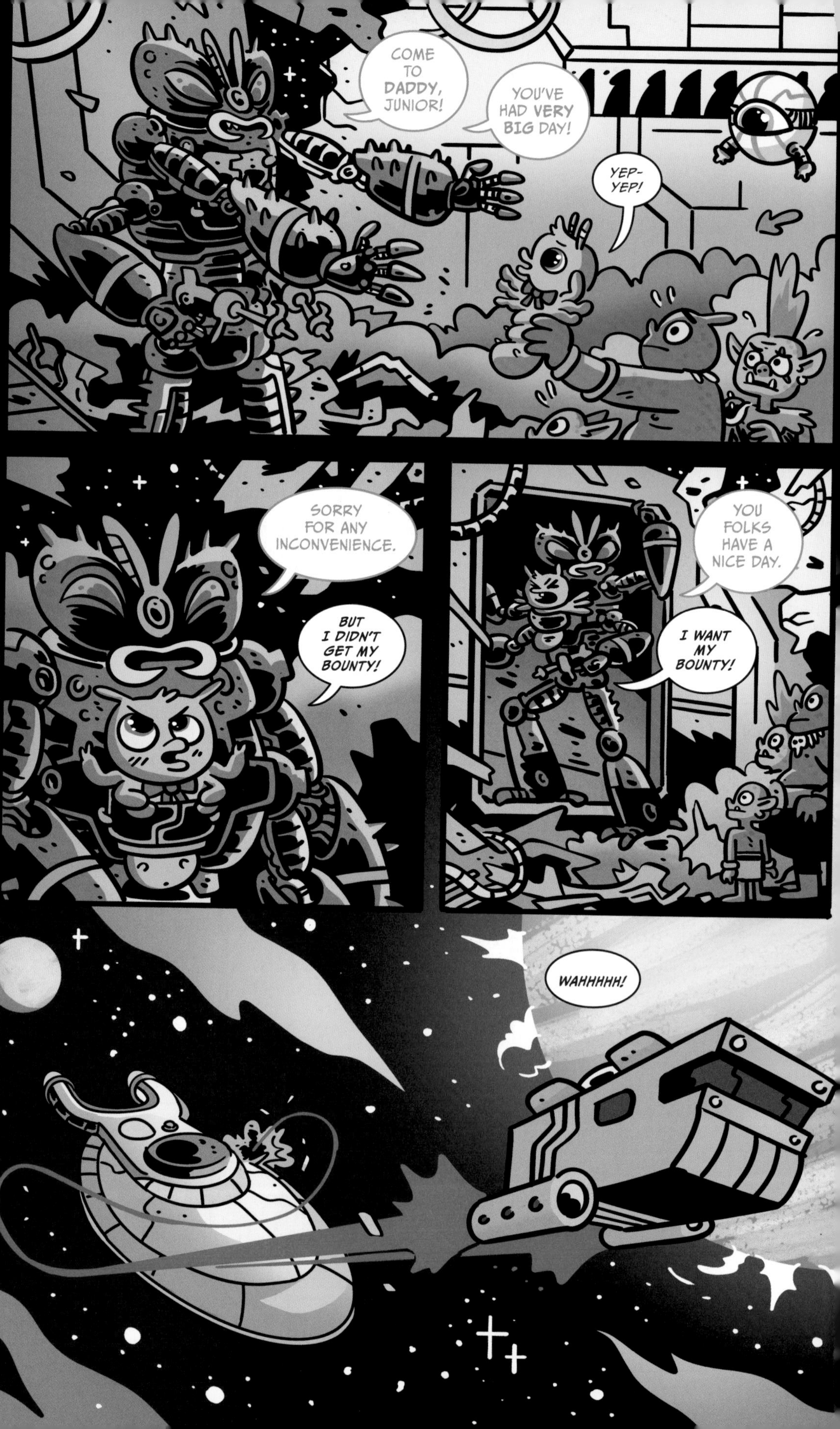
COME TO DADDY, JUNIOR!
YOU'VE HAD VERY BIG DAY!
YEP-YEP!
SORRY FOR ANY INCONVENIENCE.
BUT I DIDN'T GET MY BOUNTY!
YOU FOLKS HAVE A NICE DAY.
I WANT MY BOUNTY!
WAHHHHH!

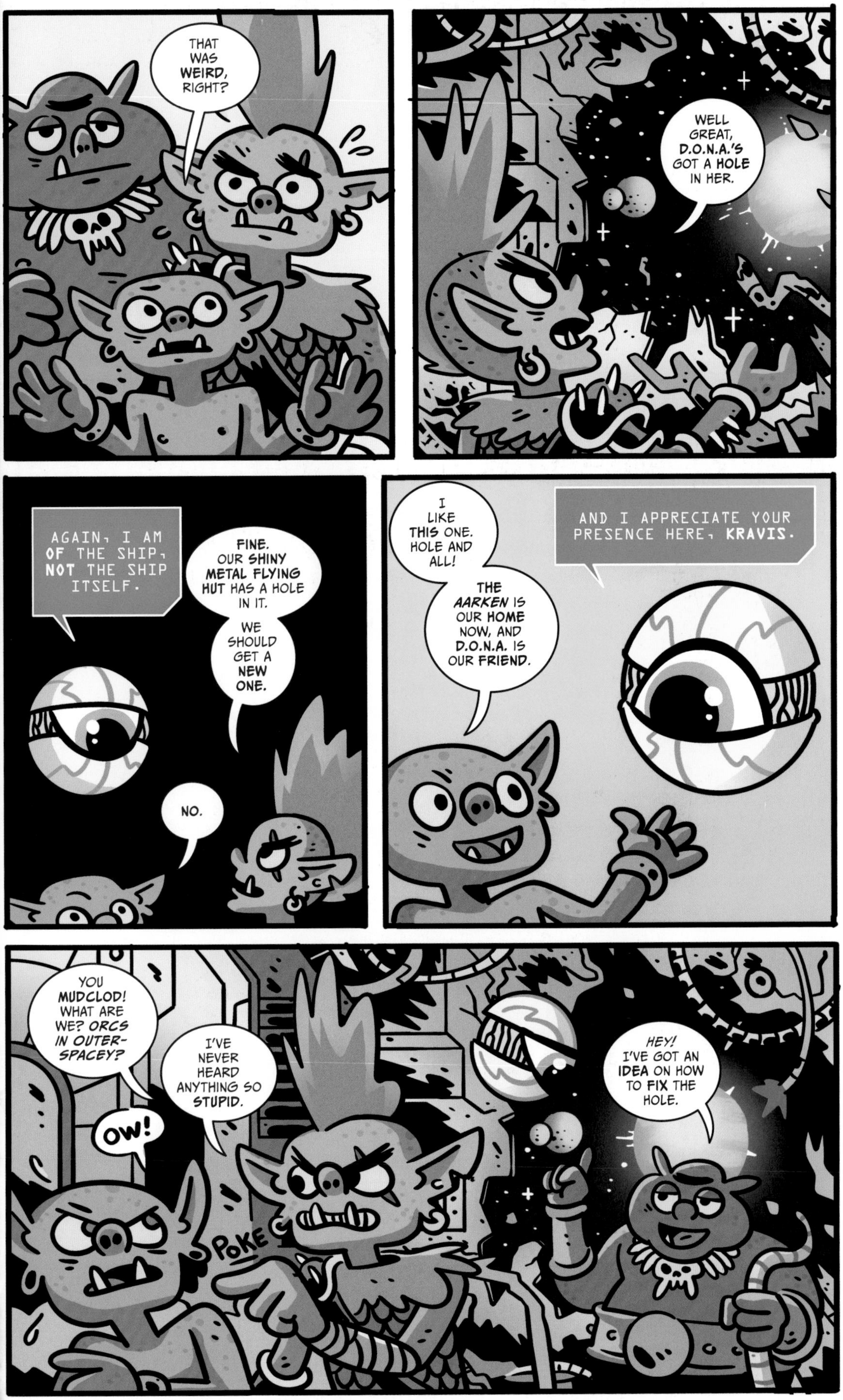

THAT WAS WEIRD, RIGHT?
WELL GREAT, D.O.N.A.'S GOT A HOLE IN HER.
AGAIN, I AM OF THE SHIP, NOT THE SHIP ITSELF.
FINE. OUR SHINY METAL FLYING HUT HAS A HOLE IN IT.
WE SHOULD GET A NEW ONE.
NO.
I LIKE THIS ONE. HOLE AND ALL!
THE AARKEN IS OUR HOME NOW, AND D.O.N.A. IS OUR FRIEND.
AND I APPRECIATE YOUR PRESENCE HERE, KRAVIS.
YOU MUDCLOD! WHAT ARE WE? ORCS IN OUTER-SPACEY?
OW!
I'VE NEVER HEARD ANYTHING SO STUPID.
POKE
HEY! I'VE GOT AN IDEA ON HOW TO FIX THE HOLE.

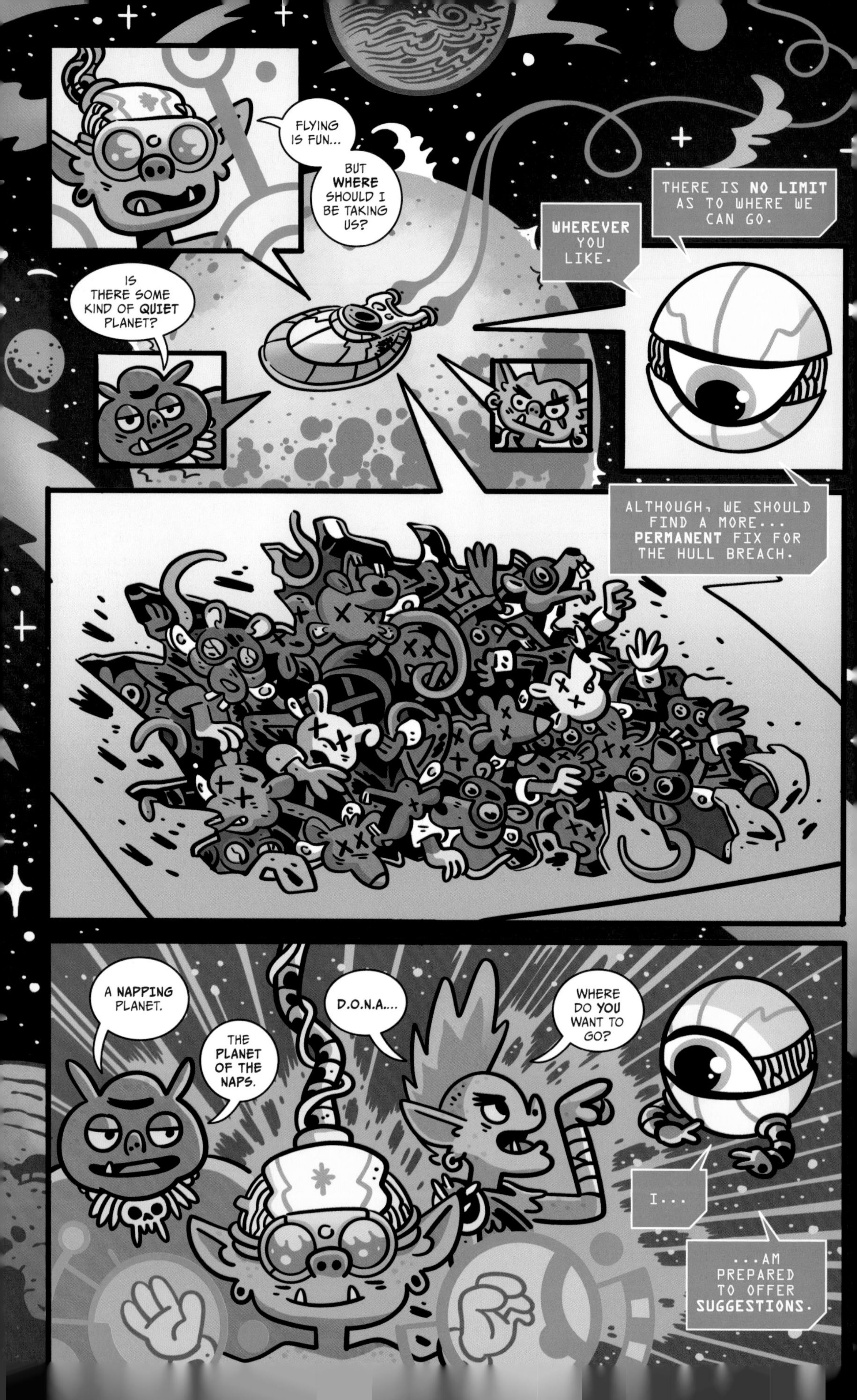
FLYING IS FUN...
BUT WHERE SHOULD I BE TAKING US?
IS THERE SOME KIND OF QUIET PLANET?
WHEREVER YOU LIKE.
THERE IS NO LIMIT AS TO WHERE WE CAN GO.
ALTHOUGH, WE SHOULD FIND A MORE... PERMANENT FIX FOR THE HULL BREACH.
A NAPPING PLANET.
THE PLANET OF THE NAPS.
D.O.N.A....
WHERE DO YOU WANT TO GO?
I...
...AM PREPARED TO OFFER SUGGESTIONS.

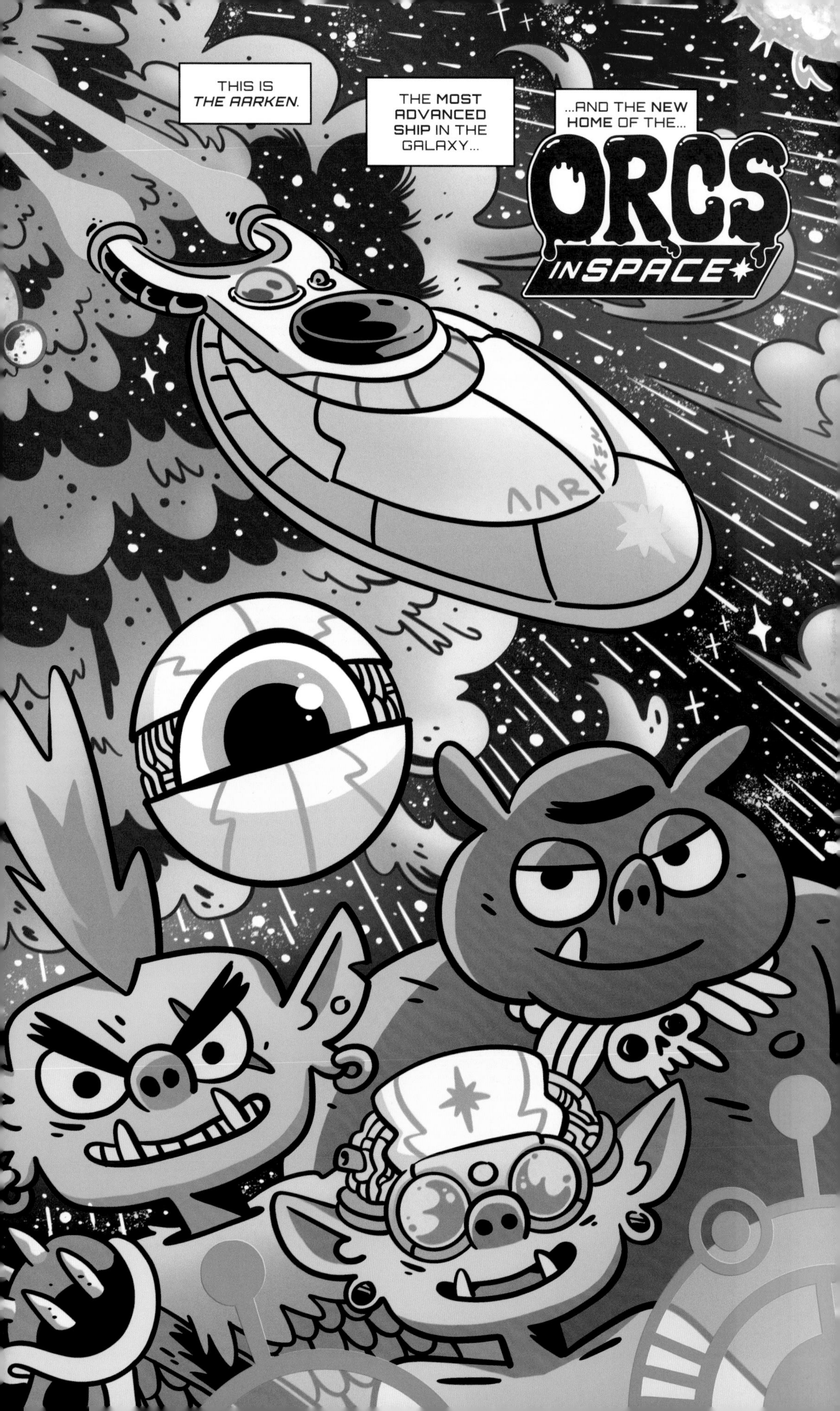
THIS IS THE AARKEN.
THE MOST ADVANCED SHIP IN THE GALAXY...
...AND THE NEW HOME OF THE...
ORCS IN SPACE

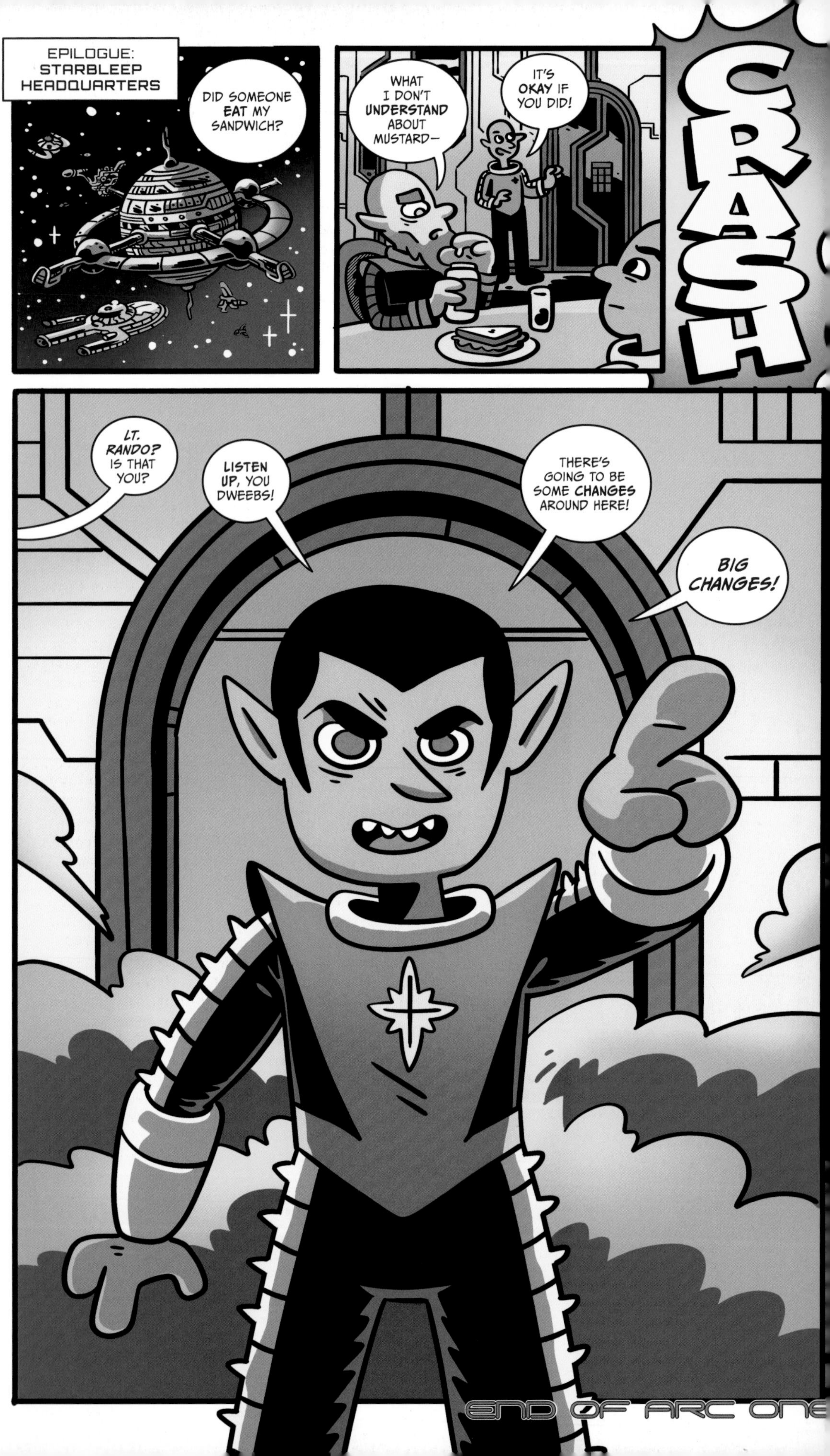

EPILOGUE: STARBLEEP HEADQUARTERS
DID SOMEONE EAT MY SANDWICH?
WHAT I DON'T UNDERSTAND ABOUT MUSTARD—
IT'S OKAY IF YOU DID!
CRASH
LT. RANDO? IS THAT YOU?
LISTEN UP, YOU DWEEBS!
THERE'S GOING TO BE SOME CHANGES AROUND HERE!
BIG CHANGES!
END OF ARC ONE

CREATOR BIOS

Mike Tanner, *writer*. Born in Great Falls, Montana, Michael Tanner kept moving west until he hit the ocean, and then he went south and stopped in Los Angeles. He has lived there longer than anywhere else, so he now considers himself an Angelino. And he truly believes it's the greatest city in the world...once you figure out how to stop getting parking tickets. Although a lifelong comics fan, he credits having an interesting hobby for getting him into the world of professional comics. For years he was a referee for the LA Derby Dolls, and his first published comic was in a derby anthology by Oni Press. Now he's done multiple stories in many anthologies and co-writes the YALSA-nominated graphic novel series *Junior Braves of the Apocalypse*. He has also been a podcaster, an actor, a comedian, as well as food blogger back when that was a thing.

Rashad Gheith, *(aka Velgamog), writer*. R.Y. Gheith is a writer who spends an unhealthy amount of time reading comics, playing fantasy online games, and planning his next step toward musical pop stardom.

Abed Gheith, *writer*. Born in the sleepy suburban town of Modesto, California, Abed Gheith grew up surrounded by He-Man toys, Jim Henson properties, and Superman comics. At a young age, he was always using his imagination to play outside by his lonesome. While other kids were getting broken legs and playing sports, he was coming up with ideas and stories and pretending he was an action movie star. Fast-forward to adulthood, Abed moved to Los Angeles at 23 with his friends Justin Roiland and Sevan Najarian. Together, they created the cult Internet sensation *House of Cosbys* for Channel101.com. This led to writing two episodes of *Rick and Morty* with his brother, Rashad. Nowadays, Abed works as a story consultant on shows for Disney and Cartoon Network, and in his spare time writes comic books. He is the inspiration for the character Abed Nadir on the NBC sitcom *Community* and occasionally co-hosts on a podcast called *Gone Riffin'* with Rich Fulcher.

Justin Roiland, *writer*. Justin Roiland grew up in Manteca, California, where he did the basic stuff children do. Later in life, he traveled to Los Angeles. Once settled in, he created several popular online shorts for Channel 101. Some notable examples of his work (both animated and live action) include *House of Cosbys* and *Two Girls One Cup: The Show*. Justin is afraid of his mortality and hopes the things he creates will make lots of people happy. Then maybe when modern civilization collapses into chaos, people will remember him and they'll help him survive the bloodshed and violence. Global economic collapse is looming. It's going to be horrible, and honestly, a swift death might be preferable than living in the hell that awaits mankind. Justin also really hates writing about himself in the third person. I hate this. That's right. It's me. I've been writing this whole thing. Hi. The cat's out of the bag. It's just you and me now. There never was a third person. If you want to know anything about me, just ask. Sorry this wasn't more informative.

François Vigneault, *illustrator*. François Vigneault is a freelance illustrator, designer, and cartoonist (not necessarily in that order). In addition to *Orcs in Space*, his work includes *Titan* (Oni Press), *13e Avenue* (Éditions de la Pastèque), and his comics and illustrations have appeared in publications such as *Planches*, *Papercutter*, *Kayak*, and *Study Group Magazine*. His work has been nominated for numerous awards, including the Joe Shuster Award, Prix des Libraires, and the Prix des Collèges. Born in the United States to immigrant parents, he has lived and worked in Montréal, Québec, since 2015.

DJ Chavis, *colorist*. DJ Chavis is colorist for *Orcs in Space* and a big ol' nerd, with an arguably unfathomable amount of ridiculous interests and hobbies. Warning: Catch him in the right mood and he might talk your ear off about said interests. Follow his work @djcolorscomics.

Dave Pender, *color flatter*. Dave Pender is one of many Daves in comics who is a comic enthusiast, flatter, and colorist who loves to collaborate. His first major credit with a major publisher is *Orcs in Space*, published by Oni Press! You can find him on Twitter @waytoomanydaves to congratulate him.

TAKE A PEEK AT FRANÇOIS VIGNEAULT'S DESIGNS!

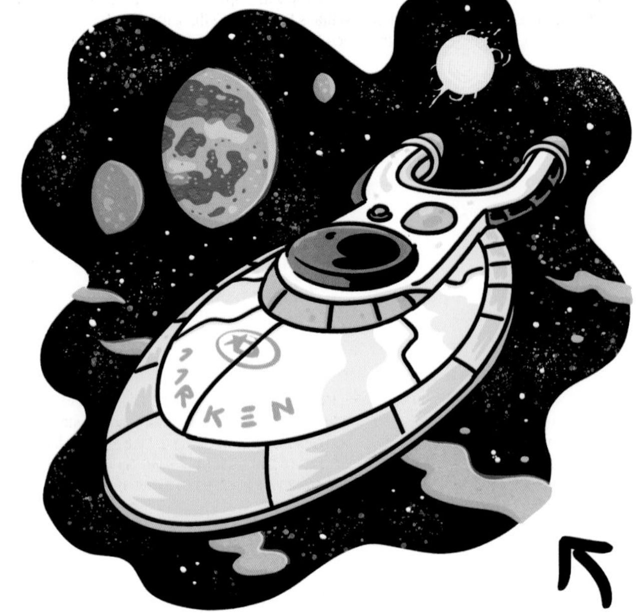

AARKEN

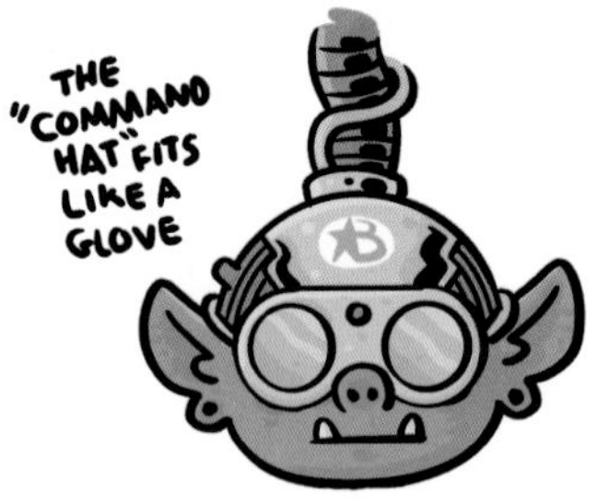

THE "COMMAND HAT" FITS LIKE A GLOVE

"The *AARKEN* is meant to be a pretty straight homage to golden age sci-fi spacecraft, sleek and geometric, but with a lot of flexibility built into it. I want the reader to have the impression that the whole thing could shift and change at a moment's notice. It has a somewhat mysterious layout that can hopefully encompass whatever the writers throw at it; someday I'll do one of those big schematic designs of the whole thing in all its glory!"

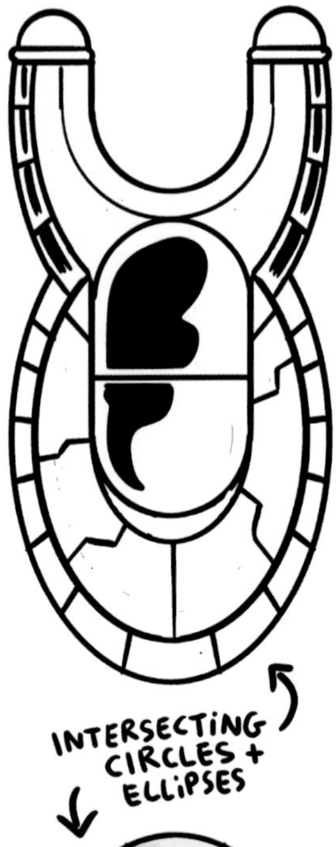

INTERSECTING CIRCLES + ELLIPSES

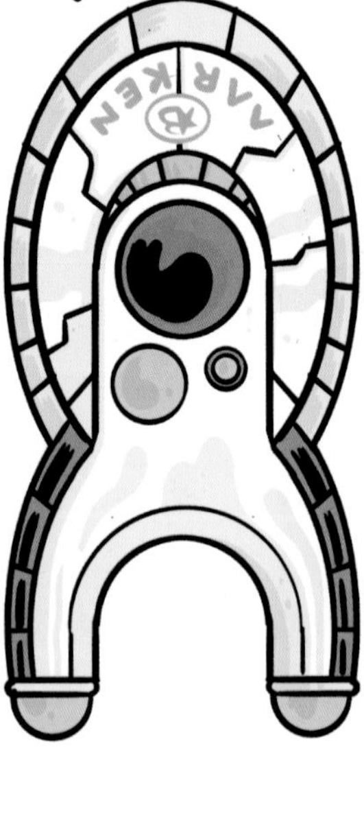

AARKEN

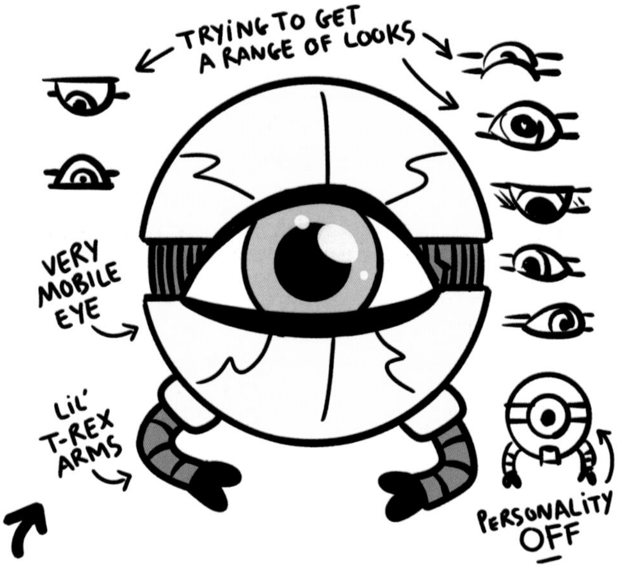

TRYING TO GET A RANGE OF LOOKS
VERY MOBILE EYE
LIL' T-REX ARMS
PERSONALITY OFF

"Like the *Aarken*, D.O.N.A. is meant to have a very high-tech, futuristic look, to contrast with the rough-and-tumble "primitive" orcs. Her eye has a very flexible aperture to give her a little flair, and like the ship she pilots, she could be hiding all kinds of secrets inside—above and beyond her arms."

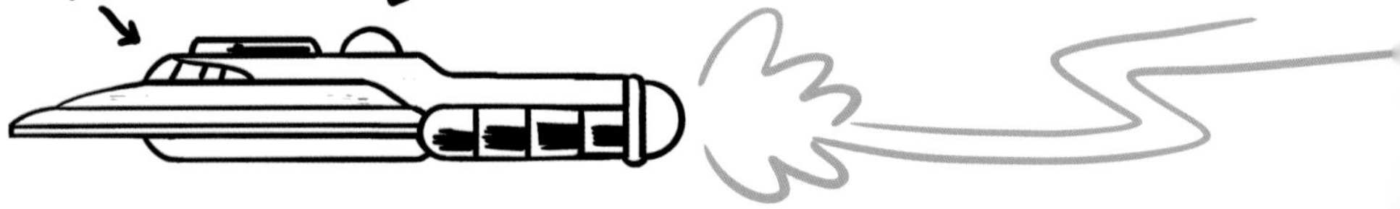

BRIDGE
ARBORETUM

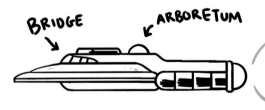

"I always liked the way orcs and goblins and such were mixed up in fantasy lore, from Tolkien to *Warhammer 40,000*. So, with the script calling for KRAVIS to be the runt of the group, I wanted to push it to the point where you wonder, is he even the same species as the other dudes? I picture Kravis as an escaped slave (you see a couple of other "Kravis-sized" orcs carrying around Velgar's throne), so I think of his cuffs as iron shackles rather than mere jewelry. Kravis's size also established a lot of the scale of the universe, since his head fits perfectly in the command hat. The StarBLEEP guys are about his same size, for instance."

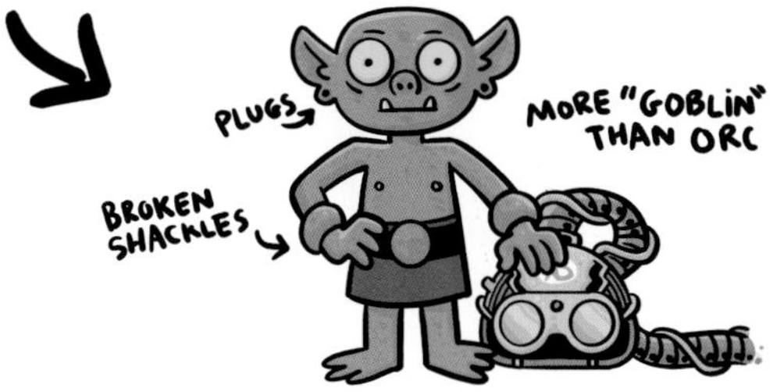

PLUGS
MORE "GOBLIN" THAN ORC
BROKEN SHACKLES

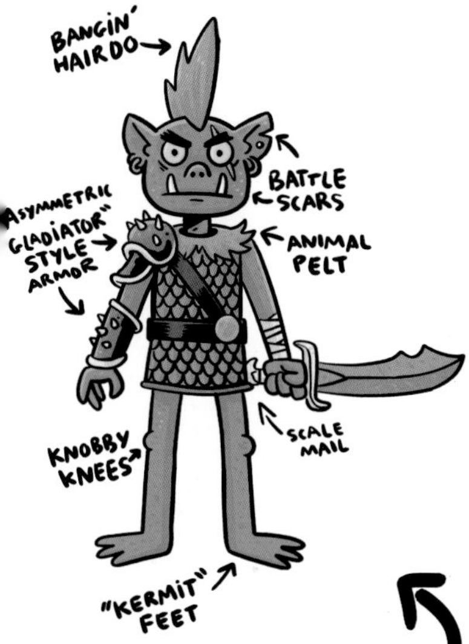

BANGIN' HAIRDO
BATTLE SCARS
ASYMMETRIC "GLADIATOR" STYLE ARMOR
ANIMAL PELT
KNOBBY KNEES
SCALE MAIL
"KERMIT" FEET

"MONGTAR is the big sleepy dude. His look pulls from a bunch of inspirations, from Obelix (gotta love the high-waisted pants and no shirt look) and the drawings of James Jarvis, to Snorlax and my childhood obsession with Garfield. Like all orcs, he's got the freckles all over (I dig the sense of texture that adds), but from his brown skin to his more cat-like features he's got a different vibe from his companions."

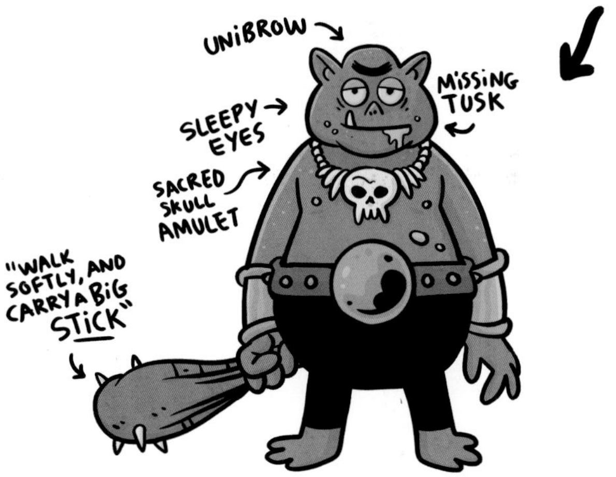

UNIBROW
MISSING TUSK
SLEEPY EYES
SACRED SKULL AMULET
"WALK SOFTLY, AND CARRY A BIG STICK"

"The guys wrote GOR as having a real chip on his shoulder, and had the hilarious idea to have his overcompensating mohawk just coming up to reach Mongtar's more impressive stature. I thought it would be funny to make Gor, the warrior of the group, a real stringy, beanpole-looking guy. His look is a mix of a Roman gladiator, a Koopa Kid, and Kermit the Frog. He's a ton of fun to draw."

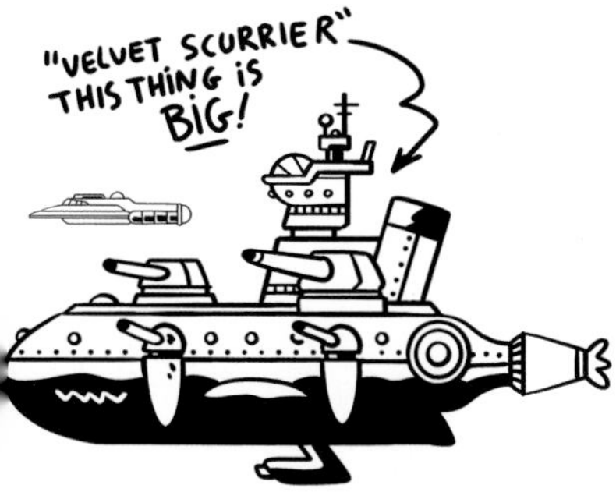

"VELVET SCURRIER" THIS THING IS BIG!

"The script called for the SPACE RATS to have a steampunk by way of the British Royal Navy look, so I aimed to deliver that, haha! I've actually had pet rats, so I have a soft spot for these scallywags. Some elements I particularly dug were the short pants (an homage to another famed sea-faring rodent), the "clockwork cyborg" elements, and all the little bits and bobs of regalia I could work in."

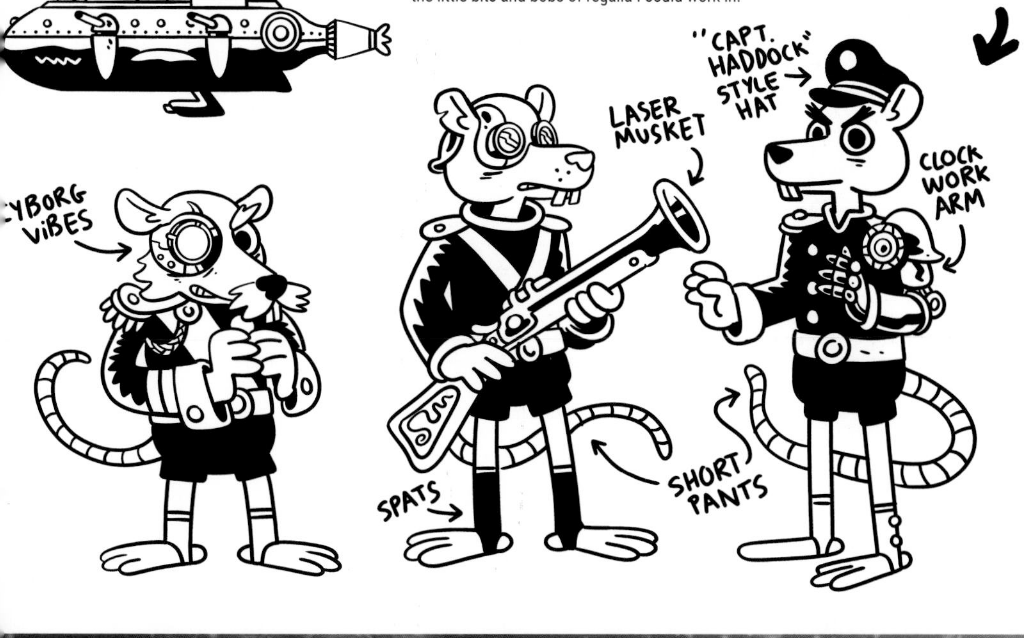

"CAPT. HADDOCK" STYLE HAT
LASER MUSKET
CLOCK WORK ARM
YBORG VIBES
SHORT PANTS
SPATS

To my mom and dad for all their support, and to my
cousin Rami for being a comic book co-pilot.

-ABED

To the Orc Lord Orcinacia.

-RASHAD